SECRET BERLIN

Tom Wolf, Manuel Roy and Roberto Sassi

JONGLEZ PUBLISHING

travel guides

After earning his PhD in philosophy, **Tom Wolf** decided to dedicate himself to writing. He has written 22 crime novels, 3 guides inviting travelers to take a fresh look on the places they visit, and a guide on wines produced in the region of Brandenburg. After spending 12 years in Berlin-Mitte and Kreuzberg, he now lives in the north of the Berlin/Brandenburg metropolitan region where he looks after his vineyard and his small craft brewery. But that story is for another time ...

Manuel Roy had been a Germanophile for many years when he discovered Berlin like a punch in the face. He had seen Germany through the verses of Schiller and the paintings of Caspar David Friedrich, and found himself in a post-apocalyptic landscape full of punks scrupulously respectful of the selective sorting of rubbish. He admits to not having understood everything straight away. Twenty years of research later, with a doctorate in philosophy under his belt, having been a Berliner by adoption since 2000, and a guide in Berlin since 2013, Manuel now thinks that he has a better grasp of the city. But amazement is never far away. Despite its recent gentrification, the city never ceases to shake him up and surprise him. And it would seem that he loves that.

Born in 1986, **Roberto Sassi** is an urban sociologist. With Teresa Ciuffoletti, he is the author of the book *Guida alla Berlino ribelle* (Voland Edizioni, 2017) (*Guide to rebellious Berlin*, not yet translated). He regularly organises travel writing workshops and works with several journals, magazines among which the journal of the Goethe-Institut Italia, and websites. He lives in Prenzlauer Berg.

We have taken great pleasure in drawing up *Secret Berlin* and hope that through its guidance you will, like us, continue to discover unusual, hidden or little-known aspects of the city.
Descriptions of certain places are accompanied by thematic sections highlighting historical details or anecdotes as an aid to understanding the city in all its complexity.
Secret Berlin also draws attention to the multitude of details found in places that we may pass every day without noticing. These are an invitation to look more closely at the urban landscape and, more generally, a means of seeing our own city with the curiosity and attention that we often display while travelling else-where ...

Comments on this guidebook and its contents, as well as information on places we may not have mentioned, are more than welcome and will enrich future editions.

Don't hesitate to contact us:
E-mail: info@jonglezpublishing.com
Jonglez Publishing, 25 rue du Maréchal Foch
78000 Versailles, France

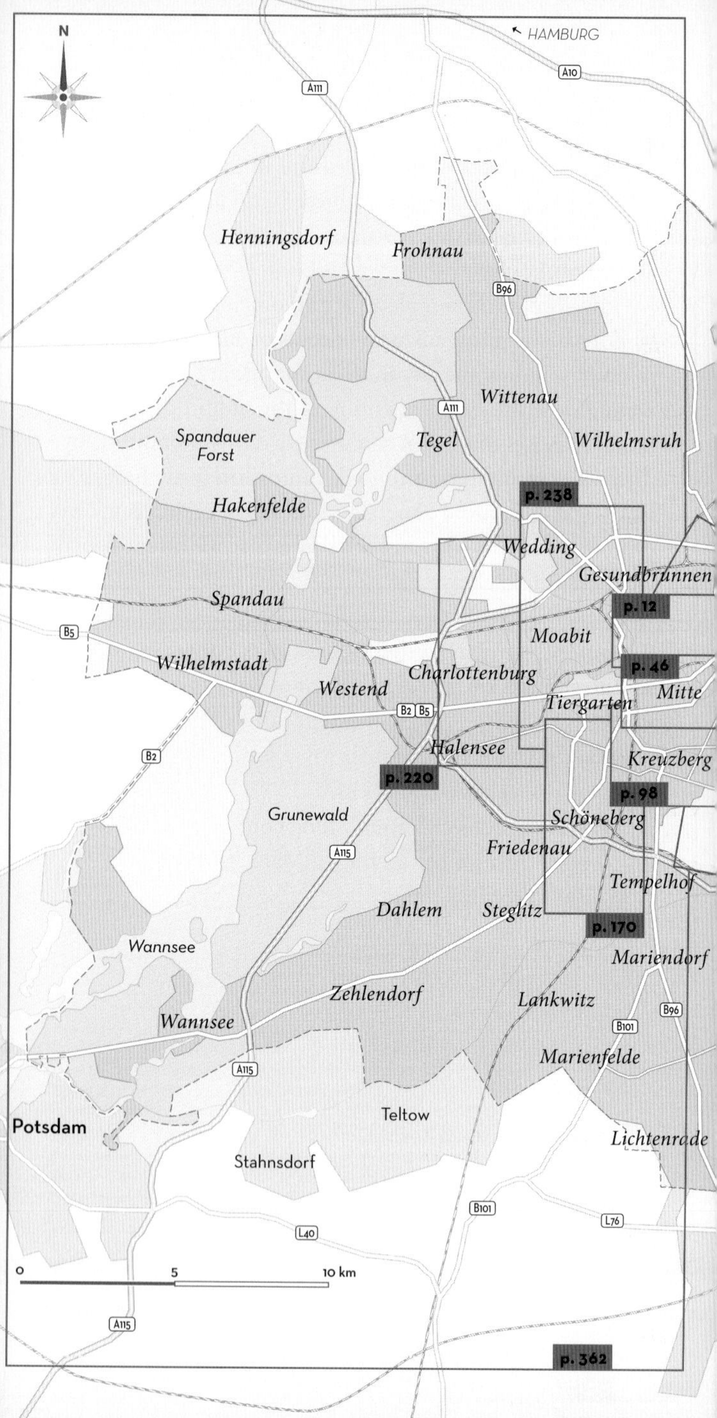
N
HAMBURG
A10
A111
Henningsdorf
Frohnau
B96
A111
Wittenau
Spandauer
Forst
Tegel
Wilhelmsruh
p. 238
Hakenfelde
Wedding
Gesundbrunnen
Spandau
p. 12
B5
Moabit
Wilhelmstadt
p. 46
Charlottenburg
Westend
Mitte
B2 B5
Tiergarten
B2
Halensee
Kreuzberg
p. 220
p. 98
Grunewald
Schöneberg
A115
Friedenau
Tempelhof
Dahlem
Steglitz
p. 170
Wannsee
Mariendorf
Zehlendorf
Lankwitz
Wannsee
B96
B101
Marienfelde
A115
Teltow
Potsdam
Lichtenrade
Stahnsdorf
B101
L76
L40
0
5
10 km
A115
p. 362

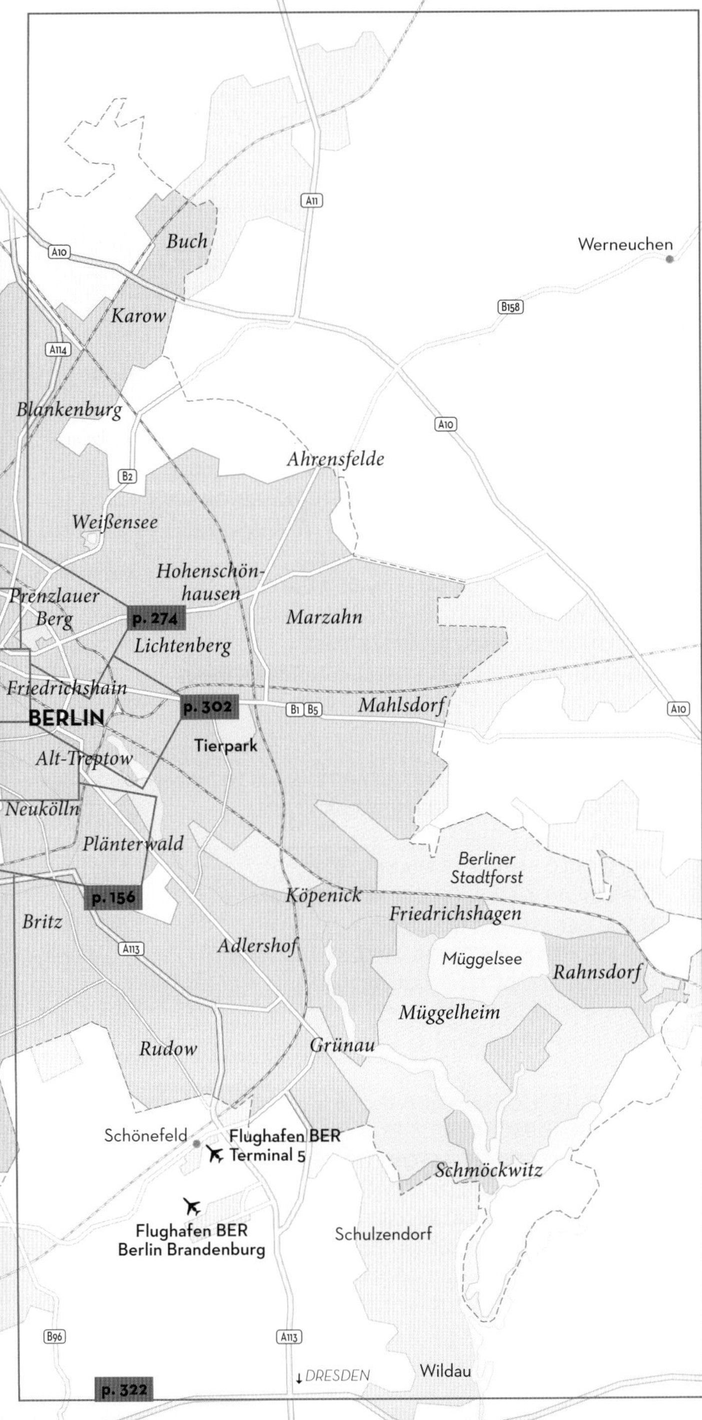
A11
A10
Buch
Werneuchen
B158
Karow
A114
Blankenburg
A10
Ahrensfelde
B2
Weißensee
Hohenschön-
hausen
Prenzlauer
Berg
p. 274
Marzahn
Lichtenberg
Friedrichshain
p. 302
B1
B5
Mahlsdorf
A10
BERLIN
Tierpark
Alt-Treptow
Neukölln
Plänterwald
Berliner
Stadtforst
p. 156
Köpenick
Friedrichshagen
Britz
A113
Adlershof
Müggelsee
Rahnsdorf
Müggelheim
Rudow
Grünau
Schönefeld
Flughafen BER
Terminal 5
Schmöckwitz
Flughafen BER
Berlin Brandenburg
Schulzendorf
B96
A113
DRESDEN
Wildau
p. 322

CONTENTS

North Mitte

South Mitte

Kreuzberg

Neukölln

Schöneberg

Charlottenburg - North Wilmersdorf

Wedding – Moabit – Tiergarten

Prenzlauer Berg

Friedrichshain – Rummelsburg

Pankow – Lichtenberg – Marzahn Hellersdorf – Treptow/Köpenick

Reinickendorf – Spandau – Grunewald Wilmerdorf – Steglitz/Zehlendorf

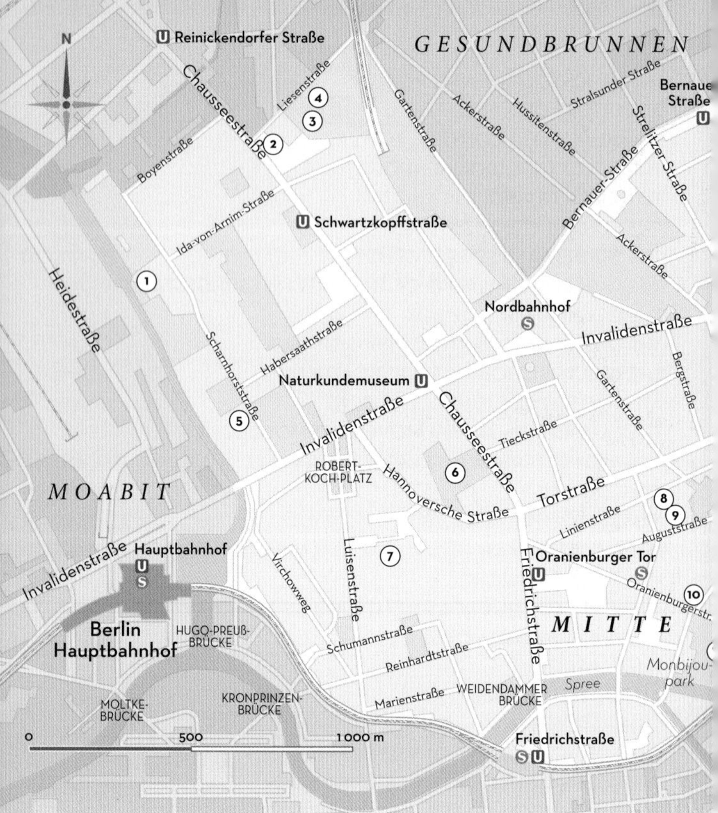

N
Reinickendorfer Straße
GESUNDBRUNNEN
Bernauer Straße
Chausseestraße
Liesenstraße
Gartenstraße
Ackerstraße
Hussitenstraße
Stralsunder Straße
Strelitzer Straße
Boyenstraße
Bernauer Straße
Ida-von-Arnim-Straße
Schwartzkopffstraße
Ackerstraße
Heidestraße
Nordbahnhof
Invalidenstraße
Scharnhorststraße
Habersaathstraße
Naturkundemuseum
Gartenstraße
Bergstraße
Chausseestraße
Invalidenstraße
Tieckstraße
ROBERT-KOCH-PLATZ
Hannoversche Straße
MOABIT
Torstraße
Linienstraße
Auguststraße
Invalidenstraße
Hauptbahnhof
Virchowweg
Luisenstraße
Oranienburger Tor
Friedrichstraße
Oranienburgerstr.
Berlin Hauptbahnhof
HUGO-PREUß-BRÜCKE
Schumannstraße
MITTE
Reinhardtstraße
Monbijou-park
MOLTKE-BRÜCKE
KRONPRINZEN-BRÜCKE
Marienstraße
WEIDENDAMMER BRÜCKE
Spree
0
500
1 000 m
Friedrichstraße

North Mitte

Bernauer-Straße
Ruppiner Straße
Wolliner Straße
Schwedter Straße
Oderberger Straße
Sredzkistraße
Knaackstr.
Schönhauser Allee
Prenzlauer Allee
Danziger Straße
Christburger Straße
Immanuelkirchstraße
Rykestraße
Kollwitzstraße
Knaackstr.
Kastanienallee
Choriner Straße
Brunnenstraße
Fehrbelliner Straße
Zionskirchstraße
Schwedter Straße
PRENZLAUER BERG
Belforter Straße
Wörther Straße
Senefelderplatz
Metzer Straße
Heinrich-Roller-Str.
Greifswalder Straße
Weinbergsweg
Lottumstraße
Straßburger Straße
Prenzlauer Allee
Torstraße
Rosenthaler Platz
Linienstraße
Prenzlauer Berg
Am Friedrichshain
Volkspark Friedrichshain
KOPPEN-PLATZ
Rosa-Luxemburg-Straße
Alte-Schönhauser-Str.
Torstraße
Linienstraße
Rosa-Luxemburg-Platz
Mollstraße
Große Hamburger Straße
Gipsstraße
Sophienstraße
Karl-Liebknecht-Str.
Wadzeckstraße
Höchste Str.
Weinmeisterstraße
Otto-Braun-Straße
Büschingstr.
Mollstraße
Dircksenstraße
Berolinastraße
Hackescher Markt
ALEXANDERPLATZ
Karl-Liebknecht-Str.
Alexanderplatz
Karl-Marx-Allee
Schillingstraße

GÜNTER LITFIN MEMORIAL FOR VICTIMS OF THE WALL

①

The brother of the first victim secures the future of a memorial

Kieler Straße 2, 10115 Berlin
May-Sept: Sat & Sun, 10am–4pm
Free
U6 (Schwartzkopffstraße) / S3, 5, 7, 9 (Hauptbahnhof)

On the corner of Kieler Straße, hidden between residential buildings built after the reunification (nearly all the buildings of Berlin Mitte give an indication of where the demarcation zone between the two borders used to be), is a watchtower typical of the former GDR. Only a few – like those on Erna-Berger-Straße and on Schlesisches Busch – still exist. This former command station (FÜST) offers the same view of the border at the canal as was seen by the East German border police. Back when the tower was not surrounded by buildings (and where the current central station now stands), the entire canal could be seen in one sweeping glance. However, it is the story behind the watchtower that makes this place so unique.

Günter Litfin (1937-1961) was gunned down in cold blood by the East German water police while trying to swim across the canal at the Humboldt harbour (near the current central station) to reach the West. Though always keen to avoid run-ins with authority, Litfin's brother Jürgen was held in custody in a Stasi cell, accused of conspiring in the escape. The Federal Republic of Germany bought his freedom, but Jürgen could not forget his brother's murder at the hands of the SED (Socialist Unity Party of Germany).

After the opening of the Berlin Wall, Jürgen Litfin came across the former command station (at the Kieler Ufer) responsible for giving the fateful orders. He moved heaven and earth to make sure the watchtower was not demolished, despite objections from real estate speculators – renting expensive apartments overlooking a frightening East German watchtower is not easy. On 24 August 2003 Jürgen Litfin inaugurated a site dedicated not only to his brother's memory, but also to the memory of all subsequent victims of the Wall. He also founded an association with a mission to ensure that the watchtower and memorial remain after he passes away. In 2017 this association entrusted the watchtower to the Berliner Mauer foundation. By ensuring its conservation, Jürgen Litfin proved that civil participation can prevent the disappearance of sites attesting to the arbitrary power and murderous terror of the former authoritarian regime.

In 1962 a commemorative stele was unveiled on the west bank of the North Harbour (Nordhafen) near Sandkrug Bridge; it was relocated in 2015 to the central station where Günter Litfin was killed.

RABBIT SILHOUETTES ON CHAUSSEESTRAẞE

②

Crossing borders in fur coats

Chausseestraße 61, 10115 Berlin
kaninchenfeld.de
U6 (Schwartzkopffstraße)

Despite all the security measures in place, the former border in the heart of Berlin was not impassable. Every day there were hundreds, even thousands, of crossings. These were not the rare and heroic crossings that occurred between 1961 and 1989, but rather the countless comings and goings of rabbits.

The demarcation between the former communist bloc and the West corresponds to a long green belt of great ecological value and rich biodiversity. During the Cold War, rabbits comfortably settled in these demarcated zones. With the end of the German Democratic Republic, everything became more complicated: cross-border infrastructures and so-called no man's lands disappeared faster than expected. The border areas were paradise: there were no hunters, nobody looking after their gardens, and no residents. For a long time, troops positioned at the borders had orders not to shoot the rabbits, and the rabbit tunnels heading towards West Germany were tolerated. It was only at the end of the German Democratic Republic that the rabbits became the victims of hunting rifles. Their population had grown to such proportions that there was a risk: by crossing the border unhindered, they could inspire men to do the same.

These days, rabbits are more likely to be spotted in one of the city's largest parks, such as Humboldthain or Tiergarten. But there is still one other place where some 120 rabbits roam around freely: the old border post between Wedding to the west and Mitte to the east.

By installing gleaming brass silhouettes of rabbits in the asphalt near number 61 Chausseestraße, artist Karla Sachse paid a special tribute in 1999 to these long-standing trans-border critters. There were initially many more of these little silhouettes, but rapid urbanisation (always a threat to art in public spaces) meant the brass rabbits ended up sharing the same fate as their organic cousins – in large cities, their numbers have also dwindled considerably, despite the ongoing efforts of the artist's friends.

THE OLD MONUMENTAL CROSS OF THE BERLINER DOM ③

But what is the old cross of the Berliner Dom doing in a cemetery?

Cathedral Parish Cemetery I
Liesenstraße 6, 13355 Berlin
Summer: 8am–6pm; Winter: 9am–5pm
U6 (Schwartzkopffstraße)

At the entrance to the Oberpfarr- und Domkirche zu Berlin (the supreme Parish and Collegiate Church of Berlin) cemetery, visitors who venture into this area, which is set apart and devoid of tombstones, will be intrigued by the presence of an impressive golden cross standing 15 metres high. This cross, weighing 12.5 tonnes, graced the dome of the Berliner Dom (Berlin cathedral) from 1981 to 2006. It was dismantled because of the rust that was corroding its gold-plated copper coating, thus jeopardising the stability of the cross, which could have toppled over in a storm or high winds: it is likely that the alloy of noble metals used in making the cross (copper and steel), and the use of sub-standard steel in particular, caused this premature deterioration.

Stefan Felmy, the architect in charge of the renovation of the Dom, insisted that the cross be placed in the Liesenstraße cemetery: it had

indeed belonged to Berlin cathedral, and had been almost completely demolished during the construction of the Berlin Wall which was to run through it (see below).

Today a plaque at the base of the cross testifies to the harrowing past of these cemeteries, in addition to the new symbolism of the cross, commemorating the victims of the Berlin Wall and those whose tombstones were demolished when the latter was built.

NEARBY

Remains of the Berlin Wall in cemetery I of the cathedral parish (4)

Part of the cathedral parish cemetery I and the two neighbouring cemeteries (the cemetery of St Hedwig and that of the French Reformed church) were surrounded for 28 years by the inner and outer sides of the Wall.

Some remains of the Wall can still be seen here. On the corner of Liesenstraße and Gartenstraße, to the east of Liesenbrücken, there is a piece of the outer side of the wall (in this case superimposed on the wall of St Hedwig cemetery).

On the eastern border of the same cemetery, a 200-metre-long section of the Wall consisting of concrete slabs supported by metal pylons has also been preserved along the railway line. Finally, a short section of the inner wall still remains standing at its western end.

THE WINDOWS OF THE INVALIDS' HOUSE

⑤

Windows for the war-wounded

Invalidenstraße 35, 10115 Berlin
U6 (Naturkundemuseum)

Frederick II of Prussia, known as Frederick the Great, might have been a wiser tyrant than many other monarchs, but that did not stop him from going to war. When they weren't killed immediately on the battlefield or didn't die in horrendous agony like one soldier that Frederick II scolded and ordered to "die with dignity", many of the king's soldiers came back wounded from the three wars he waged against Austria to reclaim Silesia, as well as the War of the Bavarian Succession.

During the 18th century, all those who came back crippled from these wars could not count on social welfare or unemployment benefits: Frederick the Great, therefore, built them a house where all their needs would be met, and in return they had to work to whatever extent they could.

The disabled soldiers made sure to keep this promise: a large part of the New Palace in Potsdam was actually built by them. The construction of the New Palace was meant to prove that, even after the third Silesian war (known throughout Europe as the Seven Years' War), Prussia had not been worn down. During the guided tour of the marble hall in the New Palace, you will notice a number of defects in the construction, such as evident cracks in the panelling, which are undoubtedly attributed to the disabled soldiers.

The Royal House of Invalids was inaugurated on 15 November 1748 in the presence of the king, who was warmly welcomed by the 631 veterans who had fought during the first two Silesian wars. Food and accommodation were provided to the boarders, who were also given clothing and attended by doctors. They could also pray to God in the chapel of their choice, Protestant or Catholic, and train to learn new trades, such as that of livestock breeder, brewer, or distiller in the various surrounding buildings. It was only later that they were requested to build the palace.

What about the soldiers who could no longer use their legs and were confined to the ancestor of today's wheelchair? In order to enable them to enjoy the view, windows overlooking the street and the courtyard were built close to floor level, as can still be seen today. According to the king, being able to look out onto what was still a bit of countryside on the doorstep of the city of Berlin had the power of "regenerating the body and the mind".

For those who were unable to follow this programme, the remaining option was the nearby Invalids' Cemetery.

LIGHTING INSTALLATION OF JAMES TURRELL

⑥

World-class contemporary art in a cemetery

Dorotheenstädtischer Cemetery I Chapel
Chausseestraße 126, 10115 Berlin
evfbs.de
Sept–May: guided tours only, see website for hours
U6 (Naturkundemuseum)

In the heart of the historic Dorotheenstadt cemetery is a rather peculiar art installation. Since 2015, the chapel located near the main entrance (near the tombs of such illustrious individuals as Bertolt Brecht, Georg Wilhelm Friedrich Hegel and Christa Wolf) has housed the work of American artist James Turrell, one of the main representatives of the Light and Space movement.

In collaboration with architects and technicians of the Lichtplaner planning office, Turrell created an impressive lighting installation that includes ten different programmes, eight of which are static and succeed each other throughout the day, illuminating the chapel in various shades. When these programmes are activated, the colour of the altar changes depending on the liturgical seasons: red for Pentecost; green for Ordinary Time; purple for Advent and Lent; and white for Easter and Christmas.

The chapel was built between 1927 and 1928 to complement the space dedicated to the cemetery; it underwent several modifications during the GDR era. Following the restructuring of the building between 2013 and 2015 by the Berlin architectural firm Nedelykov Moreira, the inside was entirely reorganised in order to adapt it to the light effects projected by Turrell.

The incredible lighting programme can be enjoyed by taking part in a guided tour, which always starts half an hour before sunset – opening times vary depending on the time of the year. The guide outlines some of the key moments of the cemetery's history, explains various technical details about Turrell's installation, and briefly recounts the artist's life. Throughout, the chapel is illuminated in blue, while the altar and the apse both change colour every two minutes.

On the second part of the tour, visitors can sit and contemplate the chapel in silence. Coloured light fluctuates at a rapid pace, which, along with the natural light filtering through the windows and the glass tympanum, produces a breathtaking vision in this sacred place.

ANIMAL ANATOMICAL THEATRE ⑦

Elevator to the final act

Philippstraße 12–13, 10115 Berlin
Tue–Sat: 2pm–6pm
U6 (Oranienburger Tor)

Hidden away in the Charité, Berlin's university hospital, the animal anatomical theatre is an impressive building built in 1790 by Carl Gotthard Langhans, who found his inspiration in Andrea Palladio's Villa Rotonda in Italy. The bull skulls among the bas-reliefs over the outer windows hint at the building's purpose.

This type of theatre emerged across Europe to satisfy the growing interest in surgery and the human body. Berlin already had the anatomical theatre of the Collegium Medico-Chirurgicum, located since 1713 in the nearby Charité building complex. However, demonstrations performed on human bodies were not sufficient to meet the needs of the army: to the ruling class, animals used for military purposes – mainly horses and bulls – were just as important as soldiers. Therefore, in order for veterinarians to acquire the necessary knowledge, a second theatre dedicated to the dissection of animals was built.

Nowadays, Berlin's human anatomical theatre and the original building of the Charité complex no longer exist, but the building still referred to in German as "TAT" gives an authentic idea of what these theatres were like. At the entrance, a small permanent exhibition details the history of the building and its architectural elements. Markings in the middle of the floor outline the area where the manually operated elevator hoisted the dead animals. And in addition to the particularly steep tiers of seats, the main attraction of the auditorium is its domed ceiling and the remarkable animal-themed grisaille paintings found there.

Since 2012, the Hermann von Helmholtz Center for Cultural Techniques (HKZ) uses the "TAT" as an innovative exhibition showroom and a centre for exchanges between scientific culture and the practice of exhibition making.

In contrast to the many human anatomical theatres (there are eight in Germany alone), there were only half a dozen animal anatomical theatres across the whole of Europe.

For more information about the theatres see the following double-page spread.

Anatomical theatres through history

An anatomical theatre (*Theatrum Anatomicum* in Latin) is a room dedicated to the teaching of human anatomy to medical students. The first ever amphitheatre was built in 1594 at the university of Padova (Italy), but Greek physician Herophilus of Chalcedon was already performing public dissections on human corpses at the Alexandria School of Medicine in Egypt in the year 300BC. These dissections were initially forbidden then later authorised again during the Renaissance in western countries.

During the 15th century, dissections were performed in small improvised rooms, such as in the former hospital of the Royal Monastery of Santa María of Guadalupe (Spain), home to a prestigious medical school that trained famous surgeons and was granted a papal bull to perform *anathomías* or dissections.

The discoveries of the great anatomist Vesalius (1514-1564) marked the beginning of a new era. During the 16th century, anatomy became a very popular discipline not only among students, but also with the wider public. The first temporary anatomical theatres in Italy were based on a structure similar to that of amphitheatres of the Roman Empire. When dissections were abolished, the theatres were systematically destroyed. French anatomist Charles Estienne – known as Carolus Stephanus in Latin and Charles Stephens in English – later introduced a new architectural style in Paris, which remained very popular until the 19th century.

As the study of anatomy evolved, permanent anatomical theatres emerged. During the 16th and 17th centuries, two different design models came to the fore: those of the university of Padova and those of the university of Bologna. While both models incorporated wooden constructions within the largest building of their university, their architectural characteristics diverged.

In 1594 the first permanent anatomical theatre of the University of Padova was created by Girolamo Fabrici of Acquapendente; it took the form of a funnel (a truncated inverted cone) and could welcome up to 200 visitors. The theatre was in use for 278 years before being transformed into a museum. It became the reference model for a number of other amphitheatres: Leiden (Netherlands, 1597); Uppsala (Sweden, 1620); Copenhagen (Denmark, 1640); Groningen (Netherlands, 1654); Kiel (Germany, 1666); Amsterdam (Netherlands, 1691); Altdorf (Germany, 1650); Berlin (Germany, 1720); and Halle (Germany, 1727).

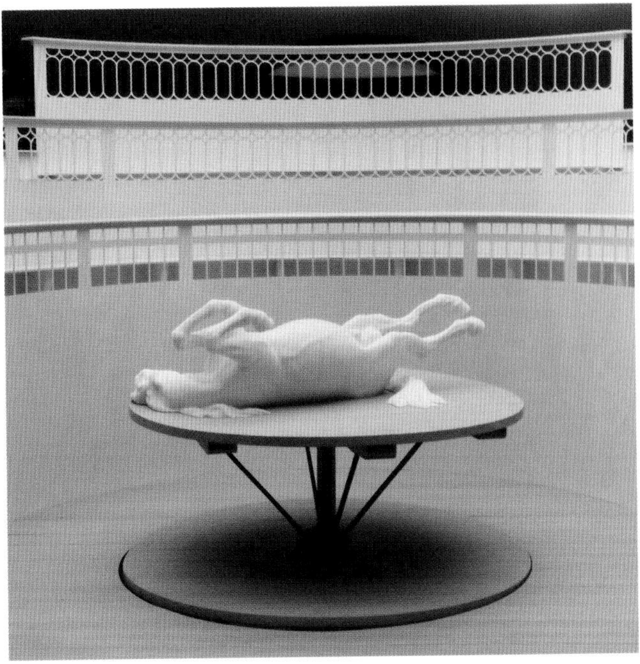

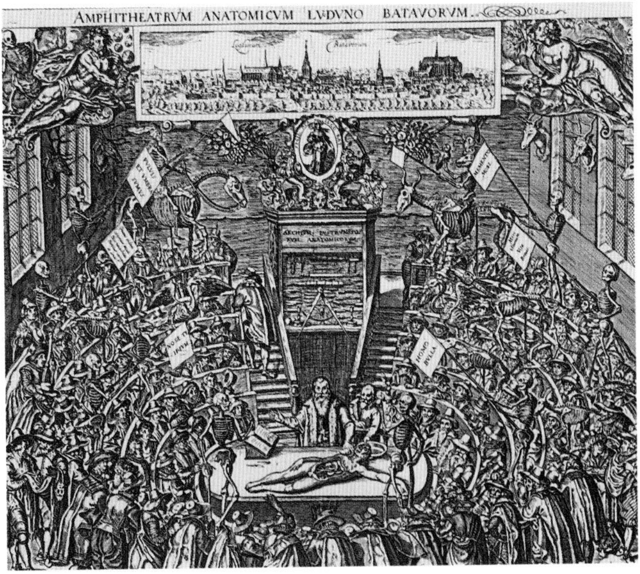
AMPHITHEATRVM ANATOMICVM LVDVNO BATAVORVM

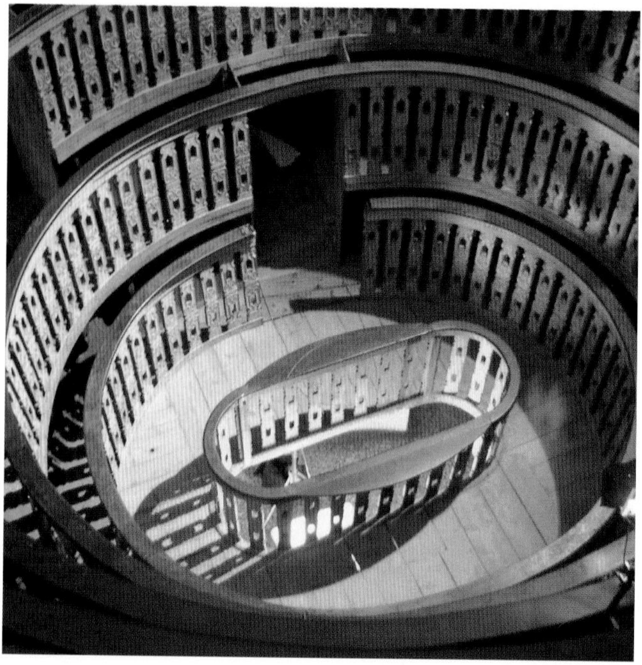

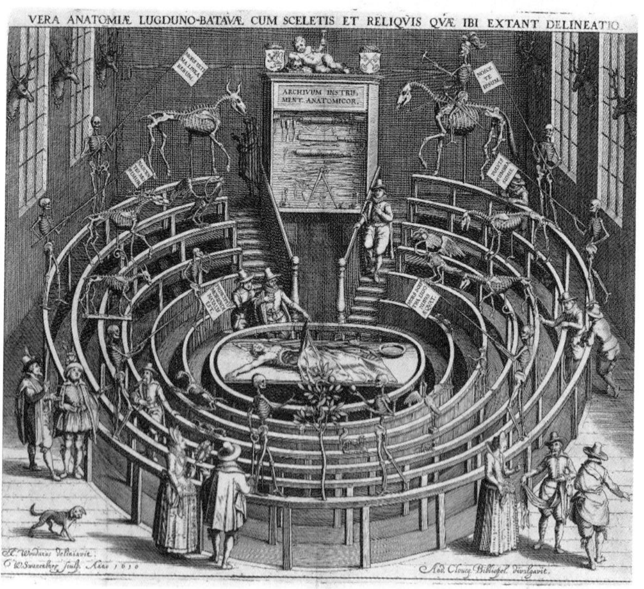
VERA ANATOMIÆ LUGDUNO-BATAVÆ CUM SCELETIS ET RELIQVIS QVÆ IBI EXTANT DELINEATIO.
ARCHIVUM INSTRU-
MENT. ANATOMICOR.
Nosce te ipsum.
And. Clouck Bibliopol. divulgavit.

The other main architectural style for permanent amphitheatres followed that of the amphitheatre of Bologna, built in 1637 by the architect Antonio Paolucci. Rectangular in shape, like many medieval meeting places, it was decorated with magnificent wooden panels and sculptures depicting famous physicians of history. One anatomical theatre influenced by the Bologna model is the theatre of Ferrare (1731).

During the 18th century, considerable modifications were made to the structure of anatomical buildings. The first autonomous anatomical theatre was built in Saint-Côme (France) by the Royal Academy of Surgery of Paris in 1694. The academy later became the *Ecole de Chirurgie* (School of Surgery) and relocated to another building built by architect Jacques Gondoin. The design of the Grand Amphithéâtre (1768-1775) was influenced by the Pantheon in Rome, particularly apparent in its cul-de-four vault and demi-rose window. It could accommodate more than 1,400 visitors. In such a monumental environment, the corpse on the table and the professor performing the demonstration appeared almost in miniature. The school building was intended to evoke a sanctuary dedicated to Asclepius, the Greco-Roman god of medicine.

New methods for the preservation of human corpses required additional space to ensure the storage, preparation, maceration, investigation and exhibition of the corpses. All these requirements meant that the relevance of the traditional *Theatrum Anatomicum* was limited.

Nevertheless, a number of notable new theatres were built during this era: Barcelona (1762); Frankfurt (1776); Mainz (1798); Montpellier (1804); London (1822); Erlangen (1826); Munich (1826); Dorpat (1827); Göttingen (1828); Tübingen (1832); Zurich (1842); Greifswald (1854); Berlin (1863); Fribourg (1867); Bonn (1872); Leipzig (1875); Prague (1876); Rostock (1876); Strasburg (1877); Breslau (1897); Marburg (1902); Basel (1921); Helsinki (1928); and Sofia (1929).

The evolution of audiovisual equipment gradually led to a revolution; anatomical auditoriums eventually became mere screening rooms. In 1872 the German physiologist Czermak (1828-1873) built what he called the "Spectatorium" in Leipzig. This institute, which comprised modern and comfortable audiovisual rooms, marked the definitive end of the traditional *Theatrum Anatomicum*.

THE MUSEUM OF SILENCE

An artistic space where silence reigns supreme

Linienstraße 154, 10119 Berlin
Tue–Sun 2pm–7pm
Free entry
S1, 2, 25, 26 (Oranienburger Straße)

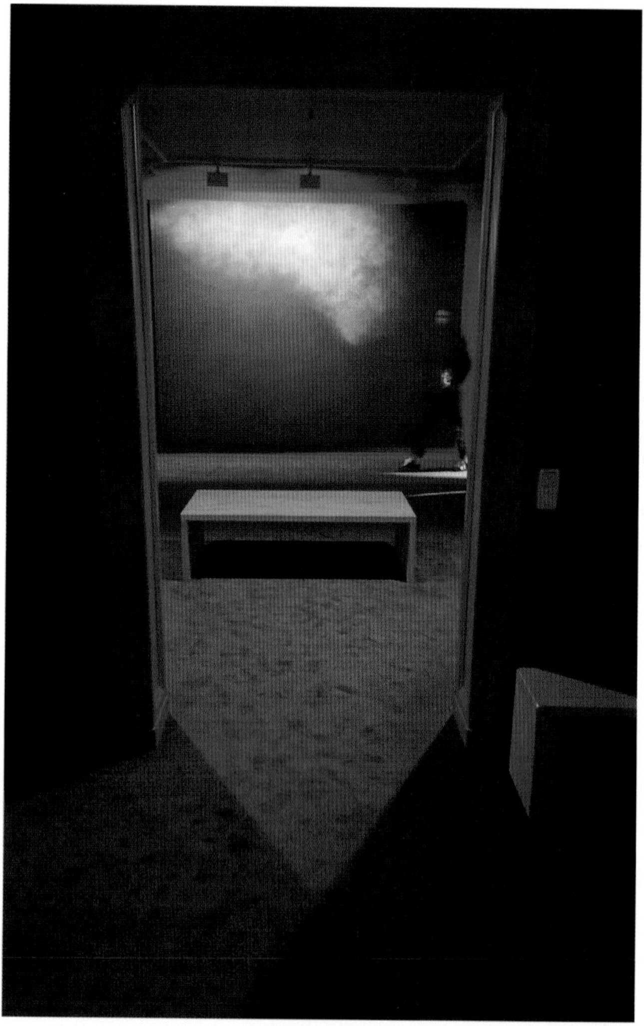

Founded in 1994 by the Russian painter Nikolai Makarov, the Museum of Silence is one of the most unique exhibition spaces in the city. This little museum located at the heart of the Scheunenviertel (the Barn Quarter), Berlin's former Jewish quarter, was designed to be a space of quiet contemplation. It is modelled on the Rothko Chapel in Houston (Texas, USA), which exhibits fourteen paintings by the artist Mark Rothko and aims to be a sacred space devoid of any specific religious connotations.

Unlike the Rothko Chapel, which is one vast circular room, the Museum of Silence is made up of three small rooms. The first room is reserved for an exhibition of seven architectural models made in 2014 by internationally recognised architects, such as Michael Marshall, Stephan Braunfels, Sergei Tchoban and Franco Stella. The purpose of each project is to further the concept of a meditative structure that can only welcome a single work of art.

The second room, and the actual heart of the museum, the Room of Silence, is hidden from sight by a curtain. Here, the walls and ceiling are entirely painted red, and a simple white bench has been placed at the centre to enable visitors to contemplate the unique painting presented here, which occupies almost the entire wall. The painting by Nikolai Makarov, an abstract landscape in sepia tones, invites the viewer to enjoy a moment of peace and meditation.

The third room is also in line with the museum's artistic philosophy and only features a single painting, also by Makarov.

Thanks to the incredibly effective soundproofing of each room, visitors are plunged into almost complete silence – a surreal sensation of isolation in the heart of a bustling city.

In collaboration with the Museum of Silence, a new exhibition space dedicated to Xenia Mawrizki, a Ukranian teacher who emigrated to Germany and spent decades promoting Russian culture, was opened to the public in 2014 on the mezzanine level of the building. The Sergej Mawrizki Foundation, which owes its name to the artist's son and whose president is Nikolai Makarov, supports artistic and cultural projects that aim to strengthen dialogue between Germany and the countries of the former Soviet Union.

THE PAVEMENT ON AUGUSTSTRAßE 69

(9)

An astonishing detail

Auguststraße 69, 10117 Berlin
S1, 2, 25, 26 (Oranienburger Straße)

Very few passers-by on the bustling Auguststraße notice a small but surprising and quirky detail on the pavement in front of number 69 : on a section a few metres long, the pavement suddenly swerves literally from its axis. It is as if a complete piece of the pavement has been pushed 7.5 degrees in a clockwise direction.

Designed by the Brazilian artist Renata Lucas in 2010, this surprising work of art was created for the exhibition of the Kunst-Werke Institute of Contemporary Art in Berlin, and was the winner of the Schering Foundation art prize. It is officially called *Cabeça E Cauda De Cavalo* (Head and tail of a horse).

THE TADSHIKISCHE TEESTUBE'S HISTORIC DECOR

A copy of the Soviet pavilion for the 1974 Leipzig Trade Fair

Oranienburger Straße 27, 10117 Berlin
0 30 / 204 11 12; tadshikische-teestube.de
Mon 4pm–10pm; Tue–Fri 4pm–11pm; Sun 12noon–10pm
S1, 2, 25, 26 (Oranienburger Straße)

Located within an elegant courtyard of Oranienburger Straße 27, hidden from the street, the Tadshikische Teestube (Tajik Tea House) is an amazing place. Amongst the charms of this oriental tea house are patterned sandalwood columns, multicoloured Persian carpets and an incredible chandelier. While the place is not a secret as such, few know about its curious past.

All the furniture and decoration once belonged to the Soviet pavilion devoted to the Central Asian republics of Tajikistan, Kazakhstan and Uzbekistan (then part of the former Soviet Union) at the 1974 Leipzig Trade Fair. While the organisers claimed to have replicated a traditional Tajik tea house, some sources have speculated that this was in fact an actual tea room that was brought from the Tajik capital Dushanbe to Germany especially for the event. Two years later, instead of returning to its home country, the Tadshikische Teestube was gifted to the German-Soviet Friendship Society and installed on the first floor of the Palais am Festungsgraben, a stone's throw from Unter den Linden, home to the organisation's headquarters in 1950. The tea house remained in the Prussian building for nearly forty years; since 1991 it has served as the restaurant of the Theater im Palais, a chamber theatre founded just a few months after the German reunification.

In 2012 the Tadschikische Teestube was once again dismantled and transferred here, next to the New Synagogue.

THE STONE OF MONBIJOU PARK

⑪

The last stone

Monbijouplatz, 10178 Berlin
S3, 5, 7, 9 (Hackescher Markt)

Two paths cross each other more or less in the middle of Monbijou Park. Nobody pays it much attention, but in the northeast angle is a large stone whose central oval medallion and symmetrical arabesques representing plants recall part of a Baroque façade. This stone is in fact the last remnant of the castle that stood here until 1951. This vestige clearly comes from the demolished façade of the castle, probably the ledge above the only row of windows, or the railing along the roof.

In the gardens of the Great Elector, where the very first potatoes of Brandenburg were planted (for their distinctive flowers), there used to be only a summer residence. In 1706 Frederick I had a small single-story castle built here for his mistress, the Duchess of Wartenberg. As of 1710, Crown Princess Dorothea, wife of Frederick William I of Prussia (the "Soldier King"), occupied this small castle. Here, her son Fritz, the future Frederick the Great, could play the flute in peace without being bothered by his father.

Once Fritz became king, he designed for his mother a beautiful park around the castle, with its own jetty where sumptuous Rococo parties were held. She nicknamed her castle and park "Mon Bijou" (from the French "my jewel").

Under Emperor William II the pleasure palace slowly decayed and was converted into a museum dedicated to the Hohenzollern royal dynasty. Like West Germany, the German Democratic Republic was keen to make a clear break from its past, and in 1951 the government had the castle demolished.

THE HANDSHAKE ON SOPHIENSTRAßE 12

Let's shake hands, comrade!

Sophienstraße 18, 10557 Berlin
U8 (Weinmeisterstraße)

With its beautifully restored façade, the house at 18 Sophienstraße stands out from its rather gloomy neighbours. It is undoubtedly due to its communist past that this house drew particular attention in the days of the German Democratic Republic: behind the arcades of the entrance porch in its inner courtyard is where, during the revolution of November 1918, the first Spartacist protests took place after Karl Liebknecht and Rosa Luxemburg made their powerful speeches. The emblem that embodies this moment, seen here on the wall above the pillar between the porch's two larges arcades, is a handshake.

The interlocked hands on the façade are only indirectly linked to those of the Socialist Unity Party of Germany (SED), formed in 1946 when the SPD (Social Democratic Party) and the KPD (Communist Party) merged. Indeed, the handshake emblem existed well before that and was linked to the Berlin Artisans' Association.

Founded in 1846, the Berlin Artisans' Association aimed to give the working classes a voice. Members voted for their own committee and together they set the association's objectives. Two years after its creation, the association already had 1,000 members. Its initial aim was the intellectual education of artisans, to enable them to think and act independently while flattering the incumbent authority so as to avoid state censorship: the association's bylaws stated that moral and intellectual life within the handicrafts sector should foster patriotism, encourage respect and compliance with the laws, as well as love for and faithfulness to the monarch. In reality, the association's original emblem represented two hands holding a sword.

With 3,000 members, the Berlin Artisans' Association was in fact a breeding ground for future revolutionaries, and it turned into a secret army of the working class, proving particularly active during the 1848 revolution. In light of the difficulties establishing a democracy during the Frankfurt Parliament, the first elected National Assembly came together in Saint Paul's Church. It quickly quenched the popular uprising that could not resist the retaliation of the King's well-armed troops. Political associations were forbidden in 1849, and it was only in 1859 that the association was allowed to reunite. On this occasion, the sword, considered too martial, was removed from the emblem above the arcades of the entrance.

Despite this, the association remained very political. In fact, as history has shown, it remained so political that the Nazis also decided to dissolve it.

THE WHITE CROSS OF SAINT MARY'S CHURCH

(13)

God does not forget

Karl-Liebknecht-Straße 8, 10178 Berlin
S3, 5, 7, 9 (Alexanderplatz)

Dating back to 1270, the medieval Church of Saint Mary is hardly a secret. But not many are aware of the discrete cross carved in white stone to the left of the main entrance.

Long ago, the rival houses of Wittelsbach and Habsburg were competing for control in the Holy Roman Empire. Pope John XXII, an enemy of the Wittelsbachs, stirred up discord across the towns within their territories. It was in this context that on 16 August 1324 (or 1325) the Provost Nikolaus von Bernau made a passionate speech in Saint Mary's Church against the young Prince Elector of the Wittelsbach family, a speech that was to prove fatal to him.

Admittedly, there is no certainty that the provost was even able to hold his sermon in the church. Was he dragged out of the building to be put to death? Did patricians close to the Wittelsbach family plan the coup and incite the people to perpetrate this abomination? Or was the assassination ordered by the margrave himself? Nobody knows for sure, but one thing is certain: Nikolaus was beaten to death by the mob and his body was burned on site. It is even said that the fire was lit a second time to get rid of the remains entirely.

The pope was furious, but it took a year for the sentence of excommunication he had promulgated in Avignon to reach Berlin. The divine services, access to the churches, the last sacraments, and the presence of a priest at weddings and funerals were now all forbidden by His Holiness. However, the Franciscans and Dominicans of Cölln were still able to perform their pastoral responsibilities to the community that had not been involved either in these quarrels or in the assassination perpetrated by a few fanatics. This time, the civil jurisdiction, which should have dealt with the case of lynching by convening a judicial assembly in the old town hall to make a court ruling, kept its silence. As a sign of repentance, a white cross and an ever-burning lamp were installed in the church.

The purchase of papal indulgences brought absolution to the city and cleared it from the smear that had plagued it up until 1345. The lamp that was supposed to burn eternally has since disappeared, leaving five small holes in the white cross.

HONI'S WINDOW

⑭

Why does this building façade only have one window?

Memhardstraße 8, 10178 Berlin
U2, 5, 8 (Alexanderplatz)

Based on the number of bells at the entrance, the block at number 2 Memhardstraße in Mitte includes 120 apartments. The "Memi" building – as it is affectionately known among its inhabitants – stands 30 metres tall and 40 metres wide. There is a legend linked to one of its windows.

Despite the hundreds of windows dotting its façades, the lone window on the eighth floor, on the side overlooking Alexander Platz, clearly stands out. If neighbours are to be believed, this window looks out of the apartment of one of the daughters of the Chairman of the State Council, Erich Honecker, who many nicknamed Honi. But did the apartment belong to his daughter Erika, born from his first marriage, or his daughter Sonja, born of an illegitimate union? Whatever the answer, the person occupying this apartment was evidently able to add a window to her initially windowless bathroom. Some even say that Erich Honecker himself monitored his people's activities from this observation post.

According to another source, the apartment in question belonged to the daughter of Erich Mielke, head of the East German Ministry for State Security, the Stasi. When asked about it, the head of the Berlin-Mitte housing association responded that the housing plans are allegedly different from one floor to another, especially among the top floors. According to him, the window has always been there. But oddly enough, he was referring to an apartment on the ninth floor, whereas the window in question is located on the eighth.

Not so long ago, drug dealers would ply their trade around the four entrances of the building and in its stairwells, which were also sought-after places to do drugs discreetly. It has been said that the problem was resolved by changing the lighting in the corridors and stairwells, making it more difficult for junkies to see their veins and inject themselves.

THE LITFAß COLUMN ON MÜNZSTRAßE 15

Monuments to a platform for exchange

Münzstraße 2, 10178 Berlin
U8 (Weinmeisterstraße)

The portrait of Ernst Theodor Litfaß engraved in the cast-iron column standing in Münzstraße near Alexanderplatz pays tribute to the inventor of other columns bearing his name. But only those of an older generation may still remember the inventor of the first advertising platform.

At a young age, Litfaß found himself at the head of a successful family printing company. He rapidly demonstrated his flair for business: remembering what he had seen in Paris during a study trip 20 years earlier, he developed a new technique to print large format (6 x 9 metres) advertising posters, which he sold to his clients along with the corresponding advertising platform. By the mid 19th century, Berlin was drowning in the vast sea of posters plastered across the city.

At the time, public urinals in the French capital were an issue. In an effort to address the problem, the city's authorities built cylindrical structures from wooden panels so that men could urinate out of sight without offending anyone. The bare outer walls of these urinals encouraged illegal flyposting. This inspired Litfaß to improve their barrel-shaped design, and the result was much more elegant than the original: a smooth column was set to the side of the urinal or the small municipal fountain installed in the middle of the structure. Litfaß presented this new concept to the head of the Berlin police, Karl Ludwig von Hinkeldey.

From that moment on, posting was only authorised on the Litfaß columns, subject to payment, and flyposting was immediately prohibited in Berlin. In exchange for this police order, Litfaß was required to post municipal advertisements free of charge, as a result of which at least ten memorials were constructed in his name, even though the 4,000 Litfaß columns that can be found all across Berlin are already, in their own way, monuments to him.

There is another tribute to Ernst Theodor Litfaß by the Hackescher Markt: a white column topped with a golden crown bearing the inscription "Litfaßsäule" (Litfaß column).

SIGNS OF RESISTANCE ON THE UMWELTBIBLIOTHEK

16

A church that truly resisted

Zionskirchplatz, 10119 Berlin-Mitte
Wed–Sat 1pm–6pm, Sun 12noon–5pm (from November to Easter, 12noon–4pm), ascent of the tower €1
U2 (Senefelder Platz)

In the gallery on the first floor, which overlooks the nave of the Zionskirche, purple, red and green marks protected by plexiglass screens are still visible on the parquet floor. They bear witness to the resistance activities of the Umweltbibliothek, founded in 1986.

This group collected books and magazines on the environment and human rights which were forbidden in the GDR, and made them available to those who were interested in their publication *Umweltblättern* (later to become the *Telegraph*). The archives of the Umweltbibliothek were stored in the cellar of the church.

As for the galleries on the first floor, they provided enough space for its members to paint a stencil of slogans for their demonstrations. With their red outline, the letters "F" and "R" (maybe for *FREIHEIT*, freedom?) can be discerned.

On 17 October 1987, East Berlin's punk group Die Firma (several members of which would later form the group Rammstein) were performing a concert in the church when it was violently interrupted by the skinheads of the Ministry of Security. On 25 November 1987, the Stasi stormed a religious building for the first time, giving a boost to the pacifist revolution in the GDR.

Another form of resistance: the Red Orchestra

At the entrance to the church, on the right at the chevet, there is a square, metal grid just above the floor near the wall. It is the ventilation grid of a cellar which played an important role in the German Resistance against the Nazis. It contained a radio which enabled Schulze-Boysen to warn the Soviets in 1942 of an imminent Nazi attack. In 1942, the organisation, which was made up of Franco-Belgian and German networks, and was referred to as the Red Orchestra by the Nazi secret services, was dismantled by the Gestapo. Around 50 members of the network's Berlin division were executed, including the Harnack and Schulze-Boysen couples.

Before the Nazis assassinated him, from 1931 to 1944 Dietrich Bonhoeffer had been the pastor of the Zionskirche, which had become a recruiting ground for the resistance. Its cellars provided an ideal hiding place. This is where, from 1940 onwards, members of the resistance regularly gathered under the leadership of Mildred and Arnd Harnack and Libertas and Harro Schulze-Boysen, to plan actions against the regime. Many artists, intellectuals, students, ordinary citizens and workers joined their ranks to set up hideouts for people on the run or in danger, and also helped by supplying them with false identity papers and money for their escape.

N
Reinhardtstraße
WEIDENDAMMER BRÜCKE
Monbijoupark
Friedrichstraße
FRIEDRIC BRÜC
Bundestag
Paul-Löbe-Allee
Spree
MARSCHALL-BRÜCKE
Dorotheenstraße
Reichstag
Dorotheenstraße
Charlottenstraße
SCHLOSS-BRÜCKE
Scheidemannstraße
Brandenburger Tor
PARISER PLATZ
Unter den Linden
Oberwallstraße
Straße des 17. Juni
PLATZ DES 18. MÄRZ
Brandenburger Tor
Französische Straße
Behrenstraße
Französische Straße
Markgrafenstraße
MITTE
Tiergarten
Ebertstraße
Hannah-Arendt-Str.
Wilhelmstraße
Jägerstraße
GENDARMEN-MARKT
Hausvogteiplat
Taubenstraße
Stadtmitte
Mohrenstraße
TIERGARTEN
Mohrenstraße
Kronenstraße
Lennestraße
Friedrichstr.
Leipziger Straße
Voßstraße
Charlottenstraße
POTSDAMER PLATZ
LEIPZIGER PLATZ
Leipziger Straße
Krausenstraße
Potsdamer Straße
Potsdamer Platz
Schützenstraße
Zimmerstraße
Stresemannstraße
Niederkirchnerstr.
Rudi-Dutschke-Straße
Linkstraße
Köthener Straße
Wilhelmstraße
Markgrafenstraße
Lindenstraße
Kochstraße/ Checkpoint Charlie
Mendelssohn-Bartholdy-Park
KREUZBERG

South Mitte

Hackescher Markt
ALEXANDERPLATZ
Alexanderplatz
Karl-Liebknecht-Str.
Schillingstraße
Karl-Marx-Allee
Weydemeyerstr.
Lichtenberger Straße
Strausberger Platz
Karl-Marx-Allee
Rathausstraße
Spandauer Straße
Grunerstraße
Alexanderstraße
Schillingstraße
Littenstraße
Klosterstr.
Singerstraße
Stralauer Straße
Jannowitzbrücke
Breite Straße
MÜHLENDAMM-BRÜCKE
Holzmarktstraße
Lichtenberger Straße
Singerstraße
Krautstraße
Andreasstraße
JANNOWITZ-BRÜCKE
INSEL-BRÜCKE
Gertraudenstr.
Fischerinsel
Wallstraße
Rungestraße
Brückenstraße
FRIEDRICHSHAIN
MICHAEL-BRÜCKE
Märkisches Museum
Spittelmarkt
Spree
Holzmarktstraße
Seydelstraße
Köpenicker Straße
Heinrich-Heine-Straße
SCHILLING-BRÜCKE
Alte Jakobstraße
Annenstraße
Sebastianstraße
Heinrich-Heine-Straße
Adalbertstraße
MICHAELKIRCHPLATZ
HEINRICH-HEINE-PLATZ
Engeldamm
Köpenicker Straße
Oranienstraße
Bethaniendamm
MARIANNEN-PLATZ
Moritzplatz
0
500
1 000 m

FRONTAGE OF THE OLD HOFBEAMTENHAUS WILHELM II

①

Signs of the times

Geschwister-Scholl-Straße 5, 10117 Berlin
S1, 2, 3, 5, 7, 9, 25, 26 / U6 (Friedrichstraße)

At number 5 Geschwister-Scholl-Straße there is a building, whose architectural style stands out among the more modern buildings surrounding it. If its neglected appearance, in the very heart of Mitte, might seem rather strange, a closer look will reveal that it is not neglect, but actually a careful renovation project.

A sign standing between two windows on the ground floor confirms this: the building was restored from 2009-2010 thanks to funding from the German State and the Land of Berlin. The originality of the project resides in the fact that the marks left by successive periods in the past have deliberately been kept visible on the original building.

The entrance gate is undoubtedly the element that bears the most historical signs of the 19th century in Berlin. Two monumental pilasters support an elegant pediment decorated with a lion's head and the imperial monogram of Kaiser William II: an entwined W and R signifying "Wilhelminus Rex", above a 'two' written in Roman numerals. The detail speaks volumes about the history of the building designed in 1903 as staff lodgings for some of the court's high-ranking officials.

Above the gate, as on other parts of the frontage, several holes can be seen which were left by projectiles during the Second World War. They were conserved during the restructuring work, as a reminder of the terrible times that the city had endured.

Some parts of the first floor, in particular the oriel window on the right, also contain bricks of a lighter shade than the rest of the rendering. These are emergency repairs made just after the end of the fighting.

Higher up, between two windows of the third floor, the building has kept traces of neglect from the GDR era. This section of the wall also suffered considerable damage and was repaired with rather basic bricks.

PIPES OF THE LUSTGARTEN RIVERBANK WALL

②

The water from the Spree which supplies the fountain and flows back to the Spree ...

Lustgarten
Unter den Linden 1, 10117 Berlin
Bus TXL, 100, 200, N2 (Lustgarten)

If, for an instant, you turn to look away from the garden and the cathedral past the Spree canal – the last section of which (from the town's old lock) is also called *Kupfergraben* – and look over to the other side, if you look for long enough, you will notice a strange flow of water which turns out to be a kind of spring, gushing out of the riverbank wall. The luscious green plants and a young tree, hanging onto the stones of the wall, thrive in the fresh water which bubbles out of a crescent-shaped, man-made hole before splashing into the canal.

As there is no stream in the park, we could easily imagine this to be the drains, but the spring water is obviously too clear for that. The reliefs of dolphins which swim round it would suggest that the spout has

a purpose. But isn't that the sound of a large fountain in the distance, attracting selfie-taking tourists, with the water, the cathedral and the ball of the television tower as a backdrop?

In order to understand what links them all together, we must go back in time to the creation of the Lustgarten by Schinkel and Lenné between 1830 and 1834, when the great fountain played a central role. An installation was built (replacing the former great bridge of Pommeranzenbrücke), and was equipped with a steam engine, which was used to pump water from the Spree and carry it to the basin of the Altes Museum. From there, pressurised water was sent down a pipe to the fountain which would project the water 13 metres into the air. The water then flowed through a ditch out of the opening with the decorative dolphins and into the canal of the Spree. In 1893, the fountain was switched off. Later, the Nazis reorganised the park to make a place for processions and events. After the fall of the Wall, Schinkel and Lenné's concept was recreated by installing modern electric pumps which supply the central fountain today. But the water must still end its course somewhere. It still flows through the old ditches which, running safely underground, like the pipes, have survived undamaged into the 21st century.

DOLPHIN SCULPTURE

③

The last remnant of a historic balustrade

Lustgarten, Unter den Linden 1, 10117 Berlin
S (Hackescher Markt) / U2 (Hausvogteiplatz)

Near the Schlossbrücke (palace bridge), on the south-west side of Lustgarten park, there stands a rather lonesome-looking sculpture of a dolphin in a rusty cast-iron frame. The Lustgarten dolphin is indeed the last of the dolphin sculptures that used to decorate the balustrades of the palace bridge after it underwent refurbishment works under the supervision of the architect Karl Friedrich Schinkel in 1824. The bridge's current dolphins are actually just copies.

Schinkel's enhancement works of 1824 were, for the most, part a response to the 1823 catastrophe that took place here (see below).

An unlikely drowning

On 16 November 1823, the Prussian crown prince Frederick William and his wife Elisabeth of Bavaria were to be married in the palace's chapel in Berlin. To celebrate their arrival at the Berlin palace, Frederick William III requested that a large parade and a party in the Lustgarten be organised. The palace's new bridge, whose balustrade had not yet been fitted, was to be inaugurated at the same time with the crossing of the royal couple in a golden carriage. Nobody thought about the audience.

Nothing more than a wooden walkway nailed to the bridge was installed to welcome the onlookers. On the other hand, the area reserved for the couple was large enough to fit seven carriages! Quarrels started to erupt for the best spot on the walkway, and the inevitable happened: the makeshift balustrade broke and the spectators fell into the canal. On top of the fact that many of them did not know how to swim, their heavy winter clothing hampered their movements. As a result, some 22 onlookers drowned that day. However, the unfortunate incident did not seem to weigh on the conscience of King Frederick William III who had none the less organised a meal for the poor as a gesture to celebrate the wedding. Indeed, on his instructions, the publication of obituaries in the local newspapers was forbidden so as not to upset the newlyweds. It is only after the families complained to the ministry in charge that the death notices were eventually authorised.

The world's largest granite bowl ④

Sometimes displaying something for all to see is actually the best way of hiding it. This is the case for the granite bowl in front of the Altes Museum.

Visitors lie down on the grass in the Lustgarten, they sit on the steps or even settle down under the sculpture without paying any sort of attention to the world's largest granite bowl, extracted in one single piece of rough stone during the Biedermeier period, a world away from our current modes of transport and stone working processes.

The huge bowl of Precambrian Swedish Karlshamm granite still has a clearly visible shine to this day. It took two and a half years to polish, and a steam engine was built especially by the Cantian marble mason workshop to carry out this incredible and unprecedented accomplishment.

The painter Johann Erdmann Hummel immortalized this feat in several of his paper and canvas colour paintings that appeared as realistic as photographs (which, at the time, produced nothing more than grey-ish smudges requiring detailed explanations).

The Berlin bowl was the result of an unofficial competition between Frederick William III, king of Prussia, and the British diplomatic envoy, William Spencer Cavendish, sixth Duke of Devonshire, who had ordered a large granite bowl from the Berlin building inspector and stone mason, Christian Gottlieb Cantian. The King of Prussia could not accept seeing his country surpassed and he in turn ordered a bowl from Cantian that naturally had to be much larger than the bowl intended for the British.

Prussia did not have any "national" granite, but as the ice age had pushed the largest blocks of granite to the north, a piece of stone was removed from the Markgrafenstein rock in the Rauhenschen mountains, near the Fürstenwalde forest.

After having been successfully transported along the Spree river and polished in Berlin, the bowl proved too big for the museum's rotunda, which is why it must now face storms, rain, and freezing temperatures outside.

The bowl, which has survived two world wars, only suffered a small fracture and a chip which have both been repaired.

Tombstone of Alexander von der Mark: Was it fratricide? ⑤

During the 19th century, the tombstone of Alexander von der Mark by Johann Gottfried Schadow was considered one of the "wonders of Berlin". Young Alexander von der Mark was not part of ancient nobility, so his tomb was initially located in Saint Dorothea's Church, before being moved during the Second World War. The church no longer exists and the tombstone is now in the *Alte Nationalgalerie* (Old National Gallery, Bodestraße 1–3). Few remember this tragic story.

Born in 1779, Count Friedrich Wilhelm Moritz Alexander von der Mark was the natural son of the Prussian Crown Prince William (who became King Frederick William II of Prussia in 1786) and his official mistress, Wilhelmine Encke, who had been granted the title of Countess von Lichtenau by her lover and lifelong friend during a trip to Italy. The handsome and bright young boy was greatly appreciated by Frederick the Great. In fact, the Latin inscription on his tombstone praises his extraordinary virtues and capacities. At the age of five he wrote a letter to his father that can be admired today in the Marble Palace in Potsdam. The King used to call him *"das Anderchen"* ("the little different one"), and preferred him to Crown Prince Frederick William III. Perhaps this is what led to the demise of the 9-year-old boy. Indeed, the people in mourning suspected poisoning.

Rumours of fratricide loomed above the sumptuous tombstone that boldly expressed the love of grieving parents for their lost child. An urn was placed in his memory in the new garden of the Marble Palace where, it is said, King Frederick William II could still hear the laughter of his *Anderchen*. When Frederick William III became king, one of his first initiatives was to arrest and exile Countess von Lichtenau. This act could easily be interpreted as proof that Frederick William III killed his much more talented and beloved brother.

THE ROSENSTRAẞE MEMORIAL

⑥

Give us our men back!

Rosenstraße 2, 10178 Berlin
S3, 5, 7, 9 (Hackescher Markt)

The Rosenstraße Memorial is a highly symbolic and important piece of political remembrance, perhaps the most important of its kind in Mitte, as it demonstrates that during times of dictatorship, civil disobedience can save lives anytime and anywhere. Carved in stone, the suffering remains palpable. The monument is chilling both in form and substance, but comes alive upon discovering the story behind it.

Until 1942 there was a welfare office and youth service for the Jewish community here. After Himmler's decision to deport all Jews living in the Third Reich to concentration camps, 2,000 male Jews living in mixed marriages were arrested – this included "Mischlings" (persons deemed to be partly Jewish). Hitler had initially granted exceptions and ordered Goebbels to spare Jews in mixed marriages so as to avoid causing a scene in public. However, these orders were ignored by Hitler's enforcers, who preferred to engage in violence and strict adherence to the cause.

The arrests caused the unrest that Hitler had feared. Despite threats by the police, many non-Jewish spouses were unintimidated, and a growing number of them protested in front of the welfare office where their husbands were being kept pending deportation. The police would push the crowds back and the women retreated to the neighbouring streets, only to come back later and demand, "Give us our men back!"

Goebbels, in his capacity as Gauleiter (head of the district), eventually gave in. He released the prisoners and ordered the return of 25 men who had already been sent to Auschwitz-III (Buna-Monowitz). In his report he wrote: "I ask the Sicherheitsdienst (the SS intelligence and policing agency) not to pursue this 'Jewish operation' during such a critical time. We prefer to leave it aside for a few weeks so we can devote ourselves to it better later."

The success of this protest spread throughout the Third Reich. A few weeks later, in Dortmund, some 300-400 people successfully protested the arrest of a soldier. After the war, journalist Georg Zivier, one of the men arrested and for whom his wife had protested, described what some thought was a simple anecdote as "a small torch in the dark that might have become a general uprising". Indeed, 98 per cent of all German Jews who survived the Nazi regime lived in mixed marriages.

THE FOUNDATIONS OF THE "ALTE SYNAGOGUE"

⑦

Traces in the greenery

Heidereutergasse, 10178 Berlin
S3, 5, 7, 9 (Hackescher Markt)

The Heidereutergasse alleyway is so small that it can probably be considered one of the smallest streets in Berlin. On the rather unkempt and dirty plot of land between Heidereutergasse and Rosenstraße, there is a sign offering snippets of information, along with stones in the ground outlining the barely recognisable demarcations of a former synagogue.

The old synagogue represented the culmination of a long-standing dream for the Jewish community of Berlin. Although 50 Jewish families found refuge in the city in 1671 after being expulsed from Vienna, it was only in 1712 that King Frederick William I of Prussia gave them authorisation to build a place of worship. A few ground rules had to be considered, the most important of which was that the synagogue could not be taller than the surrounding wealthy middle-class houses. Unlike other newcomers who were warmly welcomed in Berlin, Jews were given neither plots of land (similar to those made available free of charge to other communities) nor construction material. In 1712, after the acquisition of two neighbouring plots, the construction of an austere rectangular hall with a vaulted ceiling began discreetly.

On 10 September 1714 the synagogue was inaugurated in the presence of the Queen consort in Prussia, Sophia Dorothea of Hanover. It was extended in 1850, but the Jewish community grew so rapidly that the synagogue quickly became cramped – by 1860 the community had 28,000 members. Once the construction of the sumptuous new synagogue on Oranienburger Straße was completed, the old prayer room of Heidereutergasse became known as the *Alte Synagoge* (Old Synagogue) and was slowly forgotten.

Hidden from view, the synagogue escaped the destructive fury of the Nazis during the pogrom of the night of 9-10 November 1938 – Kristallnacht. The last service took place in 1942 while deportations were already underway, and in February 1945 the building was bombed by the Allies. Under East Germany, the ruins were cleared, but the site was left untended. It was only in the year 2000 that the foundations were uncovered.

FOYER OF THE BERLIN COURTHOUSE

(8)

Incredible architecture inside and out

Littenstraße 12–17, 10179 Berlin
Mon–Fri 9am–1pm; ID card required
U2 (Klosterstraße)

While the *Landgericht Berlin* (Berlin Regional Court) courthouse may not be a secret, few are aware that it houses one of the most beautiful interiors in the city.

After security checks at the entrance on Littenstraße (a passport or ID card is required here), visitors are treated to a spectacular sight: a 30.5 metre-high circular foyer richly adorned with eclectic decorations. A sandstone colonnade with shades of red and green surrounds a large central space. Columns on the ground floor and two spiral staircases are embellished with colourful drawings of knights in armour bearing shields. The terracotta floors are decorated with different types of tiles, many of which date back to when the building was built and represent the coats of arms of the royal crown. Twisting figures typical of *Jugendstil* (Art Nouveau) make up the white wrought iron railings of the staircases and balconies, while elsewhere the banisters are decorated with Rococo motifs.

Head upstairs for a closer look at the magnificent chandelier hanging in the middle of the room, and the decorative ceiling arches whose shape and colour recall the canons of Gothic architecture. Measuring nearly 1,000 square metres in total, the foyer can be viewed in all its glory from the upper floors.

Construction work led by architects Paul Thoemer, Rudolf Mönnich and Otto Schmalz began in 1896, and the building was inaugurated in 1904 (written above the entrance gate). The building was intended to house the Civil Chamber of the Berlin Regional Court and the High Court of Mitte. With a total of five kilometres of corridors and 3,000 windows, it used to be one of the biggest buildings in the city. Its façade follows the Baroque style common throughout Southern Germany, with two square towers neatly framing the building on the side of Neue Friedrichstraße (now Littenstraße).

The courthouse suffered serious damage during the bombings of the Second World War and was largely rebuilt during the post-war era. Although not at all damaged, an entire wing of the building was demolished in 1968-69 to create a street: Grunerstraße. During the years of separation, the building was also the GDR's Supreme Court.

Today, several Civil Chambers of the High Court are located at this address, along with the Berlin Regional Court, the largest court in Germany by number of employees.

©Ansgar Koreng

REMAINS OF THE CITY WALLS

⑨

The last traces of the old city wall

Waisenstraße 14–16, 10179 Berlin
S3, 5, 7, 9 (Alexanderplatz) / U2 (Klosterstraße)

The limits of the old town of Cölln run south from Alexanderplatz, and, if on foot, traces can be seen of the oldest constructions in today's Berlin.

Go past the 13th century Notre-Dame church before walking left around Rotes Rathaus, then go down the Jüdenstraße and across the Grünstraße. The centre of the former Jewish quarter, the Große Jüdenhof, is now a car park in the town centre.

If you walk down the Grünstraße to the left, you will come to the church of the Franciscan monastery, in ruins since the last war – traffic drives over its foundations today.

Turn right into a quiet street called Littenstraße to discover the oldest traces of Berlin's architecture that are still standing: the remains of the medieval city wall built around 1250 and which measured 2.5 kilometres in those days, surrounding the 70 hectares of Cölln and Berlin.

On the small section where the streets of Littenstraße and Waisenstraße run parallel to each other, these remains were uncovered

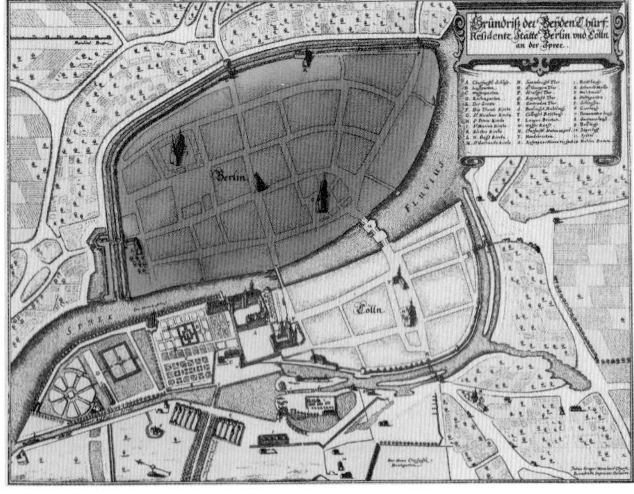

when the ruins of the bombed houses covering them were cleared away in 1948. The Zur letzten Instanz inn building was also part of the old city walls and was used as a *Wiekhaus*, a type of lookout post which was sometimes built into the wall. In 1621, one of the Prince Elector's grooms set up an inn there, the earliest ancestor of the current café-restaurant.

We can get a closer look at what remains of the first walls in the front, back and inside the café: 3 to 6 feet thick (around 1 to 2 metres), they have vertical parts which were added over time and were built either on relatively rough stones or slotted tightly together. The bricks were used to raise the part of the original wall (around two metres high), which is made up of stone rubble taken from fields, giving it a total height of four or five metres.

Some crenelations were added here and there. In addition to the many *Wiekhäuser*, towers measuring up to 25 metres high were built randomly along it, providing a lookout to spot approaching enemies.

In front of the new wall (near today's Littenstraße), two 15-metre wide ditches, separated by ramparts of 7.5 to 10 metres wide, were dug to slow down enemy advances.

As with all urban defence systems, there were *trous-de-loup* (in German, literally "bear traps" – for the future heraldic animal). Some years ago, it was still possible to see traces of the prints of small carnivores, which had been cooked into the red bricks of the monastery. Today, they are being slowly worn away.

THE CRYPT OF THE PAROCHIALKIRCHE

⑩

A perspective of eternity

Klosterstraße 66, 10179 Berlin
0 30 / 526 802 - 135
crossroads@besondere-orte.com
crossroads-berlin.com
Guided tours must be booked at CROSS ROADS (Berlin mit anderen Augen Evangelischer Kirchenkreis Berlin Stadtmitte)
Booking by email or phone
U2 (Klosterstraße)

The crypt can be reached by a narrow, stone spiral staircase a few yards away from the vast nave of the Baroque parish church (Parochialkirche) on Klosterstraße, which was built between 1695 and 1703.

The only crypt in Berlin containing the tombs of lesser nobility and wealthy bourgoisie, its cross-shaped aisles follow the same pattern used in Baroque religious buildings. Stemming from the axes of the cross, some thirty tombs are arranged down the sides. Each burial vault is closed by a simple wooden, slatted gate, giving a glimpse of the interior and allowing some ventilation.

The good ventilation system, which made the Parochialkirche crypt special from the very beginning, has, in fact, largely mummified the fully dressed remains of those who had paid for their resting place there. The

mummies were discovered during the restoration of this crypt which is the only one of its kind in Europe. On the guided tours, visitors can get a closer look at the burial vaults with their stone tombs and wooden coffins and some photos explaining the mummies in more detail.

Visitors can also see the very modern dress, made in a golden-coloured silk satin fabric, with its plunging neckline that was worn by Baroness Louise Albertine von Grappendorf (who died around 1750 at the age of 24). As her funeral took place in winter, her fragile skin was not perforated by maggots.

There is also the cat (also mummified) – lying in the arms of Lorenz Christoph Schneider, the commissioner of the Mint who died in 1715, or the area filled with children's coffins and a vault with a coffin with a window, which had been added to overcome the fear of being buried alive.

During this tour, the macabre story of Else the Red is also referred to. If ever the annual payment (the equivalent of about 40,000 Euros today) was not paid, the bones were buried during the night in the little parish cemetery, where commoners are covered with earth and where robes, as precious as they may have been, turn into humus.

During the 20th century, the crypt, which was not protected, was desecrated countless times. Grave robbers in search of jewellery cut through the gloves of the mummies and the students at the Charité Hospital, encouraged by their professors, used it as a free supply of human skulls. The crypt was finally walled up, which prevented the air from circulating and caused mould to form that archaeologists sometimes refer to as "the pharaoh's curse".

THE GESCHÄFTSHAUS TIETZ 

A rare example of Jugendstil architecture in Berlin

Klosterstraße 64, 10179 Berlin
U2 (Klosterstraße)

At number 64 Klosterstraße, opposite the huge Altes Stadthaus, the Geschäftshaus Tietz represents a splendid example of early 20th-century Berlin architecture.

Visitors strolling down this old street in the historic centre will be surprised by its original sandstone façade.

The unusual aspect of this building is undoubtedly its pillar structure, a type of construction that emerged during the 19th and 20th centuries, and which made it possible to incorporate a large number of windows. Even the ground floor has four windows, which separate the six pillars and let in the light, producing a bright interior environment.

The cornice mouldings, found mainly on the central block, are particularly interesting. They include floral motifs and stylised faces of men and women with Ionic and Corinthian capitals.

These decorative elements, just like the decorations on the wrought iron main door leading to the inner courtyards, are typical of German Jugendstil architecture (an architectural style related to Art Nouveau).

The Geschäftshaus Tietz was built between 1904 and 1906 based on the designs of the architect Georg Lewy. It is one of the rare buildings in the area not to have suffered damage during the Second World War.

Berthold, Georg and Heinrich Tietz, three entrepreneurial brothers in the textile industry, ordered the construction of the building. The words Gebr. Tietz (Tietz Brothers) are carved above the entrance gate while the sides bear the words Berlin and Annaberg, a town in Saxony where the family was originally from (the brothers are not to be confused with the founders of the famous Tietz department store).

The premises of the building were initially rented out to textile companies and used by the owners as a place to resell trimmings until 1933 when the Nazi regime began to attack the Jewish community, to which the Tietz family belonged.

This is where, in 1940, the armed forces set up their headquarters; after the war, the building was used to house the East Berlin land registry offices.

Today, the Geschäftshaus Tietz is protected as a cultural heritage site and provides offices for several small and large businesses.

THE WUSTERHAUSISCHER BÄR

The last witness of Berlin's fortifications

Am Köllnischen Park 5, 10179 Berlin
U2 (Märkisches Museum)

A curious little tower of bricks stands proudly in Cöllnischer Park. The sculpture, which is capped with a roof in the shape of a salad bowl, is no more than 5 metres high from top to bottom. Its modest interior is closed off with a gate and cut open with an arrow slit. The inscription "Wusterhausischer Bär 1718", which was put there in the days of the Prussian king, Frederick William I ("soldier king" and father of "Old Fritz"), does not seem to mean very much. Like most of the sculptures and other architectural remains from old Berlin which are gathered in this park, it no longer stands on its original spot. This place is used as a refuge for stone artefacts which have had to make way for others, without being given a new space in the buildings of the Märkisches Museum (the museum of Mark Brandenburg) or in its interior courtyard.

In the year 2000, visitors could still see an authentic brown bear, the heraldic animal of Berlin, in the bear pit in this park at mealtimes. But the "Bär" (which means bear in German and is pronounced "Behr") of the sculpture has absolutely nothing to do with bears. It would seem that the etymology of the word "Bär" comes from the medieval Latin *barra* or "barrier". They are constructions that were part of the defensive arsenal that was also called "Wehr" in German. A "Bär" was a specific dam of fortifications around Berlin. The dams were set up in the moats, the walls of which were equipped with a defensive tower which were used to protect these moats and block any attacks or sieges that were waged on the fortifications. The tower covered the entire length of the dam, from one side to the other, so effectively that whoever tried to get round it would invariably fall into the water. Of the three pseudo bears ("Bären", in fact "Wehren" and therefore dams) which were operating in Berlin's defensive moats, it was the Bär of Wusterhausen which best stood the test of time. The fortifications were taken down in the 18th century, but the dam continued to operate in the moat known as the green moat (Grüner Graben) by regulating the water coming into the mill. As the dam was on the road to the small town of Königs Wusterhausen, it was called the Wusterhausischer Bär. When the green moat and the dam were filled in, in 1883 and 1884, the tower known as the Wusterhausischer Bär was the only thing left standing in the new Jakobsstraße street. In the plan of conservation measures recommended by the Märkisches Museum, it was dismantled and rebuilt in Cöllnischer Park. This was added to the inscription of 1718: "built in the middle of the first green moat behind bastion VI".

The Bär/Wehr/bear is today the last trace of the, once immense, fortifications of Berlin, which were so impenetrable that they never suffered attacks or sieges.

ERMELER HOUSE BAS-RELIEF

13

Slaves to enrich Berlin

Märkisches Ufer 10, 10179 Berlin
U2 (Märkisches Museum)

Located on the Friedrichs-Gracht quay, the Ermeler House was named after an old tradition typical of port cities. The beautiful bas-relief above the main entrance door depicts a tropical landscape and half-naked men and women harvesting tobacco by hand.

Berlin merchants made a fortune from the tobacco trade. Wilhelm Ferdinand Ermeler, who bought this house in 1824 from a tobacco trader named Neumann, wrote in his diary: "I started with 100 thaler and now, at the age of 56, I already have more than 200,000 [...] Fully deserved."

Along the bas-relief, which already existed at the time Ermeler bought the house, images show tobacco being imported by ships, themselves guarded by white Europeans.

To the right, the two churches of the Gendarmenmarkt indicate that the leaves were destined for sale in Berlin. In the 1690s alone, slave traders in Berlin (the place of residence of prince-electors and where

slave trading had been authorised since the days of the Grand Elector in the 17th century) deported more than 20,000 men, women and children from Africa and sent them to plantations in the southern colonies of the United States.

For a while, Prussia even outnumbered its Dutch and French competitors in terms of human trafficking. At the time, Berlin's rich merchants viewed Africans as savages, animals that could be captured and exploited without remorse. This is in fact what Pastor Gossner used to do through his missions with the (Moravian) Bohemian Bethlehem Church in Berlin.

This work of art, along with the street name that caused controversy in the 1990s (Mohrenstraße), is now considered by many to be racist. Indeed, the term "mohr" in German has the same negative connotation as the word "nigger" in English.

Built during the 18th century at number 11 Breiten Straße, the Ermeler House was destroyed in 1966-1967 and rebuilt in its current location in 1968-1969. During its reconstruction, the original bas-relief was replaced.

THE COMMEMORATIVE STONE OF FISCHERKIEZ (14)

The destruction of a "scruffy district"

Fischerinsel 5, 10179 Berlin
U2 (Märkisches Musuem)

The old sculpted stone on the wall of the enormous prefabricated building on the Friedrichsgracht (an arm of the Spree River) has bewildered many a passer-by. No explanations are given to curious visitors who might wonder what the Berlin bear is doing above a man in uniform wearing a hat and holding a fish in each hand. The name of the street, Fischerinsel (meaning Fisher Island), is enough to indicate that it referred to a former city district. Indeed, there used to be a district here that owed its name, Fischerkiez, to fish. But by the early 19th century, fishermen no longer played an active role in this area of Berlin.

The district used to be called Speicherinsel (meaning Granary Island) due to the enormous granary that once stood here. With its rather outdated and picturesque appearance, it was considered the oldest and most "rural" district in Berlin, and was notably home to the traditional restaurant Zum Nussbaum, recommended to intrepid tourists by Karl Baedeker. The Milljöh, which, out of a sense of nostalgia, was meant to be rebuilt in 1987 on a vacant lot surrounding the remains of St Nicholas' Church, had a similar reputation.

During the 1920s the district was considered a scruffy area that needed to be destroyed. On the other side of the Spree, a similar district, the infamous Krögel, disappeared in the 1930s to give way to the construction of the Reich's mint. Speicherinsel, however, survived the destruction of the Second World War.

Following the example set by West Germany with its "Interbau" exhibition of modern and functional architecture and the futuristic district of Hansa, the East was ready to emulate its counterpart. But the buildings on the southern bank of Spreeinsel (the historic district of Cölln) were a cause for shame. While half of them were renovated, the conservation and construction plans were quickly forgotten by those seeking swift change, and even the safeguarding of monuments was not enough to prevent the demolition of the 30 old buildings.

THE REMAINS OF CÖLLN TOWN HALL ⑮

History beneath our feet

Scharrenstraße 22, 10178 Berlin
U2 (Spittelmarkt)

It seems to be the ambition of Berlin to become the city of archaeological windows. They can be found in Gesundbrunnen, at the Mauerbrunnen, and at the Rotes Rathaus metro station. The largest is on Petriplatz and still in the planning stage, while one of the oldest and most discrete is at the Capri by Fraser Hotel at the crossroads of Scharrenstraße and Breite Straße.

The structure of the Capri by Fraser – as impersonal as the surrounding hotels – is intended to reflect the cubic style of the former Cölln Town Hall, the medieval town hall that presumably once stood here. The second town hall, built in Baroque style, was also located here until it was demolished in 1900.

Archaeologists examining the site before the construction of the current hotel, which is much smaller than the previous town hall, discovered below the Baroque building foundations and cellars belonging to bourgeois houses dating back to the late Middle Ages. These houses were built on what was once the major trade route crossing the city of Cölln.

Hochtief, the company in charge of the hotel construction project, was required to conserve these archaeological findings; it integrated a 41 square metre glass panel into the floor of the hotel lobby. After reading some explanatory notes, visitors can descend a staircase to the very heart of the German capital.

Initially built to administer the cities of Cölln and Berlin after their reunification in 1709, Cölln Town Hall never fulfilled its original purpose. Although Frederick William I of Prussia – the "Soldier King" son of King Frederick I – oversaw the construction of the town hall until 1723 (minus the construction of the tower), the cities were managed and governed from Berlin's former town hall until the construction of the Rotes Rathaus, Berlin's current town hall.

NEARBY

Doors of the public library (16)

Breite Straße 30–36, 10178 Berlin

Though many visitors have pushed open the heavy doors of the old library of East Berlin, few have noticed that these doors are covered in squares bearing the letter A in 117 (9 x 13) different styles. The artist responsible is Professor Fritz Kühn, whose work using squares can also be found on the coloured doors of the old State Council building, at the entrance of the Leibniz room in the Parliament of Lower Saxony, and in the Leineschloss castle in Hanover.

MUTTER HOPPE RESTAURANT BAS-RELIEFS

(17)

Evidence of the history of communism

Rathausstraße 21, 10178 Berlin
U2 (Klosterstraße)

On the border of *Nikolaiviertel* (Nicholas' Quarter) is an apartment block; its portico is topped by six concrete bas-reliefs, built to echo the stone chronicle of the Rotes Rathaus, Berlin's Red Town Hall, located some 200 metres away. The work is entitled "The fight of progressive forces and the fate of the city."

Above the arcades of the Mutter Hoppe restaurant (which dates back to 1987 and is not as traditional as it would have us believe), the history of communism is displayed with unusual pride. The bas-reliefs were created by Gerhard Thieme, who also created the sculpture of the pigeon on the neighbouring building and the famous sculpture of the construction worker in Karl Liebknecht Street. Typically, there is no information about this significant GDR-period work of art spanning the façade of the building.

The fresco begins with the creation in 1919 of the KPD, the Communist Party of Germany, and its founders Rosa Luxemburg and Karl Liebknecht, along with the unmistakable flag and castle in the background. The speech of Ernst Thälmann, the leader of the Communist Party of Germany, is also represented. Completing the first bas-relief is a

diorama, a three-dimensional model of the heavy-handed crackdown on KPD demonstrations in May 1929 during the Weimar Republic.

The second bas-relief immortalises the years of Nazi dictatorship, with representations of the Reichstag fire, the burning of books, concentration camps, resistance movements, bombings during the war, and the liberation of Berlin by the Red Army. The third is a representation of the post-war period: the creation of the SED (the Socialist Party of Germany) and the GDR in 1949, the highly stylised emblem of which is easily recognisable and no longer found today.

The fourth bas-relief highlights key events that occurred between 1950 and 1968, such as the redevelopment of Alexanderplatz, and the remarkable victory of East Berlin athletes at the Olympics Games in Mexico. The fifth continues with communist events marking the period between 1970 and 1986: the World Youth Games, the construction of the Marzahn district, the 25th anniversary of the GDR, and the legendary German-Soviet flight aboard the Soyuz 31 ship that moored at the Soviet space station Salyut 6. United by strong brotherly ties, the two cosmonauts, Waleri Fjodorowitsch Bykowski and Sigmund Jähn, appear triumphant.

Günther Stahn, the architect responsible for the district, knowingly built these concrete bas-reliefs in the same style as the town hall's large fresco. His aim was to create a contrast and to highlight the superiority of this new form of society based on communism.

On leaving the restaurant, be sure to stop and thank Marx and Engels on the eponymous square located a few minutes' walk away.

PLAQUE OF THE PALAST DER REPUBLIK

18

The last vestige of the Palast der Republik

Rathausstraße 53A, 10178 Berlin
U2 (Klosterstraße)

At the north-west end of Nicholas' Quarter, a discrete plaque secured to the wall of the house with the dove of peace bears the monogram PdR. The plaque is the last vestige of the once famous Palast der Republik, and this is where the ticket office used to be. From the 1980s, people came here to buy tickets to the popular shows staged at the palace.

Opened in 1976 where Berlin Castle once stood, the palace served as the *Volkskammer* (the "People's Chamber" – i.e. the parliament of the German Democratic Republic) and was an important cultural meeting point. It was demolished between 2006 and 2008.

Despite the astronomical cost of its construction, the palace quickly became a meeting place for all generations; parties were organised for special occasions, and East Berliners proudly brought visitors from the West.

The palace looked fantastic, boasting a restaurant, milk bar, and wine bar, along with a large hexagonal room that could welcome up to 4,500 people. The hall was equipped with hydraulic devices to move elements on stage or adjust the rows of seats.

Tickets to concerts were inexpensive and highly sought after. It was not permitted to buy more than four tickets per person, so the entire family had to participate. Waiting in line was an integral part of German Democratic Republic culture, though it was possible to jump the queue by standing next to someone you knew. Camping and bringing along folding chairs was the norm, and the simple fact of being in line was a cause for celebration in itself. Many musicians from the West performed at the palace; during one concert by Tangerine Dream, queues were more than 500 metres long, although only a few lucky ones were able to get in and enjoy the show.

On cold days, the palace staff would serve free coffee ... those were the good old days.

THE ARM OF THE STATUE OF THE FORMER STATE COUNCIL BUILDING ⑲

A brazen falsification

Schlossplatz 1, 10178 Berlin
U2 (Hausvogteilplatz)

It is said that authentic remains from the façade of Berlin Palace are now hanging on the former State Council Building, the Staatsrat, which was Chancellor Gerhard Schröder's official residence after the fall of the Wall whilst a chancellery was being built.

At first glance, it does indeed look authentic, especially in the evening, when the sunlight gives the Hermes sandstone a golden hue. The sign claims that it is the window that was used for the emperor's speeches and from which Karl Liebknecht proclaimed the "Free Socialist Republic of Germany" on 9 November 1918, in the wake of the storming and looting of the castle. It would therefore seem to be part of the GDR Socialist family's legacy, hung there in 1963 on the red façade like a banner stolen from the enemy. But just how much truth is there to all this?

The castle, which was scheduled for demolition in 1950, had five entrance gates. The idea was to hang two of them, the fourth and the fifth, on the State Council Building to decorate the front and back of the building. The plan was to firstly dismantle entrance number five and the window with the balustrade from which Liebknecht had spoken. To cushion the impact when it fell, straw was placed on the ground, but things did not go to plan and all that remained of Liebknecht's authentic façade after the attempt to take it down, was a pile of rubble. Number four was, however, dismantled and passed off as number five by putting it back together by hand, and stone by stone. The back of the State Council Building remained surprisingly empty, making it one of the first rather unsuccessful demonstrations of Modernism in the East.

And the plot thickens. Not only is it the wrong gate, but it has also been brazenly falsified. If we are to compare the Atlas on the right to the one shown on old photos, we can see the strange position of the fist, which is not anatomical at all. More effort was spent working on the ornate interior decoration, where a superb earthenware tile, and also a multi-coloured glass picture signed by the GDR's leading artist, Womacka, are a celebration of "life in the Democratic German Republic". Under the silhouettes of Rosa Luxemburg and Karl Liebknecht the expression that is always used to detract attention from a lie or a swindle shines out: "All the same!"

ALLEGORICAL SCULPTURE OF THE SPREE

⑳

One of the last remaining elements of the memorial to William I

Unterwasserstraße, 10117 Berlin
U2 (Hausvogteiplatz)

From the Schinkelplatz, looking in the direction of the Humboldt Forum, the platform on the right is all that remains of the pedestal of the former 1897 national memorial to William I (see picture opposite). On the left of the platform, an arched pontoon is decorated with a small sculpture of a slender feminine silhouette draped in reeds and holding a

fish in her arms. This charming and rare allegorical representation of the Spree River is one of few still remaining in Berlin.

As for the memorial, the tribute to the beloved emperor was not actually wanted by the people; the city was already crowded with such memorials. The idea came from the emperor's son, William II, who also became emperor and was more than happy to squander the people's money. This project gave him the opportunity to demolish Schlossfreiheit Square, the privileged district of the German nobility, whose architecture he strongly disliked but couldn't avoid seeing from the windows of his nearby palace.

The Zoo of William II

The huge monument was quickly mocked and nicknamed "The Zoo of William II".
A satirist at the time counted on the memorial 21 horses, 2 bulls, 8 sheep, 4 lions, 16 bats, 6 mice, 1 squirrel, 10 pigeons, 2 crows, 2 eagles, 16 owls, 1 kingfisher, 18 snakes, 1 carp, 1 frog, 16 crabs, and 32 lizards – a grand total of 157 animals.

The other remains of the memorial

Only two lions and an eagle have survived (along with the carp in the allegorical arms of the river). The lions were moved to the zoo in East Berlin (see page 336), while the eagle was relocated to the courtyard of the Märkisches Museum.

Several other Baroque buildings, such as Café Josty and Café Helms, also fell victim to the emperor's destructive urges.

HISTORICAL MILESTONE ON DÖNHOFF PLATZ

(21)

Berlin's level zero

Leipziger Straße 49, 10117 Berlin
U2 (Spittelmarkt)

At number 49 Leipziger Straße, in front of the Spittelkolonnade of Dönhoff square, stands a good-sized obelisk which is often overlooked, however, as passers-by think it is part of the Spittelkolonnade.

This obelisk, dating from 1979, is in fact a copy of a level "zero" milestone (*Null-Meilenstein*) which indicated the point from which the Prussian postal service calculated its distances from Berlin. The original milestone was installed in 1730 a few metres away from where it stands today. At the end of the Thirty Years' War (1618-1648), desolation reigned in Brandenburg. Berlin's population was decimated, falling from 13,000 to a mere 4,000 inhabitants. Brandenburg's economy was in serious decline. To save it, Elector Frederick William of Brandenburg (1620-1688) drew up postal routes lining the main trade routes of the region. Some of these axes can still be seen today and have even become the famous federal roads in the German capital (notably numbers one and five, inaugurated respectively in 1646 and 1660).

The region's first milestones, used for precise calculations depending on the distance to be driven, delivery deadlines and postage costs, also date back to this time. They also indicated the postal charges, as the post was delivered by the famous "stagecoaches" (*Postkutsche*) used by travellers. From 1800, these roads became paved streets known as "Chaussees" (the name given to Chaussee Straße in Mitte, one of the capital's first two paved streets, with Bundesstraße 1 leading to Potsdam, a section of which still bears the name Potsdamer Chaussee). All the users of these fast roads, except for the sovereign and the postal service, were charged a tax based on the military milestones.

Distances were calculated from so-called "zero" points, indicated by granite obelisks that were placed at different entrances to the city, which, surrounded by moats and bastions, then stretched for only a few square kilometres. Although it is difficult to be absolutely sure, it would seem that there were in fact at least two "zero" points: one in the north of the city, in front of the Oranienburg gate, and one in the south.

The obelisk on Dönhoff Platz originally stood on the south-west side of the city, in front of the Leipzig gate (which gives its name to today's Leipziger Straße, onto which this gate opened out).

Starting from these obelisks, the milestones were placed at intervals of one mile and half a mile (and, according to some records, a quarter of a mile). The Prussian mile measured 24,000 footsteps (around 7.5 km), in other words, the average distance originally travelled by a stagecoach in two hours.

For more information about where to find the military milestones in Berlin, see the following double page.

Berlin's other military milestones

In addition to the copy of the Null-Meilenstein on Dönhoff Platz, twelve military milestones still stand discreetly in the streets of the German capital:

1. At 63 Hauptstraße, Schöneberg
2. At 44 Potsdamer Str, Zehlendorf
3. At 42 Königstraße, Wannsee
4. At 7 Spandauer Damm, Charlottenburg
5. In front of 220 Spandauer Damm, Ruhwald
6. On the Lichtenberg bridge (Lichtenberger Brücke), Lichtenberg
7. On Alt-Mahlsdorf street (in front of 109, on the other side of the street), Mahlsdorf
8. On the corner of Gabrielenstraße and An der Mühle, Alt-Tegel
9. On Ruppiner Chaussee (in front of 377a, on the other side of the street), Hennigdorf
10. On the corner of Falkenberger Chaussee and Pablo-Picasso-Straße, Neu-Hohenschönhausen
11. At 169 Waltersdorfer Chaussee, Rudow
12. Opposite 66 Buschkrugallee, Britz

III
MEILEN
von
BERLIN

THE MICHAELSEN PALAIS

A beautiful example of German Art Nouveau

Schützenstraße 6–6A, 10117 Berlin
U6 (Kochstraße Checkpoint Charlie)

The Michaelsen Palais at number 6 Schützenstraße, also known as the Hotel Roter Adler, is one of the most distinctive examples of *Jugendstil* architecture in the centre of Berlin.

Its imposing façade, decorated with patriotic sculptures, is a true manifesto of German Art Nouveau. Among the many characters depicted, two familiar figures are seen standing just below the huge painting of Greek god Hermes: Charlemagne (on the left) and Emperor William I (on the right). Between them, encompassed within a medallion, is Saint George fighting a dragon (symbolising the conflict between good and evil), while the bust of "Iron Chancellor" Otto von Bismarck is clearly visible a little lower and to the right near the pediment.

The entrance gate also merits special attention; with its floral decorations and gargoyles it is one of the most beautiful gates in the city.

The building was built by and named after Berlin architect Otto Michaelsen between 1903 and 1907. Michaelson was commissioned by the contractor Emil Voigt, though barely a year after construction finished, Voigt was forced to sell the property due to financial issues. The building was then purchased by Swiss insurance company Winterthur and used as offices.

Partially destroyed during the Second World War, the Michaelsen Palais was used during that period as the headquarters of the public prosecutor, the criminal court, and a luxury hotel.

At the time of the German Democratic Republic, the indoor areas were occupied by the civil engineering and road construction bureau, before once again becoming the property of Winterthur after the fall of the Wall.

The building as it stands today underwent considerable restructuring at the beginning of the year 2000, which ensured the conservation of some original architectural elements, along with the reconstruction of the wing on the corner of Charlottenstraße that suffered bomb damage.

©Marek Sliwecki

THE BUILDING AT 8 SCHÜTZENSTRAẞE

(23)

An astounding copy of the Farnese Palace in Rome

Schützenstraße 8, 10117 Berlin
U6 (Kochstraße Checkpoint Charlie)

On Schützenstraße, just a few hundred metres from the popular tourist area of Checkpoint Charlie, stands a façade unlike any other in Berlin. Architecture enthusiasts will notice that its Renaissance-style composition recalls another very familiar building. It is in fact a copy of part of the inner courtyard of the Farnese Palace in Rome, built

by Antonio da Sangallo and completed by Michelangelo in 1550.

The masterpiece of Italian Renaissance was reproduced in the centre of Berlin by the Italian architect Aldo Rossi, who was in charge of designing the entire district of Schützenstraße at the beginning of the 1990s.

Built between 1995 and 1997 in what used to be called the "death strip" (the long strip of land that separated East and West Berlin), the building complex is composed of four inner courtyards, one octagonal in shape; it is an homage to the architecture of 19th-century Berlin that was largely destroyed during the bombings of the Second World War.

Aldo Rossi, in collaboration with the architect's studio Bellmann & Böhm, was directly inspired by pre-war buildings on the streets of Schützenstraße, Mark-grafenstraße, Zimmerstraße and Charlottenstraße. Rossi even integrated into the façade the remains of one of the buildings that had survived the war. The shapes, colours and materials of the new construction make this one of the most original architectural projects of post-reunification Berlin.

ALFANDARY HOUSE BAS-RELIEFS

(24)

Mythology on ceramics

Zimmerstraße 79–80, 10117 Berlin
U6 (Kochstraße/Checkpoint Charlie)

Just a few metres away from Checkpoint Charlie, and swamped with hordes of tourists, stands a house built of partially vitrified bricks known as "Dutch" or "clinker", the main attraction of which is a narrow frieze on the front. Before reunification, this house was the editorial office of East Berlin's newspaper *Neue Zeit.*

After the Second World War, it was also home to the Union Verlag publishing house's readers' office. The writer Johannes Bobrowski worked there for a while. One wall of the house was part of the border between East and West Berlin and faced part of a demarcation zone.

Today, the advertising sign for the *Neue Zeit* no longer shines on the front. The house has been painstakingly restored to its 1914 original condition, except the last floor that was added under the rafters with windows overlooking Zimmerstraße.

In those days, this building which was built for the Sephardic Alfandary family, who ran an import-export business, caused a real sensation. In Berlin's directory, the Alfandarys (Jacques manager for

Istanbul, Moïse dealing with London, Salomon and Raphaël with Berlin) advertised "Persian rugs, wholesale embroidery and products imported from the East."

The German architect, John Martens, who was the project manager for the work, specialised in construction ceramics and had developed a new manufacturing process which made it particularly weather resistant. He used it to make the decorative frieze on the front of the house. Its main role was to detract attention from a certain aesthetic imbalance: to the right, four doors were added to the two floors, opening out onto the warehouses. Two, barely perceptible, women were also added to the central mullion of two of the windows on the second floor.

Hans Schmidt, who designed this frieze, placed characters and symbols side by side like hieroglyphics. The characters – three women and a man – are depicted lying down as there was not enough space to show them standing.

They are interspersed with symbols of perseverance and economic activity (a hive) and abundance (a basket of fruit). A child brings flowers, and a small pet dog lies near a sunflower; the second (Leda?) raises her hand against a swan; the third seems to be facing a goat (maybe a satyr). The divinities are represented by a large head, containing another small one in its mouth. The sleeping man at the far righthand end seems to be dreaming of a golden age: a gnome holding a coconut tree palm in his hand and pulling a minecart full of ore.

MEMORIAL TO KARL LIEBKNECHT ㉕

Forgotten in no man's land

Potsdamer Platz 10, 10785 Berlin
S1, 2, 25, 26 (Potsdamer Platz)

In front of number 10 Potsdamer Platz, stands a grey cubic block of stone identified by a small plaque as "the first stone of the monument in memory of Karl Liebknecht". Liebknecht was a former member of the Social Democratic Party of Germany and co-founder of the German Communist Party, and was assassinated in 1919. Who wanted to dedicate a monument to the former communist amidst this temple of consumerism? Well, nobody to tell the truth. In fact, this gigantic base was never used for the statue of Liebknecht. The monument base dedicated to the communist is only tolerated on Potsdamer Platz today because it fills the role of a somewhat "performative" monument: it represents the way Germany deals with the socialist and antimilitarist traditions of its past.

On 1 May 1916, Karl Liebknecht (1871-1919) and Rosa Luxemburg (1871-1919) called for the immediate cessation of the First World War during a demonstration that was held in this very spot, near the Potsdam train station. Behind them stood the old building of the Imperial German Treasury for Warfare. Liebknecht was immediately arrested and sentenced to four years and one month of imprisonment, of which he served two. In 1951, for the 80th anniversary of the birth of Liebknecht, and as part of the third World Festival of Youth and Students for Peace and Friendship, Friedrich Ebert, the mayor of East Berlin, decided to lay the first stone of the monument's base in this historic place. However, ten years went by without any sculpture of Liebknecht being erected on top of the base. Located in the demarcation zone by the wall, the monument base was soon forgotten after 1961. With the collapse of the Berlin wall, a construction site barrier kept the base company for a little while. Given that plans for new construction did not incorporate the base, it was dismantled and stored in a warehouse in the district of Marzahn where most of the East's embarrassing monuments ended up. However, this situation was not to the liking of the Berlin Commission of Commemorative Plaques, and on 20 November 2003, by regional government decision, the monument base regained its original location on Potsdamer Platz. This time, however, as a "unique element of the topography of Cold War monuments".

The marble panels of the Mohrenstraße metro station 

Until 1950, the Mohrenstraße metro station was called Kaiserhof (imperial court), after a famous hotel located above it and that had been damaged, just like the access to the metro platforms. The hotel was knocked down and the station was renovated.

Poor old Wilhelmstraße, which had been more or less cleared of rubble, hosted the seat of the GDR government, whilst Goering's Ministry of Aviation became the GDR's "House of Ministries". Below ground level, the restorers of the station made an emphatic architectural gesture.

The opportunity was taken to honour the former chairman of the German Communist Party by renaming the station Thälmannplatz. The walls were clad in marble panels of royal red (or something that looked like it).

Ironically, these ornamental stone panels were taken from the quarries of Saalburg in Thuringia, the very quarries from which Hitler had ordered an ersatz of local marble for the dining room in the neighbouring Neue Reichskanzlei.

He had, however, chosen "light shades of pink", a difference in colour that has sufficed to discredit stories told by many guides, claiming that the marble of the Reichskanzlei was reused for the metro station. This was, in fact, just a rumour that was launched by the weekly news magazine *Der Spiegel*.

The final phase of the work had the makings of a truly impossible task: it is said that the last panels were delivered the night before the inauguration, planned for the sixth anniversary of the assassination of Thälmann in the Buchenwald concentration camp.

After receiving urgent instructions from the highest echelons, the quarries put a large order from the planetarium of Saint Petersburg on hold, so that they could send the marble slabs to Berlin. During the opening ceremony of the station on 18 August 1950, after only 108 days of work, the Berliner Zeitung called it "the capital's most beautiful metro station".

Irma Thälmann, the daughter of the "great leader of German workers", was there and it was before her that, in the name of the young, Alfred Sichert, a train traffic operator, took an oath to the Republic to loyally serve the station in memory of Ernst Thälmann.

With such promises, what could possibly go wrong?

N
MITTE
Potsdamer Platz
Niederkirchnerstr.
Wilhelmstraße
Friedrichstraße
Zimmerstraße
Alte Jacobstraße
Oranienstraße
Linkstraße
Stresemannstraße
Ritterstraße
Mendelssohn-Bartholdy-Park
Potsdamer Straße
Schöneberger Straße
Lindenstraße
Alte Jacobstraße
Lobeckstraße
Hallesches Tor
Gleisdreieck
Möckernbrücke
Kurfürstenstr.
Park am Gleisdreieck-Westpark
Gitschiner Straße
Prinzenstra
Obentrautstraße
KREUZBERG
Park am Gleisdreieck-Ostpark
Möckernstraße
Mehringdamm
Urbanstraße
Yorckstraße
Yorckstraße
Blücherstraße
Gneisenaustraße
Hagelberger Str.
Gneisenaustraße
SCHÖNE-BERG
Kreuzbergstraße
Bergmannstraße
Südster
Katzbachstraße
Victoria Park
Mehringdamm
Fidicinstraße
Platz der Luftbrücke
Dudenstraße
PLATZ DER LUFTBRÜCKE
Columbiadamm
0
500
1000 m
TEMPELHOF

Kreuzberg

FRIEDRICHSHAIN
Berlin
Ostbahnhof
Heinrich-
Heine-Straße
SCHILLING-
BRÜCKE
MICHAELKIRCH-
PLATZ
Köpenicker Straße
Mühlenstraße
Warschauer
Straße
Waldemarstraße
Manteuffelstraße
Moritzplatz
ORANIEN-
PLATZ
Oranienstraße
OBERBAUM-
BRÜCKE
Stralauer Allee
Spree
Schlesisches Tor
Görlitzer
Bahnhof
LAUSITZER
PLATZ
Kottbusser Tor
Schlesische Straße
Wrangelstraße
Görlitzer Straße
Görlitzer
Park
Kottbusser
Straße
Manteuffelstr.
Lausitzer Straße
Reichenberger Straße
Wiener Straße
Schönleinstraße
ALT-
TREPTOW
Grimmstraße
Graefestraße
Kottbusser Damm
Hobrechtstraße
Landwehrkanal
Ratiborstraße
Lohmühlenstraße
Kiefholzstraße
Urbanstraße
Fichtestr.
Pflügerstraße
LOHMÜLEN-
BRÜCKE
Reuterstraße
Dannierstraße
Harzer Straße
Bouchéstraße
Wildenbruchstraße
Hasenheide
Sonnenallee
Hermannplatz
Weigandufer
Weichselstraße
WILDENBRUCH-
BRÜCKE
Elsenstraße
Volkspark
Hasenheide
Karl-Marx-Straße
Sonnenallee
Weserstraße
NEUKÖLLN

“PEACE BE WITH YOU” MURAL ①

The snake charmer of the Rudi-Dutschke-Haus

Rudi-Dutschke-Straße 23, 10969 Berlin
U6 (Kochstraße/Checkpoint Charlie)

Without careful manoeuvring, the work of art on the façade of what was once the main building of the *Tageszeitung* (*TAZ*) newspaper is barely visible from Rudi-Dutschke-Straße. But the image packs quite a shock, even for a city like Berlin: a man strides purposefully forwards, completely naked except for his glasses, socks and shoes, his cobra-headed penis extending up towards the sky, seemingly entranced by the flute of a penis charmer seated near the top. The title of the mural is inscribed above: "Peace be with you".

The windows on all four floors of the building divide this monstrous phallus into slices, like curry sausages – a Berlin speciality. The message is not immediately apparent, but the procession of characters represented in the first third of the work gives a clue; the tiny naked men standing side by side carry placards bearing titles originally published in *Bild* magazine, such as: "Viagra boom during crisis"; "Federal Court: it is now permissible to say *Pimmel* (dick)"; "I'm disclosing Klatten's sex photos"; "First goal scored with the penis"; and "Emasculated by his mother-in-law's basset hound". At the bottom left is the headline "More than 65% of men think their penis is too small". The common denominator is the naked penis.

For a long time, *Bild* was the highest circulation newspaper in Germany. But between 2001 and 2015, sales fell by 65 per cent. Its historical editor-in-chief was Kai Diekmann, the main character in the mural.

For Peter Lenk, the author of the work (which was inaugurated in 2009), it is artistic therapy for the penile fixation held by *Bild* and its main shareholder Friede Springer, the snake charmer in the image.

The fresco illustrates the climax that *TAZ* and *Bild* had reached on this subject.

An explanatory panel located near the mural provides further information.

DIASPORA GARDEN

②

A stunning and symbolic garden

Fromet-und-Moses-Mendelssohn-Platz 1, 10969 Berlin
Mon & Wed 10am–7pm; Tue, Thur & Fri 10am–6pm
Free entry
U6 (Kochstraße Checkpoint Charlie)

Located opposite the Jewish Museum, the W. Blumenthal Academy – the museum's research and training centre – is often overlooked, yet it houses a stunning artificial garden that is home to a rich variety of

plants and flowers from all over the world.

Created by the Atelier Le Balto, a landscape architecture studio specialising in gardens, this Diaspora Garden is highly symbolic. Here, vegetation that has literally been uprooted from its natural habitat flourishes, and many of the plants present have a strong link to Jewish history and culture.

Bathed in the soft natural light pouring through the large skylight, the plants are set out on big metal tables. Most of the them grow in a soil bed and are irrigated artificially.

This unique garden is a metaphor for the diaspora; just like the Jewish community, these plants have had to abandon their homeland and learn to adapt in a new environment.

Some of the species in the garden are directly linked to relevant Jewish figures or play a fundamental role in Jewish religious festivities, while others owe their names to anti-Semitic sentiments.

Covering a total surface area of 500 square metres and home to more than 200 plants from various climatic zones, the Diaspora Garden is divided into four sectors, each enriched with informative material.

The W. Blumenthal Academy is not only home to the Diaspora Garden, it also houses a library with a public reading room, archives, an auditorium, and several seminar spaces. It provides educational programmes that enable participants to discover the characteristics of various plants and seeds through hands-on exercises.

Between 2010 and 2012, this building, which used to be the Blumengroßmarkthalle (Flower Market), was entirely renovated by architect Daniel Libeskind, the man behind the Jewish Museum.

The main entrance is particularly original; a portion of the wood-panelled cube that forms the entrance is oddly sunken into the pavement and embedded in the façade.

STAIRCASE OF THE GERMAN STEELWORKERS UNION

③

An unknown masterpiece by Erich Mendelsohn

IG-Metall-Haus, Alte Jakobstraße 149, 10969 Berlin
0 30 / 253 87 - 0
igmetall-berlin.de
Mon, Tue & Thur 8:30am–12noon and 12:30pm–5pm; Wed 8:30am–12noon and 12:30pm–4pm; Fri 8:30–12noon
Free entry
U1, 3, 6 (Hallesches Tor)

On the corner of Alte Jakobstraße and Lindenstraße, the House of the German Steelworkers Union (IG-Metall-Haus) does not tend to capture the attention of passers-by unless they are passionate about architecture.

Accessible to the public during working hours, the building has a spectacular staircase that stretches from floor to ceiling and measures five metres in diameter. Along with its magnificent brass railing that emphasises the spiralling effect, its plunging lighting system also extends the entire height of the structure; on each floor a bunch of light bulbs is enclosed in an elegant glass sphere.

Designed by famous German architect of the time Erich Mendelsohn, briefly assisted by R.W. Reichel, the building was completed in August 1930. Its construction, which began in 1929, had been disrupted by the Great Depression of that same year, as well as a four-week strike by workers requesting more pay.

The building exhibits outstanding examples of architectural detail heralding the new Art Deco style: the gold lettering of the word "Metall" and its typography are typical of the 1920s; the bronze finishes on the windows and the corners of some travertine walls; and the particularly unusual inwardly curved main façade.

Other notable constructions of the expressionist architect Erich Mendelsohn include the Schaubühne, an avant-garde Berlin theatre built in 1928 on Kurfürstendamm Avenue, and the spectacular Einstein Tower in Potsdam.

REMAINS OF THE STRESEMANNSTRAßE RAILWAY LINE

④

The railway line that once connected Berlin's train stations

Stresemannstraße 37, 10963 Berlin
U1, 3, 6 (Hallesches Tor)

At the corner of Stresemannstraße and Großbeerenstraße, on the central space separating the two pavements, there is a piece of railway line protected by railings. A sign reveals that this is a very rare relict of the first railway line that connected Berlin's train stations to each other.

The city today is essentially a result of changes that occurred during the industrial revolution. At the beginning of the 19th century, Berlin – then the capital of Prussia – was home to a few hundred thousand inhabitants. One hundred years later, the city became the capital of the new German Empire following the political unification of Germany in 1871, and its population reached 4.5 million. As the leading industry of continental Europe, it was the third largest city in the world after New York and London. Above all, the arrival of the train led to the emergence of large industrial centres like Berlin, as high concentrations of production meant that raw materials could be transported to unique processing locations, and the produced goods could be quickly and affordably distributed across the country.

However, as they were so noisy and polluting, trains could not easily cross the city, which was already congested. Train stations called "railheads" (the railway line did not cross the city and only stopped at certain Berlin stations) were initially built at the gates of the city, itself surrounded by a customs wall (*Zollmauer*, see following page). The railway network of the German Empire resembled a giant spider's web, at the centre of which stood Berlin. This presented a major problem: how to transfer the merchandise from one railhead to another as it transited through Berlin between opposite ends of the Empire. This was the original function of the *Ringbahn*: the S-Bahn line running around the historic centre, which was originally called the *Verbindungsbahn* (or junction line).

Redesigned during the 1860s to accommodate the growing number of stations, the current trajectory of the *Ringbahn* dates back to 1871. With its reduced perimeter, the first connection line, inaugurated in 1851, ensured the transit between the stations of Stettin (now the park of the northern railway station, the *Nordbahnhof*), Hamburg (which became the Museum of Contemporary Art in 1996), Potsdam (now the *Tilla-Durieux* park just by Potsdamer Platz public square), Anhalt (now the parks of *Lilli-Henoch*, *Elise-Tilse* and *Gleisdreieck*), and Frankfurt (later called the Silesian railway station, now the *Ostbahnhof*, the east railway station – the only former railhead still in use).

Since its creation, this ancestor of the *Ringbahn* has nearly entirely disappeared from the Berlin landscape. All that remains is the small section found on the Stresemannstraße that connected the stations of Potsdam and Anhalt.

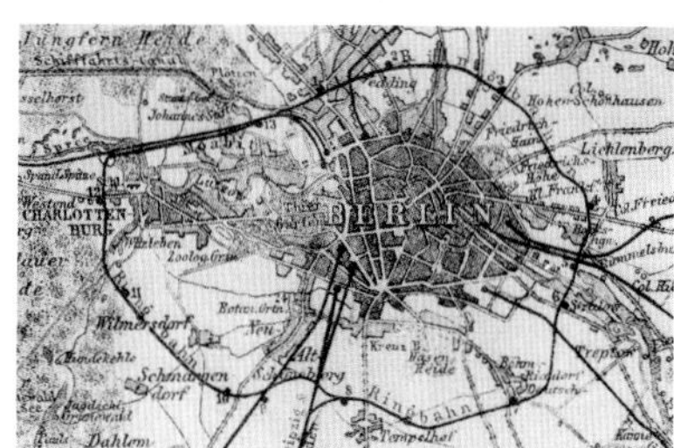

The other relict of the Verbindungsbahn

The passing-by of the 1851 Ring railway line is also evidenced by the name of a street in Kreuzberg that pays tribute to it: the *Eisenbahnstraße* ("road of the railway line") was the street along which the connection railway line passed as it transited between Görlitz (built subsequently in 1866-1867) and Frankfurt.

In fact, where the road meets the River Spree, it lines up with the remains of the *Brommybrücke*, an old bridge whose ruins can be found at number Brommystraße 1 (see page 148).

THE TOLL WALL

5

The last remnants of Berlin's customs clearance wall

Stresemannstraße 66–68, 10963 Berlin
S1, 2, 26, 26 (Anhalter Bahnhof)

In the middle of Stresemannstraße, the small piece of wall which is still standing at numbers 66–68 is not the remains of a building destroyed during the last war, but the remnants of a toll wall (used for collecting customs taxes) that surrounded Berlin from the 18th to the 19th century, the partial outline of which can still be seen on Stresemannstraße, Linienstraße and Torstraße.

It was in 1987 that a section of this toll wall was reconstructed here from the original foundations.

For Frederick William I of Prussia, the "soldier king", the city wall of Berlin (his home city and garrison town) served primarily to protect the local economy from cheap foreign products, but also to hinder

smugglers who had absolutely no intention of paying the taxes due on leaving the city. It was also used to fill the coffers of the state and to stem the number of desertions within the army's ranks, as most of the Prussian troops were poorly paid, ill-treated and even kidnapped or forcibly conscripted.

The tax wall was dotted with 18 gates which were used to carry out customs controls on merchants coming into the city. Today, 17 of them are little more than a name on maps of the city.

In the 18th century, after going through the first customs control at the city's gates, the carts and wagons had to go to the Packhof (the customs warehouse) to unload their contents and pay customs on their goods.

In the days when the territory of the city went beyond the wall, this warehouse was demolished, and the customs control was moved to customs tax offices which were built well in advance of the city walls.

One of these toll barriers has been preserved: the Royal Waters Inspection pavilion on the island of Lohmühle.

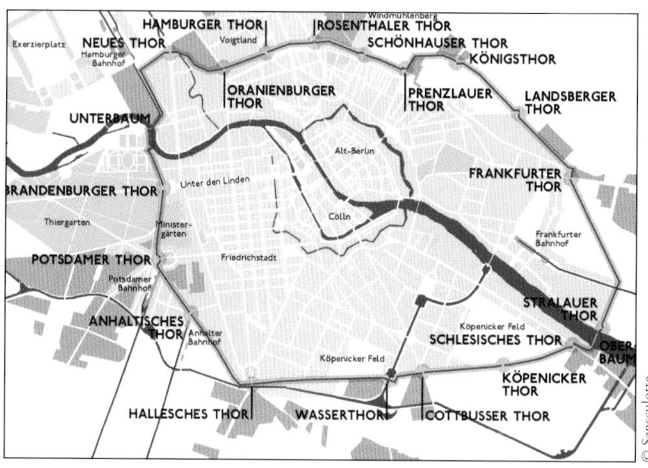

A toll wall which affects the location of stations

The toll wall even affected the location of the first stations, called terminus, where the new railways began: each of them was built outside the toll wall.

THE UNDERGROUND HOUSE

When the underground goes through a house ...

Dennewitzstraße 2, 10785 Berlin
U1, 2, 3 (Gleisdreieck)

The house located at number 2 Dennewitzstraße is a real curiosity: this old building is perhaps the only building in the world to be directly traversed (one could even say cut through) by the underground.

The (indirect) cause of this peculiarity was a serious accident on 26 September 1908, when two underground trains collided head-on in Gleisdreieck, probably due to a signalling error.

The accident claimed the lives of 18 people and left the whole town in mourning. In order to prevent such a tragedy from happening again, an alternative route was devised, but its construction was postponed in the mid-1920s due to the First World War.

At that time, the Berlin Public Transport Authority (BVG) had acquired 30 plots of land along with the buildings on them. Instead of demolishing them, the decision was made to build new underground tracks that would cut through the houses – it was simply the cheapest solution. Most of the houses that were tunnelled through disappeared after the Battle of Berlin in 1945, but the house in Dennewitzstraße survived the war.

Since 1926, excluding the effects of air-raid warnings and driver strikes, trains on the U1 line have gone through this house 444 times a day every working day (222 times in each direction).

After crossing the park on the metal bridge, the rails of the underground train pass through a covered ramp that enters the house. For its occupants, who have often been interviewed by the local press, it begins with a distant roar that seems to come from the bowels of the building like the depths of a mine. The noise becomes louder and turns into a roar: it sounds as if the ceilings are starting to vibrate. Rat-a-tat! The tiles on the floor echo and the noise then quickly fades away before disappearing entirely. All along this ramp, as well as in the house, the rails are enclosed in double-walled concrete casings to mitigate the unwanted noises that obviously accompany an underground train.

It must be noted that to attract occupants, rents in this house are particularly low.

Berlin 1905, Dennewitzstraße

CONCRETE PILLARS OF YORCKSTRAẞE

⑦

The difference between old and renovated bridges

Corner of Yorkstrasse and Bautzenerstrasse, 10829 Berlin
S1, 2, 25 / U7 (Yorckstraße)

The attentive passer-by may notice that the pillars of only some of the bridges in Yorckstrasse are wrapped in concrete bases. This difference separates those bridges that have been renovated since construction work began in 2011/2012 and original ones from the late 19th and early 20th centuries.

The extra concrete was poured during the Second World War to prevent the piers from slipping out of their pivot point in the event of shock waves caused by bombs: these so-called "pendulum piers" (*Pendelstützen*) are not attached to the bridge deck above, but simply support it by means of ball and socket joint systems on which the deck is placed.

Nowadays, these concrete bases are used instead to stabilise the structure should a heavy vehicle hit the pillars. Since renovated bridges are now modified in such a way that the piers are no longer load-bearing, the concrete base has become redundant.

The oldest metal bridge in Berlin

Until the Second World War, 40 bridges overlooked Yorckstrasse, compared to 30 today.

Of these bridges, 26 are originals. Since 1992 they form a listed ensemble, a genuine open-air museum of the technical evolution of metal bridges from 1875 to 1934.

The oldest is bridge number 5 at the corner of Bautzenerstrasse. It is the oldest metal bridge in Berlin.

Berlin, the European capital of bridges

There are an astounding number of bridges in Berlin – about 2,700. The website brückenweb.de lists them all. Contrary to popular belief, that's more than in Hamburg, which has less than 2,500, and more than any city after New York. Built on wetlands, Berlin is among the many so-called "Venice of the North" towns. Some 450 bridges in Berlin cross a watercourse – that's more than in Venice!

Why is there a sharp bend in Yorckstraße?

If you look closely at Yorckstrasse on a map of Berlin, one detail is rather striking: Gneisenaustrasse, which becomes Yorckstrasse further west, is exactly in line with Bülowstrasse, Kleiststrasse and Tauentzienstrasse on the other side of Gleisdreieck Park. However, at the level of this park, Yorckstrasse bends sharply to the south before going up and back to its original axis as Bülowstrasse.

To celebrate the end of the Napoleonic occupation, it was decided in the middle of the 19th century to create a long avenue that would cross the city from west to east in a straight line between two churches also built as part of this project: the Garrisonkirche of Südkreuz, not far from the new Berlin Garrison Cemetery (Columbiadamm 122-140), where the soldiers who fell at Dennewitz and Großbeeren during the liberation wars against Napoleon are buried; and the Kaiser Wilhelm Memorial Church, celebrating William I, the founder of the German political unity that the liberation wars had prepared.

Tribute was also paid to the great Prussian generals of the

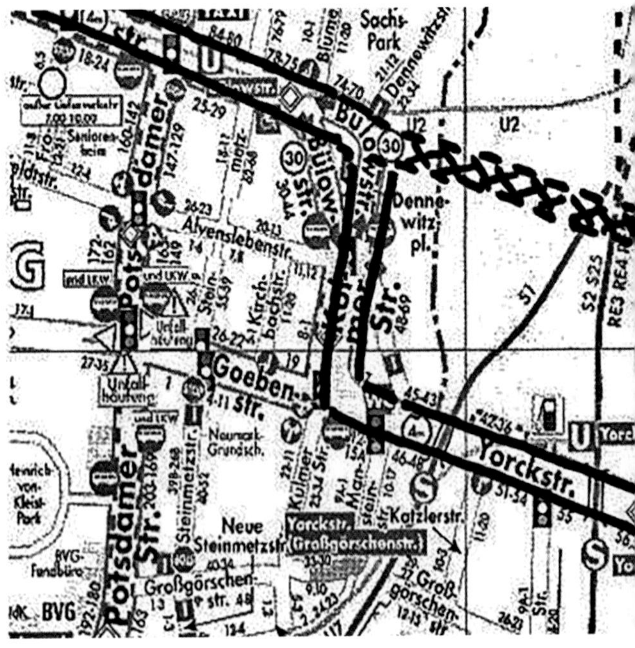

liberation wars by naming the *Generalszug* ("Parade of Generals") after Generals Yorck, Bülow, Kleist and Tauentzien. The names of the squares that punctuate this avenue (Dennewitz, Nollendorf, Wittenberg) are those of the cities where these generals won decisive victories.

However, conceived in the midst of the Industrial Revolution, the project posed a major problem: it had to cross the numerous north-south railway tracks of the Potsdam and Anhalt lines, to which the tracks of the Schöneberg military station and the Dresden line were soon added – all of which converged on Gleisdreieck.

The city insisted on creating an avenue without a level crossing. This meant considerable backfilling work that the railway companies refused to take on. After several years of negotiations, a compromise was reached: taking advantage of the Teltow plateau slightly further south, the *Generalszug* was lowered by 400 metres in order to use the natural slope of the land, which greatly reduced the amount of work required. This also explains why there are so many bridges crossing Yorckstrasse at this point.

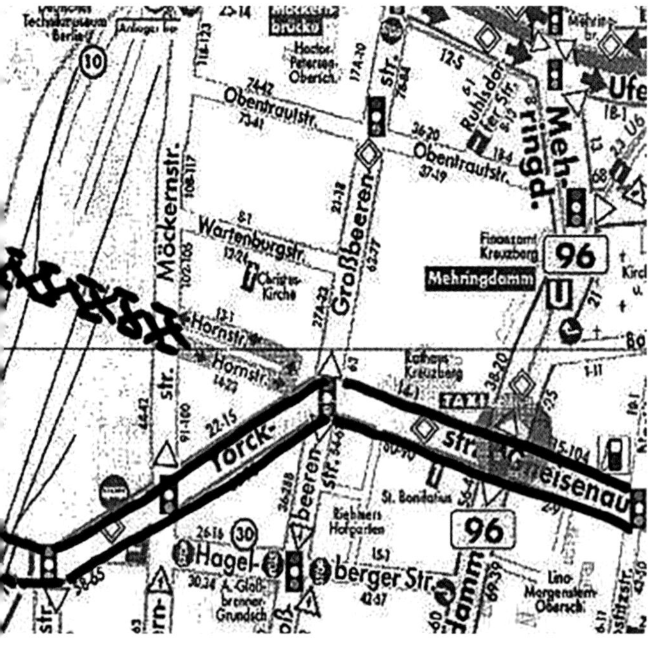

LAPIDARIUM

One of Berlin's great secrets

Viktoriapark
Monument of the wars of liberation (Napoleonic German campaign)
10965 Berlin
0 30 / 50 58 52 - 32
Two-hour guided tour (in German only) once a month from May to October
Tickets on sale at the Friedrichshain-Kreuzberg-Museums (FHXB), Adalbertstraße 95A
It is not possible to make prior bookings
U6 (Platz der Luftbrücke)

In the Viktoriapark, behind the national monument of the wars of liberation (on the northern side of the park), a discreet metal gate opens out onto one of Berlin's great secrets: a collection of plaster cast moulds and copies of the characters represented in the monument, and also the original of the frieze of the Mint, a work by Johann Gottfried Schadow who was Karl Friedrich Schinkel's master.

This frieze was used to decorate the former Mint (Alte Münze) of the Werder market in the historic district of Friedrichswerder. The 37-metre-long reliefs relate the economic history of humanity. The new Mint, of the Schwerin Palace, on Molkenmarkt square, only possesses a copy of this frieze.

On the guided tour we learn that, for example, Queen Luise (the

wife of Frederick William III, the king of Prussia who often fell from his horse) briefly joined ranks with Napoleon after the Prussian defeat of Jena and Auerstedt before finally defeating him by being part of the Sixth Coalition.

A worldwide first

As the complete church that had originally been planned would have been too costly, the only thing that was actually built was this spire, which is why it looks very much like a belltower. At the time, this cast iron spire was the first of its kind in the world to be placed on a monument.

NEARBY

Plaque of the emotionally advanced android ⑨

At the foot of the National Monument, immediately on the right at the beginning of the waterfall, an important event is indicated on a discreet plaque fixed to a tree stump: "In this park took place the contemplation of the N44 V864 962, the first emotionally advanced android. He observed a leaf for 2357 hours, deducing its atomic structure as well as its function within the all. 12th September/19th December 2313". Good luck with that ...

ENTRANCE HALL OF THE BUILDING AT KREUZBERGSTRASSE 29

The four seasons in Kreuzberg

Kreuzbergstraße 29, 10965 Berlin
Politely ask a resident for access
U7 / S1, 2, 25, 26 (Yorkstraße) / U6 (Mehringdamm)

The rather banal façade of the building at Kreuzbergstraße 29 does not suggest anything out of the ordinary, but its entrance hall conceals some charming paintings by Berlin artist Wilhelm Wiegmann. A polite request to a resident is usually enough to gain access. Wiegmann specialised in historical paintings and mosaics; his contributions to the mosaics of the Memorial Church and the decoration of the now defunct Hotel Bristol (Unter den Linden 5-6, as it was formerly known) are famous. The paintings created here by Wiegmann represent valuable period documents: four landscapes depicting the four seasons of Kreuzbergstraße as it appeared to the inhabitants of the building when it was inaugurated in 1888.

On the left, a winter landscape shows the southern slope of Kreuzberg before Victoria Park and the waterfall, both inaugurated in 1894. At the top of Kreuzberg is the Friedrich Schinkel National Monument of 1821 and the slope of the snow-covered hill, where children can be seen playing with sledges. To the right, a second painting depicts Kreuzberg in spring. The same hill can be seen again from slightly further away, from the corner of the Kreuzberg and Großbeerenstraße. In addition to the children playing on the slope and the people strolling around the monument, part of the street includes a horse-drawn carriage (the electric tram was still new at the time, see page 416), a few passers-by, and the Richter Villa, which was demolished to accommodate the waterfall in 1893. On the other side, a third painting clearly represents the summer. It depicts the sunlit Kreuzberg hill against a blue sky. On the cobblestone street (*Kopfsteinpflaster*) a man is riding a penny-farthing – the first bicycle with spoked wheels, developed by the Englishman James Starley in 1870. On the hillside, the now defunct Villa Naundorff is difficult to distinguish, unless it is actually the National Monument seen from the top of the hill, in which case the view would be from the corner of Kreuzberg and Möckernstraße.

The fourth painting depicts an autumnal evening. A couple walking under the streetlights is hailed by another couple seated on a bistro terrace.

OLD GAS STATION

Remnants of the former Translag transport complex

Mehringdamm 20–30, 10961 Berlin
U6, 7 (Mehringdamm)

Few customers of the organic supermarket at the intersection of Mehringdamm and Obentrautstraße in Kreuzberg notice that the entrance to the shop incorporates the remains of a petrol station.

Petrol pumps under the large flat roof were supported by four pillars. On either side of the entrance, the two small modern annexes once served as ticket counters.

The main building, which was originally closed at the side (under the roof), served as a car wash; cars entered through a rear door (now walled up) and exited to the side of the shop window facing the Mehringdamm.

The petrol station and its car wash were part of the gigantic Translag (Transport und Lagerhaus) car transport complex.

Developed in the 1920s, it included a dealership, a car repair service and a fleet of 600 delivery vehicles.

The company was located on the former grounds of the German cavalry (the Dragoon Guard).

While 500 soldiers were originally housed at Mehringdamm 22, the four long buildings that can still be seen at the rear housed 700 horses.

After World War I, Germany was demilitarised and the cavalry disbanded. The Kreuzberg Finanzamt moved into the barracks and the Translag into the stables.

Seen from the outside the stables appear somewhat banal, but their ceilings are impressive: the three series of ribbed vaults supported by two rows of cast-iron pillars earned them the nickname “horse cathedrals”. An ideal way to admire them is from the organic market, whose rear wing occupies part of the former stables.

THE TOMB OF ARCHDUKE LEOPOLD FERDINAND OF AUSTRIA ⑫

The extraordinary life of a rebel archduke

Cemetery III of the Jerusalem Church,
Mehringdamm 21
Daily: Jan & Dec 8am–4pm; Feb & Nov 8am–5pm; Mar & Oct 8am–6pm; Apr & Sep 8am–7pm; May–Aug 8am–8pm
U6, U7 (Mehringdamm)

Near the entrance of Cemetery III of the Jerusalem Church, a tomb stands out from the others: a rectangular block of cement supports a wrought iron golden cross, under which is the funerary plaque of Leopold Wölfling.

©Jörg Zägel

This type of grave is generally reserved for people of the church, yet the man who lies here was not known for his unshakable faith or moral correctness. Leopold Wölfling is not even the man's real name; it is Leopold Ferdinand Salvator Marie Joseph Johann Baptist Zenobius Rupprecht Ludwig Karl Jacob Vivian of Austria.

It was only in 1902, at the age of 34, that Leopold Ferdinand, son of the last Grand Duke of Tuscany, renounced his rank as an archduke to embrace a life far removed from the comforts of the royal court and the military career for which he was destined. Free from oppressive family obligations, he married Wilhelmine Adamovicz, a young woman who, according to his contemporaries, made ends meet through prostitution.

The flamboyant couple married in Switzerland in 1903 and moved to the Swiss canton of Ticino, which, at the turn of the century, was home to a colony of nudists and vegetarians. However, their time in this community was brief and Leopold abandoned his wife just two weeks after arriving. In 1907 he married another young prostitute, Maria Magdalena Ritter, acquired from a procurer in Munich, Bavaria. The former archduke travelled to Paris with her, but this second relationship also ended after a few years.

The advent of the First World War and the fall of the Austro-Hungarian Empire meant that Wölfling lost his monthly allowance. Back in Vienna, he opened a delicatessen and worked as a tour guide in the imperial palaces.

However, his wanderlust got the better of him. He moved to Berlin, where he was employed as the narrator for a silent film on the Habsburg royal family, and as a doorman at the *Rakete* cabaret. There, he also played the role of a prince in a comedy set within the Austro-Hungarian Empire.

He later dedicated himself to writing and published an autobiography in both Czech and in English, along with a book of anecdotes about the Austrian royal family. He also collaborated with the daily newspaper *Berliner Morgenpost*, publishing a series of articles on the empresses he had met.

In 1933, at the age of 60, he married Klara Pawlowski, a much younger Eastern European woman with whom he lived at 53 Belle-Alliance-Straße (now 119 Mehringdamm) until he died, penniless, in 1935. Klara, the third and last wife of the former archduke, rests opposite her late husband's tomb.

GRAVE OF THE MÜHLENHAUPT FAMILY (13)

Hats of the Resistance

Bohemian-Lutheran Bethlehem Cemetery, Mehringdamm 21
Dec & Jan 8am–4pm; Feb & Nov 8am–5pm; Mar & Oct 8am–6pm;
Apr & Sept 8am–7pm; May–Aug 8am–8pm
U6 (Mehringdamm)

The gravesite of the Mühlenhaupt family is by far the most original in the Bethlehem Cemetery in Kreuzberg. It features four stelae cast in concrete, each decorated with a colourful portrait of a member of the family: on the left, Kurt Mühlenhaupt and his wife Friedel; on the right, Kurt's siblings Wilhelm and Margarete.

The stones were made by Kurt Mühlenhaupt (1921-2006) himself, a naïve artist nicknamed the "painter of love", who was easily recognisable by the bright red wide-brimmed hat that he never took off — it can be seen on his own gravestone. The hat originated from the deep indignation Mühlenhaupt felt as a child when a teacher hit a Jewish classmate who had the audacity to keep his school cap on as the children sang their daily national anthem. All members of the family are depicted here wearing a hat.

Along with Günter Grass, Kurt Mühlenhaupt was a member of the Berlin society of poets and painters founded in 1972 in Kreuzberg, where he lived for most of his life, not far from the cemetery where he wished to be buried. When his brother Wilhelm died in 1977, Mühlenhaupt made four stelae of precious metal, which he set with enamel portraits. In 1981 Mühlenhaupt said of them: "For the people of Kreuzberg the cemetery is a kind of park. In order to brighten it up a bit, I have placed my own gravestone there, as well as those of my wife, sister and brother. Only my brother lies in his grave for the time being." Stolen in the mid 1980s, the metal stelae were replaced in 1988 by the concrete ones seen there today.

NEARBY

The Mendelssohn-Bartholdy family exhibition room

Cemetery I of the Holy Trinity (adjacent to the Bethlehem Cemetery)
Opening hours as above

In the former chapel of the Holy Trinity Cemetery I, on the south wall that runs along Baruther Straße, an exhibition pays homage to the German-Jewish Mendelssohn-Bartholdy family. The location was chosen because it is in this cemetery that the family's most eminent member, the composer Felix Mendelssohn (1809-1847) – known as the "Mozart of Hamburg" – is buried among his many relatives. Felix was the grandson of Moses Mendelssohn (1729-1786), a major philosopher of the German Enlightenment and the initiator of an impressive lineage that excelled in finance as well as in the arts and sciences.

MAUSOLEUM OF THE OPPENFELD FAMILY ⑮

A surprising Egyptian-style burial place

Dreifaltigkeitskirchhof II Cemetery, Bergmannstraße 39-41, 10961 Berlin
Daily 8am–8pm
U7 (Gneisenaustraße)

In the eastern part of the Dreifaltigkeitskirchhof II Cemetery (on the left when entering from *Bergmannstraße*) is a surprising tomb: with its

overhanging roof, sloping walls, brightly coloured trapezoid entrance, and floral fluting, the Oppenfeld mausoleum is a magnificent example of Egyptian-style architecture.

The mausoleum was built in 1828 according to the wishes of Georg Moritz and Carl Daniel Oppenfeld, two prominent members of the eponymous line of Berlin bankers. The former Oppenheim family had received permission to change its name to Oppenfeld just one year earlier, on 22 September 1827. This change was due to Georg Moritz's decision to abandon the Jewish faith and convert to Catholicism. In 1822 he received the sacrament of baptism and renounced his Jewish name of Moses.

The reason why the banker wanted an Egyptian-style tomb remains unclear. Was it simply a response to the fashion triggered by Napoleon's Egyptian campaign between 1798 and 1801, which had aroused immense interest in the country across the Old Continent? In any case, this architectural choice is not due to the fact that Georg Moritz is related to famous Egyptologist and writer Georg Ebers, the son of one of his cousins. The scholar was born in 1837, several years after the construction of the mausoleum.

TOMB OF ERWIN REIBEDANZ

An astonishing expressionist comet

Luisenstadt Cemetery, Südstern 8-12, 10961 Berlin
Lot 10 – in the middle of the east side (left as you enter)
Dec & Jan 8am–4pm; Feb & Nov 8am–5pm; Mar & Oct 8am–6pm; Apr & Sept 8am–7pm; May–Aug 8am–8pm
U7 (Südstern)

In the Luisenstadt Cemetery, the grave of businessman Erwin Reibedanz (1878-1919) is one of the strangest in Berlin. It depicts a comet knocking over a cross as it rises from the ground. The comet is carved out of a limestone called *Muschelkalk* ("shell limestone"), and constitutes a spiked ball that has a long rectangular tail adorned with rays trailing behind it.

Although it now looks rather dull, it was originally a bright polychrome work of art; surrounded by a hedge of red roses, the base and the cross were painted in dark blue-grey and the lower part of the tail was an intense blue, while the star and the reliefs of the rays were golden. As soon as it was unveiled it was met with strong protests that quickly got the better of this wild array of colours.

Some see in this work an expression of Christian belief, with the comet being the triumphant spirit of death, itself represented by the cross that it tips over. However, it is more likely that the sculpture is a reference to Halley's Comet, which shocked the world when it passed by a few years earlier in April 1910. Reibedanz, who was close to the most avant-garde architects of his time, commissioned the comet in the expressionist style from Max Taut, a pioneer of expressionist architecture and the brother of the famous modern architect Bruno Taut.

There were fears that Halley's Comet – the leitmotif of the expressionist worldview – would annihilate all life on Earth by enveloping it in a cloud of poisonous gas. In this regard, the tombstone would therefore celebrate the overthrow of religion through the passage of the comet.

Other expressionist works in Berlin: see pages 236 and 406.

What is expressionism?

Expressionism appeared at the beginning of the 20th century in Northern Europe, particularly in Germany, and is an artistic current that spanned many fields: painting, architecture, literature, theatre, cinema, music, dance, etc.

Condemned by the Nazi regime as "degenerate art", expressionism tends to distort reality in order to inspire an emotional reaction in the viewer. Representations are often based on anguished visions and reflect the pessimistic view that expressionists had of their time, which was threatened by the First World War, itself heralded by the passage of Halley's Comet in 1910.

As photographic techniques improved and the relationship between art and reality was profoundly modified, expressionism also broke with impressionism (which described physical reality) in a rather aggressive manner through the use of vivid colours and sharp lines. Expressionism is not really a movement or a school, but rather a reaction against academism and society.

Der Blaue Reiter ("The Blue Rider") and *Die Brücke* ("The Bridge") are the two best known groups of expressionist-inspired artists. "The Scream" by painter Edvard Munch and Franz Marc's "The Blue Horse" are two of the most famous paintings of this genre. In music, Dmitri Shostakovich's symphonies were expressionist in spirit from the late 1920s onwards.

THE BIEDERMANN TOMB 

A magnificent mosaic of the garden of Paradise

Luisenstadt Cemetery, Südstern 8-12,
10961 Berlin
Dec & Jan 8am–4pm; Feb & Nov 8am–5pm; Mar & Oct 8am–6pm; Apr & Sept 8am–7pm; May–Aug 8am–8pm
U7 (Südstern)

At the back of the Luisenstadt Cemetery in Kreuzberg, against the south wall along Züllichauerstrasse, is the Biedermann family tomb.

Although it has seen better days, it is one of the most remarkable in the cemetery. Constructed from panelled masonry and massive stone blocks – sandstone and *Muschelkalk* ("shell limestone") – the tomb is an alcove with a galvanised vaulted roof.

The opening is flanked by two statues depicting a seemingly restless man and an overwhelmed woman. For some, these statues are allegories of morning and evening. On closer inspection, however, the precise cause of the man's agitation is hidden behind the climbing ivy: on his right shoulder is the writhing body of a snake. The missing reptile's head can be seen clearly in older photos. It is therefore quite obvious that the two statues represent Eve, who, as a result of her mistake, finds herself grappling with the snake, while an angel adorning the keystone looks on.

The interior of the alcove is dominated by a large stone throne – a symbol of the divine kingdom. It is overhung by a magnificent brightly coloured mosaic and strewn with golden tesserae representing a delicious garden; in the centre of the garden is a fountain, from which two doves are drinking – an image of regained paradise, the fountain a source of youth from which pure hearts drink in the Beyond.

The mosaic bears an inscription in ancient Greek attributable to Menander, a 4th-century dramatist: Ον γαρ οι Θεοί φιλούσιν, αποθνήσκει νέος ("He dies young, he who is loved by the gods"). The quotation refers in this case to Liza Biedermann, who died in 1901 at barely 20 years old.

The tomb seems to have been stripped of its metal parts; there was probably a lamp hanging from the ceiling, a few statues or urns placed in the niches, a gate blocking the access, ornaments on the throne, on either side of which were the death plaques. Presumably made of bronze, it is likely that they were taken during the Second World War for the production of weapons.

COLUMBIAHAUS CONCENTRATION CAMP MEMORIAL

(18)

The largest concentration camp in Berlin

Columbiadamm, corner of Golßener Straße, 12101 Berlin
U6 (Platz der Luftbrücke)

At the northern corner of Columbiadamm and Golßener Straße, there is a small, easily overlooked monument made of oxidised metal. It depicts a house, roughly 2.5 metres high, containing three cells. One of the walls appears to be set back; it recalls a gravestone and serves as a memorial plaque. The ensemble pays a discreet tribute to the victims of the Columbiahaus concentration camp, which was located across the street between March 1933 and November 1936.

From 1920, between Friesenstraße and Golßener Straße, a 19th-century complex housed a division of the Berlin Police. Originally used as barracks, it had its own prison, containing 156 cells and known as the Columbiahaus, located directly opposite, where Hangar 1 of the former Tempelhof airport now stands. In 1933 this detention house was assigned to the SS, who turned it into an extension of the Gestapo Central Prison at Prinz-Albrecht-Straße 8 (on the premises of the

Prussian Secret Police, on which the Gestapo initially depended), as it was soon overwhelmed.

While the other concentration camps set up in 1933 in the heart of the German capital generally depended on SA paramilitary troops, the Columbiahaus camp was special in that it was under SS control from the outset and thus survived the neutralisation of the SA movement at the turn of the year 1933-1934.

The Gestapo became an independent police body and was given exclusive control of the internal threat. The terror of improvised camps gave way to systematic terror in the mode of the Dachau camp. In this respect, Columbiahaus was the only official concentration camp in the capital, the second of its kind after Dachau. It was the largest camp in Berlin and housed 8,000-10,000 political prisoners and opponents, several hundred of whom were tortured to death. As a first concentration camp model, Columbiahaus, like Dachau, was not only a place of detention and torture, but also a place for experimentation and the training of SS officers, on the basis of which subsequent camps were organised.

The Columbiahaus camp was dissolved in November 1936, and the building itself was demolished in the spring of 1938 to make way for the Tempelhof airport building, which was then under construction.

For the other concentration camps that existed in Berlin, see page 202.

The origin of the name Columbiadamm

Originally Prinz-Ausgust-von-Württemberg-Straße, the street was renamed Columbiadamm in 1927 in honour of the aviation pioneer Clarence D. Chamberlin. On 4 June 1927, aboard the Miss Columbia (America's other name, in reference to Christopher Columbus), Chamberlin and his co-pilot Charles Levine set out to break the record for the longest transatlantic flight, which, at the time, was held by Charles Lindbergh.

After a flight of nearly 6,295 kilometres in 42 hours and 45 minutes from New York, they made a crash landing at Eisleben, a few hundred kilometres south of Berlin, breaking Lindbergh's record by 480 kilometres. The next day they landed at Berlin's Tempelhof airport, where they were greeted in triumph by a crowd of 150,000 people.

THE MURAL FRESCO OF FICHTESTRAßE 2

19

A beautiful mural fresco hidden in a backyard

Back yard of Fichtestraße 2, 10967 Berlin
0177 304 0630
nele.wasmuth@gmail.com
Sun 11am–4pm; guided tours on request
U7 (Südstern) / U8 (Schönleinstraße)

Invisible from the street outside Fichtestraße 2 in the district of Kreuzberg is an incredible mural fresco that dates back to the construction of the building in 1890; it covers all the firewalls of the left side of the courtyard – a total surface area of more than 300 square metres.

During Berlin's industrial period, space in working-class districts was at a premium. The capacity of new buildings had been maximised to such an extent that the windows of some inner courtyards overlooked the firewalls of neighbouring constructions. In order to minimise the claustrophobia felt by residents, these walls were often covered with frescoes depicting landscapes with distant horizons.

According to the German Foundation for Monument Protection (DSD – *Denkmalschutz Deutschland*), 25 of these frescos still remained in the courtyards of Berlin in the 1980s. Sadly, around 60 per cent of them fell victim to renovations. The fresco on Fichtestraße was saved and restored in 2018 thanks to the intervention of residents living in the building, in particular Nele Wasmuth, who undertook the steps necessary to finance the operation.

The fresco, composed of large blurry areas, was created in a style recalling that of impressionist painter Edgar Degas. Some see in the fresco scenes of Mozart's Don Giovanni, while others believe it represents a South American landscape at the turn of the 17th century; attentive viewers will notice a Spanish conquistador helmet worn by a horse rider accompanied by a dog.

THE TOAD AT PRINZENSTRAẞE UNDERGROUND STATION

20

The Toad Prince of Prussia

Gitschiner Straße / Prinzenstraße intersection, 10969 Berlin
U1, 3 (Prinzenstraße)

Coming from Kottbusser Tor underground station, at the beginning of the north platform of Prinzenstraße station, it's easy to miss the small sculpture of a toad with a golden crown on its head. The little amphibian, who has been in the station ever since its inauguration in 1902, is a delightful little nod to three things: the name of the station (Prinzenstraße); the Frog Prince (*Der Froschkönig oder der eiserne Heinrich*) from the fairy tale by the Grimm brothers, in which a prince is transformed into a toad; and to the prince who gave his name to the street – William, Prince of Prussia.

The sculpture was created by the Royal Porcelain Manufactory KPM, which has its headquarters not far away at Wegelystraße 1, near the Tiergarten. It has been stolen several times, but fortunately, the underground company had commissioned several copies.

During the recent construction of the new glass entrance, the toad was put safely away in a cupboard; once the works were completed, it was simply forgotten. However, its absence did not go unnoticed for long. After a complaint from several young users, the toad was given a new home in the station – in a hard to reach place to avoid further thefts.

NEARBY

The Stehfisch sculpture (21)

Wassertorstraße 65, 10969 Berlin

It is easy to miss the surprising statue in the small park on the corner of Wassertorstraße and Gitschiner Straße. The Stehfisch sculpture (which literally means "standing fish") by Ernst Baumeister depicts a figure half-man and half-fish or half-whatever-you-want (torpedo?). It is part of a 2004 programme aimed at encouraging the development of art in public spaces.

THE RITTERHOF

(22)

A Gewerbehof *that survived the war*

Ritterstraße 11, 10969 Berlin
U8 (Moritzplatz)

The Ritterhof is one of the few buildings on this street to have survived the destruction of the Second World War. Dating back to the early 20th century, the magnificent dark red glazed brick façade of the former *Gewerbehof* (industrial complex with housing) is certainly worth a detour.

The name Ritterhof appears in large print above the entrance in reference to the street where the factory was built. In German, *Ritter* means "knight", which is why in the middle of the façade, embedded in a niche, is a knight with a sword. The word Hof means "courtyard" and refers to the typical way in which industrial and commercial complexes in Berlin were divided into courtyards.

Further up, above the tiny single balcony with the red railing, there is a horse rearing up – another element that recalls the building's name. And on the entrance portico is a high relief of a man and a woman carrying out their work, representing the primary function of this place.

Built in 1906-07 according to the plans of architects Walter Schilbach and Heinrich Schweitzer, the Ritterhof was commissioned by the heirs of the Scheck'schen family of entrepreneurs.

In the 1930s, before war broke out, no less than 30 companies operating in various fields had their headquarters on the premises of the three inner courtyards. These companies included the Eulen publishing house and the Böhm lighting factory.

The entire complex was restored at the beginning of the 1990s and is now listed as a protected building.

NEARBY

The façade of the Pelikan-Haus

Ritterstraße 9–10, 10969 Berlin

Next to the Ritterhof, the pretty Pelikan-Haus (commissioned by the German banker Georg Solmssen) was built between 1902 and 1905. On the fourth floor of the building there are statues of four Atlanteans, while in the centre there is a gold medallion bearing the logo of the famous stationery company Pelikan. The company had its headquarters there in the early 1930s and lent the building its name.

BAS-RELIEFS OF THE ENGELBECKEN HOF

23

A reminder of the site's industrial past

Leuschnerdamm 13, 10999 Berlin
U8 (Heinrich-Heine-Straße) / U1, 3, 8 (Kottbusser Tor)

The Engelbecken Hof is a building of eye-catching elegance, most notably due to its gable, where two golden suns throw their rays onto the year the building was inaugurated: 1904. Halfway up the building, the corbelled balconies (oriels) display two pretty reliefs depicting a ship and a train, both flanked by helmeted figures with ropes, possibly sailors. They remind us of the building's industrial past.

Built for Kessel & Röhl, a German-Swedish company specialising in cutting and polishing granite, the building was located just in front of the former Luisenstadt Canal, which connected the Landwehr Canal and the Spree. Its location was not chosen randomly; working with stone requires a lot of water.

Imported from Sweden, the stone carved on site was occasionally delivered directly to the gates of the Engelbecken Hof by train, but mostly by boat. The bas-reliefs of the oriels hint at this priceless logistical advantage.

The Luisenstadt Canal, which was drained between the two world wars, became the promenade we see today, with the Engelbecken being the only remaining water source.

It is also worth noting that the front part of the complex is much more elaborate than the rear, as it used to fulfil functions that would now be performed in different places. The Vorderhaus, which faces the street, was used as both offices and a shop. Typical of turn-of-the-century department stores, it was mainly built in the Berlin Secession style; the enormous gable added a medieval touch. The workshops, which revolve around six inner courtyards, were designed in a much simpler contemporary style.

NEARBY

A Jugendstil *lift*

Just after the entrance to the building, on the left before the first inner courtyard, there is a magnificent period lift decorated with *Jugendstil* (Art Nouveau) floral motifs.

Why the name Engelbecken?

The basin over which the Leuschnerdamm flows was named Engelbecken ("Angel Basin") after the archangel St. Michael, who is pictured above the porch of the neighbouring St. Michael's Church.

Until the creation of Greater Berlin in 1920, the canals to the north and south of the city (*Spandauerkanal* and *Landwehrkanal*, both dug for logistical reasons) corresponded exactly to Berlin's boundaries. The entire city was served by sea and had numerous ports, including Humboldthafen in the north-west and Engelbecken in the south-east.

SLABS OF BITUMEN ALONG THE LEUSCHNERDAMM

(24)

Remnants of the third-generation Wall

Between Leuschnerdamm 1 and 19, 10999 Berlin
U7 (Südstern) / U8 (Heinrich-Heine-Straße, Moritzplatz or Schönleinstraße)

Along the Leuschnerdamm, between Bethaniendamm and Waldermarstraße, an attentive walker may notice that several series of paving stones have been replaced by slabs of bitumen; these are very discreet remnants of the Berlin Wall, and correspond to holes made in the street in the late 1960s to drive in the pylons that supported the concrete slabs of the third generation of the Wall.

The East German regime never stopped trying to perfect the Wall: by the time it fell, phase five of its construction was about to begin. Walls built during phase four, which date back to 1975, are generally the most common.

They consisted of two walls separated by a buffer zone averaging 80 metres wide. The outer wall was topped by an asbestos-concrete tube 40 centimetres in diameter, composed of L-shaped concrete elements almost four metres high.

The first generation of the Berlin Wall was completed in two stages. The first phase of the operation consisted of closing the border with barbed wire fences; this was completed on 13 August 1961.

During the night of 17-18 August, work began on replacing this simple fence with an actual wall, roughly shoulder height. It was made of building blocks and cement and was topped with Y-shaped metal pieces supporting several rows of barbed wire.

The second-generation Wall, built in 1962, added a second so-called "inner" wall to the existing one adjacent to the political border, so as to create a buffer zone fraught with obstacles, which was harder to cross and easier to monitor.

Erected between 1965 and 1968, the third-generation Wall was the first version with a uniform appearance, whose sides, already topped with the characteristic concrete pipe, were composed of nine horizontal concrete slabs embedded one on top of the other in H-shaped concrete or steel pylons.

This explains the missing paving stones of the Leuschnerdamm, where the pylons of this third version of the Wall were drilled into the ground.

RELIEFS ON THE FAÇADE OF ADALBERTSTRAßE 79

(25)

A building that was "de-stuccoed" then redecorated

Adalbertstraße 79 and Waldemarstraße 46, 10997 Berlin
U1, 3, 8 (Kottbusser Tor)

At the corner of Adalbertstrasse and Waldemarstrasse is a building dating from the Industrial Revolution; its smooth façades are enhanced with reliefs and painted motifs.

Between the windows on the ground and first floors is a string of ceramic figures depicting scenes of children playing in a park; they are doing somersaults, running, playing tug-of-war, hopscotch ... One child watches his balloon take off a few floors up.

The cornices of the roof are covered with friezes and medallions representing various characters, including a naked woman. The windows are highlighted with a fine line of colour drawn with a brush. Some, which appear to be chosen randomly, are more lavishly decorated and set with enamels.

They are reminiscent of the German architect Hundertwasser's "window right", which urged inhabitants to embellish the space around their windows "as far as the arm could reach".

These listed decorations are the work of Yater Hanefi, an artist of Turkish origin who received part of his education at the Academy of Art in Berlin (West) during the Cold War.

He created these façades in 1984 as part of the International Architecture Exhibition (*Internationale Bauausstellung*, IBA), a federal institution aimed at promoting the urban, social and ecological development of German cities.

It is perhaps surprising that the building, which dates back to 1864-1866, does not have the typical Neo-Baroque façades of the time. They were in fact "de-stuccoed" from 1920 onwards following the advent of modern architecture in Germany (see opposite).

Stucco from Berlin's façades was removed

Until the Second World War, the façades of buildings in Berlin were over-embellished. In the industrial megalopolis suffering from unimaginable social inequalities, this exuberance displayed the pomp of the rich as much as it concealed the misery of the working class. Austrian architect Alfred Loos was the first to denounce this love of artifice and the need to display so-called superiority through external signs. This was the birth of modern architecture, which set out to fight ostentation and lies. By the end of the Second World War, this architectural revolution had become so successful that everything that was not immediately functional seemed ridiculous and outdated, both in the east and in the west. Post-war Germany was rebuilt with ruthless pragmatism. Entire districts that had survived the bombing were demolished to make way for the modern city. Of the 1.5 million dwellings from the late 19th or early 20th century still inhabited in post-war Berlin, only a third are still standing. Half of them have had the stucco of their façades removed to bring them up to date. Between 1920 and 1979, 1,400 buildings in Kreuzberg alone were de-stuccoed. Legend has it that the Berlin de-stuccoers were even paid by the kilo. It was not until the late 1960s that voices began to be raised in favour of the preservation of this architectural heritage. In West Berlin, investments were first made in the renovation of certain streets that were particularly representative of the Wilhelmian era: Planufer and Chamissoplatz in Kreuzberg, Reformationsplatz in Spandau, and Schloßstrasse and Christstrasse in Charlottenburg were the first to find favour with the authorities. In the east it was much later, on the occasion of the 750th anniversary of the city in 1987, that the idea was born to turn the districts of Kollwitz and Helmholz on Prenzlauer Berg into a kind of open-air museum in memory of what the working-class areas of Berlin used to be like. Today, there are neighbouring buildings all over Berlin, some of which have been deprived of their stucco, and others that have not. In Kreuzberg, for example, heading to Planufer from the Admiralbrücke, you can walk along the Landwehrkanal and admire the opulence of the many ornate façades ... until you reach number 96, where the charm comes to a sudden halt. Unlike its neighbours, it was the target of the prevailing policy in post-war Germany to remove stucco. Another example is in Prenzlauer Berg: at the corner of Esmarchstrasse and Käthe-Niederkirchnerstrasse there are two identical buildings facing each other that date back to 1903. While it appears that the stucco of one has been removed, the other has not suffered the same fate. And the difference is rather spectacular.

THE FAÇADE OF THE BETHANIEN HOSPITAL ㉖

Inspired by the Ducal Palace of Urbino

Kunstquartier Bethanien
Mariannenplatz 2, 10997 Berlin
U1, 3, 8 (Kottbusser Tor)

Just a few metres from Saint Thomas' Church on Mariannenplatz, the former Bethanien Hospital is one of the most important art centres in Berlin. This old deaconess hospital was built between 1845 and 1847 on what used to be called the *Köpenicker Feld* (Köpenicker Field); it represents only a fraction of the important urban planning work intended for the Prussian capital, which was experiencing rapid growth at the time. The construction was championed by King Frederick William IV of Prussia, who entrusted Ludwig Persius – court architect

© Jörg Zägel

and student of famous Prussian architect Karl Friedrich Schinkel – to complete it. Some theorise that the king (an expert in architecture) had a hand in defining the aesthetic lines of the hospital complex.

The façade of the hospital was built in the *Rundbogen* style (semicircular arches), an obvious nod to the Renaissance. According to several experts, Persius found his inspiration in the splendid Torricini Façade of the Ducal Palace in Urbino, which comprises a central block flanked by twin towers. The Prussian architect was particularly fascinated by Italian architectural models, and in 1845 (the year he died, aged 42) he set off on a long journey through Italy, visiting several cities, including Rome, Naples, Venice and Verona.

The Bethanien was not his only project inspired by Italian architecture: the same year, construction began on the *Friedenskirche* (Church of Peace) in the park of the Sanssouci Palace in Potsdam. The church is inspired by the Basilica of Saint Clement in Rome. In this specific case, Persius worked from sketches drawn by King Frederick William IV.

© Sailko

THEODOR FONTANE'S PHARMACY

27

A travel through time

Mariannenplatz 2, 10997 Berlin
Tue & Thur 2pm–5pm; Wed 11am–5pm
Free entry
U1, 3, 8 (Kottbusser Tor)

The façade of the Bethanien Hospital may be unusual even by Berlin's diverse architectural standards, but this art centre has something truly unique: along the right wing of the ground floor is the Theodor Fontane Apotheke, the hospital's old pharmacy. The pharmacy is just as it was when its doors closed sometime between 1848 and 1849: wooden apothecary cabinets, obsolete equipment and shelves of bygone vials. It is here that Theodor Fontane, one of the most important German-language realist poets, worked as a pharmacist.

Son of pharmacist Louis Henri Fontane, Theodor arrived in Berlin in 1845 and initially worked in the Polish pharmacy of Dr. Julius Eduard Schacht. Two years later, he received his license as a first-class pharmacist and was hired at the Bethanien Hospital, which had opened its doors just a few months earlier. During his time at the hospital, Fontane was also in charge of training two deaconesses, the first in Berlin to learn this trade, which had until then been the exclusive reserve of men.

Fontane lived in the hospital building – as commemorated by a plaque at 3 Mariannenplatz, near one of the entrances. At that time, he was also a committed revolutionary activist. Although his place of work was built by King Frederick William IV of Prussia, Fontane actively took part in the revolutionary riots of March 1848, fighting for German national unity and against the power of the monarchy.

His experience at the Bethanien Hospital was Fontane's last as a pharmacist. The following year, he abandoned his career to dedicate himself entirely to writing and journalism.

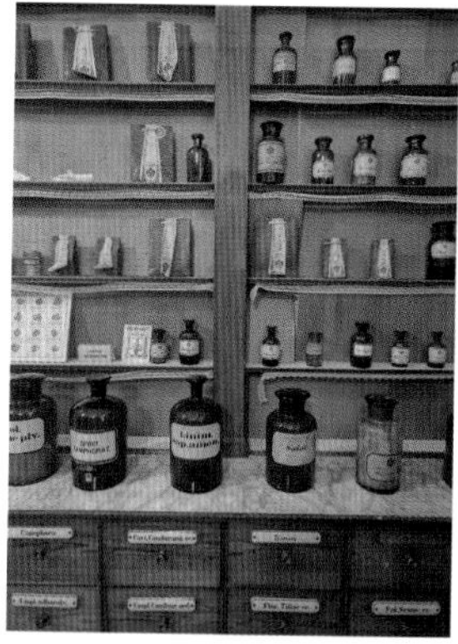

In his autobiography *Von Zwanzig bis Dreißig* ("From Twenty to Thirty") he wrote a few pages about his two years at the Bethanien; in particular, he gave a detailed account of his encounter with Emmy Danckwerts, one of the two deaconesses he had trained.

The hospital's former pharmacy was managed by the Friedrichshain-Kreuzberg Museum (Adalbertstraße 95a) – a museum dedicated to the historical and cultural memory of Berlin's Kreuzberg and Friedrichshain districts.

REMAINS OF THE BROMMY BRIDGE

28

One of the last relicts of the 1851 Verbingdungsbahn

Brommystraße 1, 10997 Berlin
U1 (Schlesisches Tor)

From the *Spreebalkon* observation deck located at Brommystraße 1, the pillar of the former Brommy Bridge, bombed by the German army in 1945 to slow down the progress of Soviet troops, can be seen emerging from the waters like a reef.

This relict is part of the very last railway bridge of the *Verbingdungsbahn*, the ancestor of the Ringbahn, which ensured the transit of merchandise between railheads at the city's gates from 1851 to 1871 (see page 106). After the inauguration of the *Ringbahn* in 1871, the old railway bridges of the former *Verbindungsbahn* became obsolete; some of them, like the Unterspree Bridge that passed slightly east of the Moltke Bridge, were simply dismantled, while others became road bridges.

The Brommy Bridge managed to survive longer for other reasons, replacing the swing bridge along which the connecting train passed as it transited from the Frankfurt train station (now *Ostbahnhof*) to the Görlitz train station (now Görlitzer Park).

The ruins of the bridge are aligned along the axis of the *Eisenbahnstraße* ("road of the railway line"), the name of which recalls the passing-by of the *Verbingdungsbahn* or junction line.

Why was this the chosen trajectory of the Verbindungsbahn?

It was decided that the Verbindungsbahn would pass along this exact trajectory, rather than further upstream or downstream, to meet the needs of the Prussian army: to the west of Brommystraße, the yellow brick complex typical of Prussian public buildings built during the Industrial Revolution corresponds to the former premises of the Heeresbäckerei, the army's bakery, which produced (from as early as 1805 and for more than 100 years) the Kommisbrot, a dark type of bread used for Berlin military provisions.

Not only did the large complex include four large furnaces to cook the bread, it also had its own silos for grain storage, its own mill, administrative buildings, and staff housing.

So the railway line could stop between Frankfurt and Görlitz, not so much to deliver the cereal to make the bread (as that tended to be shipped), but rather to load the tens of thousands of portions of bread that were produced daily, and to ensure their distribution across the city.

For this reason, as well as to deliver the coal used to produce gas on the opposite river bank (where Energieforum currently stands), this part of the railway line remained in use even after the former connection line was decommissioned and the new Ringbahn was inaugurated in 1871.

This swing bridge was too low to let boats pass by underneath and hindered maritime traffic. It was replaced by a higher road bridge, inaugurated in 1909.

The Brommy Bridge was named after an officer of the German marine, the Rear Admiral (Konteadmiral) Karl Rudolf Brommy (1804-1860).

ABANDONED LOHMÜHLENINSEL PETROL STATION

(29)

One of the oldest petrol stations in Berlin

Vor dem Schlesischen Tor 2, 10997 Berlin
U1, 3 (Schlesisches Tor)

The abandoned Art Deco petrol station at Vor dem Schlesischen Tor 2, right next to a second functioning station, is easily passed by. It's not the oldest in Berlin, but according to the current owner, who bought and faithfully renovated it, this beautiful petrol station is all that remains of a larger site formerly devoted to the automobile industry.

The site once included a car workshop, garages (housing 104 sliding door boxes from the Heinrichs company), and a restaurant. It was built in 1928-29 according to plans by Paul Schröder and Max Pohl at the same location as Gustav Ruflair's Stadt-Park-Theater in Lohmühleninsel. The owner used to live on the first floor.

On the side facing the road, the large canopy that was once the station's most striking feature has unfortunately disappeared.

The petrol pump was perfectly situated; in the 1930s, the Schlesische Straße, which runs through Lohmühleninsel and follows the Spree, was essential for traffic leaving the city in the south-east. As its name suggests, it leads to Silesia via Cottbus and Warsaw.

The ancient fountain in Görlitzer Park: a tribute to the thermal springs of Pamukkale in Turkey

Created at the end of the 1980s on the site of the former Görlitzer Bahnhof station, Görlitzer Park is home to a series of concrete terraces, most of which are tagged. They are the last physical remains of a forgotten fountain.

Designer Wigand Witting had imagined a fountain in the middle of the Turkish Quarter, composed of several giant terraces that were supposed to recall the famous thermal springs of Pamukkale, Turkey.

After three years of work, the fountain was inaugurated in the summer of 1998. Unfortunately, the first frosts ruptured part of the structure that was in contact with water. The water supply was cut and for safety reasons the site was fenced off, eventually to be sealed completely. Today, the concrete foundations remain but very few people know the story behind them.

ART INSTALLATIONS ON REICHENBERGER STRAßE

30

In memory of the district's industrial past

Reichenberger Straße 140–151, 10999 Berlin
U1, U3 (Görlitzer Bahnhof)

On the corner of Reichenbergerstraße and Manteuffelstraße in Kreuzberg, the mindful passer-by will notice that incorporated in the pavement's paving stones is a piece of railway a few metres long in which a series of horseshoes are arranged. Further down Reichenbergerstraße going east, several mosaics and 16 cement slabs, in which various tools and mechanical parts have been cast, are visible among the stone slabs.

These installations were made after the fall of the Berlin Wall at the beginning of the 1990s and are the fruits of an artistic project begun in the 1980s. As part of the 1986 International Building Exhibition Berlin (IBA), the Kreuzberg district city hall organised a competition aimed at improving the image of this street – given its notorious filthiness – by recalling its glorious pre-war past.

Following the political division of Germany and the creation of West Berlin, the western part lost its status as capital and became a rather poor city full of artists, baby boomers and rebels. Surrounded by the Wall on three sides, the famous SO36 (South West 36, a district named after the postal codes of West Berlin introduced after the construction of the Wall), the part of Kreuzberg located north of the Landwehr Canal, became the dodgiest area in Berlin, full of squats. In contrast, district 61 in the other part of Kreuzberg was deemed bourgeois. As the saying went: *"36 brennt, 61 pennt"* – 36 burns, 61 sleeps.

Until the Second World War, this was a vibrant working-class neighborhood in continental Europe's most populous and industrialised country. For example, Carl Lindström (Schlesischestraße 26) became Europe's number one manufacturer of records and gramophones. In this regard, Reichenbergerstraße was a typical road. Of the 15 art installations that were apparently intended to grace the wide pavements, at least 10 were completed, some of which are now unfortunately in a poor state or even unrecognisable.

Follow the instructions below to find them:

- In front of Reichenbergerstraßc 153, not far fiom Manteufelstraße and on the north side, is a partly damaged mosaic of an unclear subject made by an unknown artist.

- On the corner of Reichenbergerstraße and Manteufelstraße, on the north side, horseshoes and rails are visible. They are a reminder that until the electrification of train lines around the end of the 19th century, a horse-drawn tramway passed by here. On the south side is another mosaic by an unknown artist. Again, the subject is unclear due to its deteriorated state (see page 416).

- On Reichenbergerstraße, between Manteufelstraße and Lausitzer-straße, on the north side, metallic tools have been cast in the 16 cement

slabs. They refer to the various workshops and factories that once occupied the courtyards.

- On the corner of Reichenbergerstraße and Lausitzerstraße, on the north side, is yet another anonymous mosaic that seems to resemble a knight in armor accompanied by a dove. This work symbolises the Saint Mary hospice located at Lausitzerstraße 44, founded at the beginning of the 20th century by catholic nuns of the congregation of Saint Mary of the Immaculate Conception.

- On the corner of Reichenbergerstraße and Lausitzerstraße, on the south side, is a mosaic by Lutz Werner Brandt entitled "Vom Milchgeschäft zum Supermarkt" – meaning "From Creamery to Supermarket". It depicts a bar code surrounded by four old-fashioned signs displaying the words Milch, Brot, Butter, and Käse – milk, bread, butter, and cheese. The work refers to the not-so-distant past, before supermarkets had invaded our neighborhoods and forced specialist shops to close.

- In front of number 64-66 on the south side of Reichenbergerstraße is an anonymous mosaic of a collapsing chimney crashing through a blue sky with a rainbow. In the spring of 1977 a group of citizens occupied the former red brick firehouse located at Reichenbergerstraße 66; they wanted to turn it into a community centre. However, the building and its big chimney were demolished by the city on 12 May 1977, shattering the dreams of those who had occupied it.

- On the corner of Reichenbergerstraße and Ohlauerstraße, on the north side in front of number 126, is a mosaic by Irene Niepel. It depicts piano keys and refers to the famous Bechstein pianos. The premises in which the pianos were produced are still visible today at Ohlauerstraße 5-11 and Reichenbergerstraße 124. With an annual production of 5,000 pianos, Bechstein was the world's leading piano producer at the beginning of the 20th century.

- In front of numbers 101 and 90 on the north and south sides of Reichenbergerstraße are mosaics of snakes, the symbolism of which is unknown, as is the artist.

- In front of Reichenbergerstraße 80 is a beautiful mosaic by Lutz Werner Brandt showing a telephone handset surrounded by wires. The work pays tribute to the company Richard Bosse and Co., located at Wienerstraße 43, one street north of Reichenbergerstraße. During the 20th century, the company proved to be a major player in the telephone industry before it was bought by AGFEO in 1978.

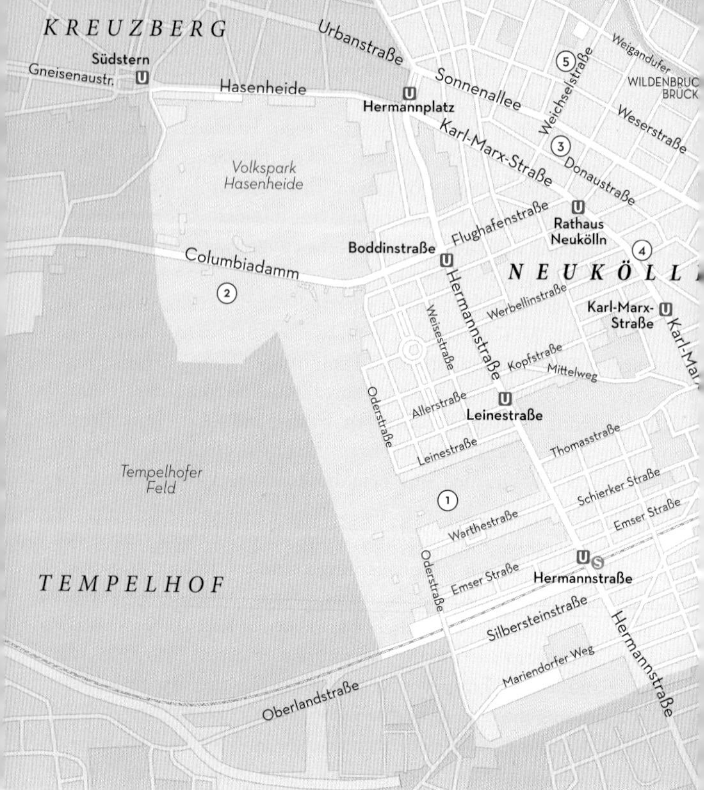
KREUZBERG
Südstern
Gneisenaustr.
Hasenheide
Urbanstraße
Hermannplatz
Sonnenallee
Weichselstraße
Weigandufer
WILDENBRUCH BRÜCK
Weserstraße
Karl-Marx-Straße
Donaustraße
Volkspark Hasenheide
Flughafenstraße
Rathaus Neukölln
Boddinstraße
Columbiadamm
Hermannstraße
NEUKÖLL
Werbellinstraße
Karl-Marx-Straße
Weisestraße
Kopfstraße
Mittelweg
Oderstraße
Allerstraße
Leinestraße
Leinestraße
Thomasstraße
Tempelhofer Feld
Schierker Straße
Warthestraße
Emser Straße
Oderstraße
Emser Straße
Hermannstraße
TEMPELHOF
Silbersteinstraße
Mariendorfer Weg
Hermannstraße
Oberlandstraße

Neukölln

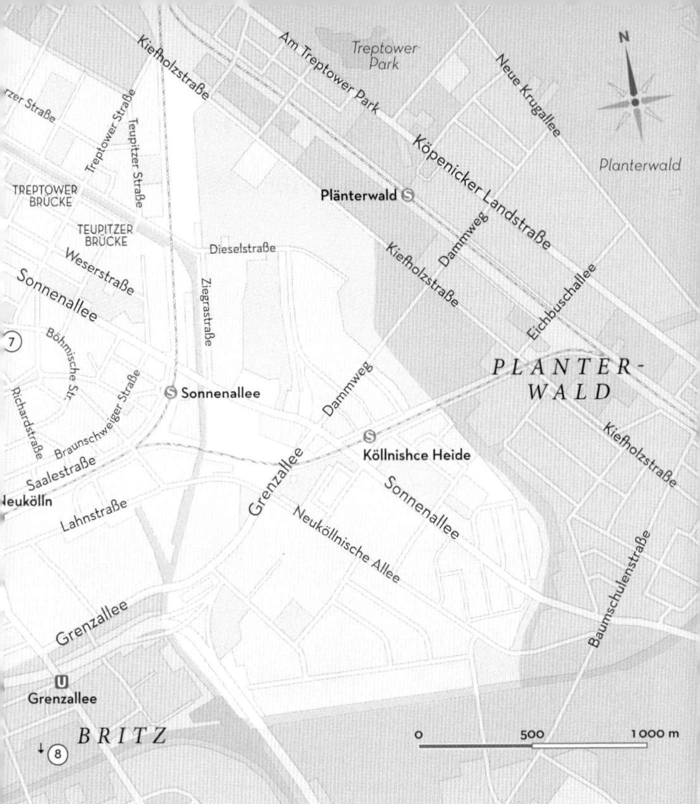
Treptower Park
Am Treptower Park
Kiefholzstraße
Neue Krugallee
N
Planterwald
Köpenicker Landstraße
Pläntерwald
Treptower Straße
Teupitzer Straße
TREPTOWER BRÜCKE
TEUPITZER BRÜCKE
Dieselstraße
Weserstraße
Sonnenallee
Ziegrastraße
Dammweg
Eichbuschallee
Böhmische Str.
PLANTER-WALD
Sonnenallee
Richardstraße
Braunschweiger Straße
Köllnishce Heide
Saalestraße
Grenzallee
Neukölln
Lahnstraße
Neuköllnische Allee
Baumschulenstraße
Grenzallee
Grenzallee
BRITZ
0
500
1000 m
7
8

REMAINS OF "THE PARISH CEMETERY LABOUR CAMP" ⓵

A forced labour camp run by the Church

Camp and commemorative stone
Jerusalems- u. Neue Kirche-Friedhof V
Hermannstraße 84–90, 12051 Berlin-Neukölln
U8 (Leinestraße)

At the back of Cemetery V of the Church of Jerusalems- und Neue Kirche, at the corner of Grüner Weg and Netzestraße (but the entrance is on Hermannstraße), the sunken remains of two buildings built in 1942 are clearly visible. Kept secret for more than 60 years, the place was the camp for the Church of Berlin's forced labour – the church

finally confessed its responsibility for this in 2012. A commemorative stone also stands here in memory of these events. From October 1942 to 1945, about a hundred men at a time were crammed into these barracks: random civilians caught by the Wehrmacht in Ukraine and then deported – 40% of them were under 20 years old, the youngest being 15.

The "workers from the East" had to remove the tombstones and dig graves in the 46 cemeteries in Berlin's parishes. They lived through apocalyptic scenes during the bombings of Berlin, which became more and more intense from 1944 to 1945. When they fell on the cemeteries, the bombs ripped apart the corpses that had just been buried and sent them flying into the trees. The prisoners had to pick up the pieces of flesh and bury them again. If they hurt themselves whilst working, they were transferred to the transit camp before being taken to an extermination camp. A simple request for more labour, and a constant supply of prisoners was assured to take their place. As they were not allowed to go to the shelters during the Allied bombings, they threw themselves behind tombstones or slid into the drains. In the days of the Nazis, Berlin had around a thousand forced labour camps, each holding an average of 100 to 200 people. Most were run by industrialists. The Church is said to have run only this one.

The information pavilion situated in the St Thomas-Kirchhof cemetery, opposite, on the other side of Hermannstraße, 12053 Berlin, provides more details of these horrific events (open from 15 April to 15 October, Wednesday and Saturday 3pm–6pm. Free entry).

THE FIST FROM THE GRENADIERS' TOMB

②

A historic military cemetery full of poetry

Columbiadamm 122–140, 10965 Berlin
Daily 8am–6pm
U8 (Boddinstraße)

Friedhof Columbiadamm is one of Berlin's most interesting and romantic cemeteries, and most of the time you are sure to be almost alone there. It was founded in 1861 for the fallen soldiers of the Berlin garrison to make up for the lack of space in the Alter Garrisonfriedhof (the former garrison cemetery, located at Kleine Rosenthaler Straße 3-7), which had become too small. The cemetery occupies an area of about 10 hectares north-east of Tempelhofer Feld. The location was not chosen at random; as early as the 18th century, this vast field on the southern outskirts of Berlin was used by Prussian troops for parades and operations.

More than 7,000 soldiers lie here. Most of them died fighting in the First and Second World Wars. After 1945, the area was almost completely flattened and only a few particularly interesting monumental graves have been preserved. As a result, visitors sometimes have the impression of being in a huge and very beautiful public garden.

Among the commemorative sculptures, the best known is the Fahnenträger (the "Standard-bearer") – a bronze sculpture created in 1888 by Johannes Boese and considered to be one of his masterpieces. It depicts a soldier slumped at the foot of an obelisk, bearing his flag for the soldiers who fell during the Austro-Prussian War of 1866 and the Franco-Prussian War of 1870-71.

A few metres away is a more sober memorial: a huge sandstone cross with a sword in the middle. It commemorates 50 French soldiers who were imprisoned and died during the 1870-71 war.

Another important memorial sculpture is the one dedicated to the fallen grenadiers of the 4th regiment of Queen Augusta's Guard. Completed in 1925 by Franz Dorrenbach in honour of one of the German regiments that suffered the most casualties during the First World War, it depicts a helmet and bayonet resting on the body of a soldier covered with a sheet.

In a dramatic and poignant manner, the soldier's clenched fist protrudes as a sign of struggle. The imposing base bears the inscription: *Wir starben, auf dass Deutschland lebe, so lasset uns leben in euch!* – "We died so that Germany might live, let us live in you!"

THE FORGOTTEN SYMBOLS OF THE IDEAL-PASSAGE

③

Inspired by the opera "Der Freischütz"

Fuldastraße 55–56 D / Weichselstraße 8–8F, 12043 Berlin
Daily 7am–8pm
U7 (Rathaus-Neukölln)

Built in 1907/08 by the architects Paul and Willi Kind for a cooperative formed by employees from the health insurance company Allgemeine Ortskrankenkasse (AOK), the Ideal-Passage (listed in 1998), linking Fuldastraße and Weichselstraße by means of three inner courtyards, is not a complete secret to the inhabitants of the area. But few realize that the complex, which became a model of social housing at the time of its construction, was built following the structure of the opera "Der Freischütz" (The Marksman), as commemorated by a plaque on both entrances.

Each courtyard has therefore been designed with reference to a scene of the opera.

The first one, near Fuldastraße, boasting an animal above every doorway, represents the "Festplatz des Dorfes", the village fairground landscaped with hedging and hornbeam thorn. In 2006, the courtyard additionally acquired the "Belles Poules", metal sculptures by the German-French artists Gabriele Roßkamp and Serge Petit. A statue of the hunter, Max, used to be in the yard depicting the "Waldhof" (forest clearing).

The second courtyard with its facade paintings of a fountain, a cock, a duck and a farmer and his wife, was destroyed during World War II, as was one of the buildings and parts of a side wing of Weichselstraße. It represented a rural village ("bäuerliches Dorf").

The third and last courtyard corresponds to the "Wolfsschlucht", the wolf's glen, Samiel's hiding place: some facade adornments represent the wild animals and spirits which appeared while Kaspar was casting the bullets.

"Der Freischütz"

Composed in 1821 by Carl Maria von Weber and considered the first romantic opera in Germany, "Der Freischütz" tells the story of the huntsman's apprentice, Max, and Agathe, his fiancée and daughter of the hereditary forester. Both have to fight for their love against Kaspar, who is assisted by Samiel.

THE STONES OF ALFRED-SCHOLZ-PLATZ

4

Mosaic of diversity

Alfred-Scholz-Platz: Karl-Marx-Straße 111, 12043 Berlin
alfred-scholz-platz.berlin
U7 (Rathaus-Neukölln)

Most people who pass through the busy Alfred-Scholz-Platz everyday do not even notice that this square is not like others: if you look carefully, you will notice that along Karl-Marx-Straße, some stones have been assembled along a line with inscriptions consisting of a name, a region of origin, and a percentage that corresponds to the percentage of residents in Neukölln who come from that region.

The square is also partly composed of coloured stones: 67.8% of these stones in the square are greywacke corresponding to the German residents, 13.6% are basalt representing immigrants from the Middle East, 9% are granite for those who came from Eastern Europe, and so on.

Across the square, some stones are marked with a discreet cross that commemorates those who actively joined the project and repaved the

square.

Called *Meinstein* ("my stone"), the mosaic was created by the artist Nadia Kaabi-Linke and represents the very diverse population of northern Neukölln.

From 2010 to 2014, the Tunisian-born artist worked together with the architectural firm el:ch Landschaftsarchitekten on the 910 square metres, placing about 150,000 stones from all over the world.

During meetings conducted by the Dutch artist Roos Versteeg in 2011, Neuköllners discussed homeland, immigration and shared their impressions regarding memory, hope, longing, anger, fear and happiness.

This information was translated into a code designed by the Berlin media artist Ralf Baecker, and later became the graphic image used for the *Meinstein* plan.

Formerly called Platz der Stadt Hof, the square was reopened in April 2014 and renamed after Alfred Scholz, the first SPD mayor in Neukölln, elected in 1919.

NEARBY

Erdemuseum ⑤

Weichselstr. 52, 12045 Berlin
Tel. 030 627 374 74
Wednesdays to Fridays 2pm–6pm or by appointment: erdemuseum.de

Opened in 2015 by Dutch artist Li Koelan, the Erdemuseum is another example of Neukölln's diversity: since 2009, Li has been collecting soil samples from the home countries of the inhabitants of the neighbourhood. Out of the 163 different nationalities living in Neukölln, Li exhibits 303 soil samples representing 120 countries in her small museum.

CAFÉ BOTANICO GARDEN

⑥

A secret permaculture garden

Richardstraße 100, 12043 Berlin
cafe-botanico.de
info@cafe-botanico.de
0 30 / 89 62 20 00 (5pm–7pm)
Tue–Fri 5pm–10pm, Sat & Sun 3pm–10pm
Garden tour: €10
U7 (Rathaus-Neukölln)

From the street, there is nothing to indicate that Café Botanico is more than a café: step inside, go through the restaurant to the inner courtyard, keep going and take the small path on the left that follows a private garden on the right. After about 100 metres, you will discover a fantastic, large permaculture garden (1000 square metres) that boasts an assortment of 200 plants, two-thirds being edible, from the exotic paracress to the familiar apple tree.

This wild garden was established in 2012 by Martin Höfft, using permaculture methods of cultivation and Masanobu Fukuoka's natural farming philosophy. The soil is fertilised by compost and plant manure made from nettle, comfrey, cabbage leaves, yaw, horsetail and other vegetable remains. Martin avoids digging and tilling, working the soil only on the surface. Chemical pesticides are completely banned. The plants should grow as freely as possible in a living and self-regulating space that welcomes bees and butterflies – a bee colony is also part of this ecosystem.

Once a month, Martin guides a group of eight people through his crops. During a one-hour tour, he explains what permaculture is and how he approaches it, tells the story of his garden and presents the best of his wild herbs, the garden's highlight.

Most of the ingredients of the café come, of course, from the garden.

NEARBY

Silent Rixdorf garden ⑦

Wanzlikpfad 3, 12043 Berlin

facebook.com/Silent-Rixdorf-Garten-333924137279861

Usually open every Wednesday from about 4pm to 6pm (confirm on the Facebook page)

Linking Kirchgasse and Donaustraße, the Wanzlikpfad is a small countryside path, a few metres from the charming Richardsplatz. Usually on Wednesdays, behind a high fence, the Silent Rixdorf garden opens its doors to the public who will get free fruit and vegetables (donations welcome), as well as flowers. A little café is also available. Activities are regularly organised. Please check their Facebook page for more information.

SRI MAYURAPATHY MURUGAN HINDU TEMPLE

⑧

Object of veneration

Blaschkoallee 48/Riesestraße 20-22, 12359/12347 Berlin
Daily 7:30am–12:30pm & 4:30pm–7:30 pm
U7 (Blaschkoallee)

The brightly coloured Sri Mayurapathy Murugan temple with its red and white stripes stands out in stark contrast in the middle of the rather banal buildings of the Blaschkoallee and the Riesestraße.

Two rainbow-coloured towers (*gorupas*) rise five or seven metres high over them and are home to a wide range of Hindu gods.

Inside the centre of this Hindu temple dedicated to Shiva, various other colourful gods are venerated. The main god in the temple is Murugan, one of Shiva's sons, just like Ganesh.

Built between 2009 and 2013 by the Indian architect Govindan Ravi Shankar, the Murugan temple is connected to the Tamils from Sri Lanka who came to Berlin in the 1980s at the outbreak of the civil war in their country. Today, there are more than 1,100 of them living in Berlin and they have recreated their country's spiritual environment in Neukölln.

Berlin has two other Hindu temples: in Hasenheide park, Indian worshippers of Shiva built a temple to Ganesh, and in the Gardens of the World Park in Marzahn-Hellersorf, the Balinese built a temple for gatherings mainly on the days of the full moon.

N
TIERGARTEN
LÜTZOW-PLATZ
Kurfürstenstraße
Lützowstraße
Potsdamer Straße
Mendelssohn-Bartholdy-Park
Tauentzienstr.
Wittenbergplatz
Kleiststraße
Augsburger Straße
Nollendorfplatz
1
Kurfürstenstraße
Gleisdreieck
Lietzenburger Straße
Martin-Luther-Str.
Motzstraße
Bülowstraße
Park am Gleisdreieck-Westpark
Geisbergstraße
Bülowstraße
KREUZBERG
Viktoria-Luise-Platz
Winterfeldstraße
Park am Gleisdreieck-Ostpark
Hohenstaufenstraße
2
Goebenstraße
Yorckstraße
5
Bamberger Straße
Gleditschstraße
3
4
Barbarossastraße
Kleistpark
Eisenacher Straße
Grunewaldstr.
Kleistpark
6
BAYERISCHER PLATZ
7
Hauptstraße
Katzbachstraße
Berliner Straße
8
Bayerischer Platz
Julius-Leber-Brücke
Monumentenstraße
Wartburgstraße
10
Innsbrucker Straße
Badensche Straße
9
Belziger Straße
Kolonnenstraße
KOLONNEN-BRÜCKE
Dudenst
Rathaus Schöneberg
SCHÖNEBERG
11
Loewenhardtdamm
Rudolph-Wilde-Park
Dominicusstraße
Feurigstraße
Cheruskerstraße
Leberstraße
Naumannstraße
Fritz-Elsas-Straße
Ebersstraße
Martin-Luther-Straße
General-Pape-Straße
Innsbrucker Platz
Schöneberg
Sachsendamm
Tempelhofer Weg
Gontermannstraße
A100
21
Handjerystraße
Hauptstraße
20
Berlin Südkreuz
13
TEMPELH
Sponholzstraße
19
A100
Hoeppnerstraße
18
A103
Fregestraße
Friedenau
Vorarlberger Damm
Rheinstr.
Rubensstraße
Schöneberger Str.
Priesterweg
Riemenschneiderweg
Eresburgstraße
14
Burchardstraße
KNAUS-PLATZ
Peter-Vischer-Str.
Grazer Damm
Bessemerstraße
Alboinstraße
Feuerbachstraße
Thorwaldsenstraße
STEGLITZ
Kaiserin-Augusta-S
Kniephofstraße
Priesterweg
17
ALBOIN-PLATZ
15
Bergstraße
Friedhof Eythstraße
Munsterdamm
Arnulfstraße
Bismarckstraße
Friedhof Steglitz
0
500
1000 m
16

Schöneberg

WINDOWS OF THE CHURCH OF THE TWELVE APOSTLES ⓵

Windows made of thousands of liquor bottles

An der Apostelkirche 1, 10783 Berlin
U1, 2, 3, 4 (Nollendorfplatz)

Inaugurated in 1874, the *Zwölf-Apostel-Church* ("Church of the Twelve Apostles") does not initially stand out from other churches built in similar Neo-Gothic style. Yet walking around the outside, it becomes clear that some of the windows are not simple panes or stained glass; they are actually made from the bottoms of more than 50,000 gin bottles.

Berlin was the most heavily bombed city of the Second World War. Official figures vary greatly, but according to some estimates, the total weight of all the bombs dropped on Berlin amounts to 450,000 tonnes. Assuming that the average bomb weighed 250 kilos, this would represent about 2 million bombs.

Unsurprisingly, Berlin suffered from a shortage of windows in the post-war period; to replace the windows of the city's various churches, the city had to make do with what it could find. So, as early as the spring of 1945, the local religious community undertook to renovate the Church of the Twelve Apostles, which had been badly damaged in the bombings of 22-23 November 1943.

The family that owned the ***GILKA*** spirits company came up with a truly novel idea, and generously offered thousands of bottles to help rebuild the gigantic windows that had been destroyed.

Renovated in 2018-19 thanks to a federal grant of 28,000, these extraordinary windows are now classified as historic monuments.

MASONIC SYMBOLS OF THE KACHELHAUS

2

A magnificent, secret façade

Goltzstraße 32/Hohenstaufenstraße 69, 10781 Berlin
U1, 2, 3, 4 (Nollendorfplatz) / U7 (Eisenacher Straße)

On the corner of Goltzstraße and Hohenstaufenstraße is a magnificent building with a façade of glazed bricks dating back to 1895. Although this is hardly public knowledge, the building's decorative ensemble was inspired by Freemasonry, which strongly influenced intellectual circles in Germany in the 18th and 19th centuries, including the likes of Frederick the Great, Mozart, Goethe and William I.

For example, just above the door at Goltzstraße 32 is an evocative relief depicting a man blinded by a bright sun. The scene takes place in a painting, itself framed by the branches of a plant emerging from a pedestal resting on two dolphins; the flower of the plant takes the form of a winged female figure. Endowed with a generous chest and crowned with nine rays, she holds two branches bearing numerous fruits.

The dolphin, a symbol of regeneration, wisdom and prudence, recalls the qualities that are necessary to reach spiritual enlightenment (wings, sun, fruits) – the ultimate goal of every true Freemason. The scene is dominated by the Egyptian deity Isis, who presides over the resurrection of the soul, and whose heirs the Freemasons declared themselves to be.

On the corner gable, almost at the top of the building, is an antique helmet decorated with feathers and marked with the enigmatic letter S. The helmet could refer to Athena, goddess of war and wisdom, who is always depicted in armour, and often associated with Isis among the Greeks.

On the frieze on the first floor, we see Ishtar, the Babylonian equivalent of Isis, whom the Romans called Venus. She is recognisable by the star on her forehead; it is the morning star (with four or eight points) to which the goddess was assimilated. The rosettes and eight-pointed buttons on the frieze are another reference to this star.

Ishtar-Venus is also accompanied by a figure with bunches of grapes hanging from his temples: this is the Greek god Dionysus. He was devoured by the Titans, who left only his heart, which Zeus then used to impregnate the virgin Semele. Dionysus is another allegory of spiritual rebirth.

Located on the first floor, a living room decorated with a frieze incorporating the theme of a bloody heart echoes this myth.

The figures of men wearing turbans, as well as the general oriental style of the façade, is probably intended to pay tribute to the Muslim world and the role it played in spreading the Egyptian initiatory mysteries. In medieval times, the Western world was dominated by a rather narrow-minded form of Christianity and sought to eradicate all traces of ancient wisdom. The Moors endeavoured to maintain this Egyptian tradition and eventually reintroduced it to Europe through Spain. At the same time, another epicentre of esoteric knowledge was developing in Italy via Greece and the Middle East: this was the beginning of the Renaissance.

For more information, see *Unusual and Secret Florence* and *Unusual and Secret Rome* from the same publisher.

THE BERLIN COURT OF APPEAL

③

An architectural jewel open to the public

Elßholzstraße 30-33, 10781 Berlin
berlin.de/gerichte/kammergericht/das-gericht/besucherinformationen
Mon–Wed 7:25am–4:20pm; Thur 7:25am–6pm; Fri: 7:25am–2:35pm
Visits to the Plenarsaal are free every first Thursday of the month: 3:30pm–5:30pm
U7 (Kleistpark)

Most Berliners are not aware of the fact that the *Kammergericht* ("Court of Appeal"), in addition to being the oldest court still operating in Germany – established in 1468 by Frederick II of Brandenburg – is also open to the public. This monumental building was built between 1909 and 1913 according to the plans of Rudolf Mönnich and Paul Thoemer, and is one of the best examples of Neo-Baroque architecture in Berlin.

The 135 metre-wide façade of this architectural gem extends to the west of Heinrich-von-Kleist Park, opposite the imposing *Königskolonnaden* ("Royal Columns"). Its central part, which includes the entrance gate, is particularly striking. The portico is similar to that of a Greek temple: it protrudes four metres from the façade, with columns that appear to rest on the second-floor balconies. The three large windows in the middle are topped with sculptures of female heads, while two eagles perch above the round windows on either side. The *Großes Wappen Preußens* ("Great Coat of Arms of Prussia"), adorned with a golden royal crown, rests in the triangular tympanum.

After passing security checks, visitors enter the *Kammergericht* and its atrium, a 17-metre circular hall as solemn as the rest of the building. A wide staircase leads to the upper floors, which are completely open and feature stone and wrought iron balconies. A series of gilded medallions near the top floor depicts ancient figures associated with the notion of Justice: Solon, Hammurabi, Solomon, Lycurgus and Aristotle. The wooden notice board that was used during the post-war period by the *Alliierter Kontrollrat* ("Allied Control Authority"), which had its headquarters in the building until 1948, is visible next to the staircase. This surprising element, vaguely reminiscent of a closet, was used to display the programme of meetings.

Inaugurated in 1917, the ceiling of the magnificent *Plenarsaal* is decorated with frescoes by German painter Albert Maennchen. The ornate balcony above the fireplace was specially designed for the Emperor to enable him to physically dominate a crowd.

The location of the International Military Tribunal that tried war criminals at Nuremberg

On 18 October 1945, the *Plenarsaal* was the scene of one of the most significant events of the 19th century: it was here that the International Military Tribunal that later tried war criminals at the Nuremberg Trial was appointed.

MOSAIC OF A COW

4

The memory of the last Schöneberg milk house

Steinmetzstraße 22, 12207 Berlin
U2, 3 (Bülowstraße)

It is a kind of tradition in Berlin – or at least common practice – to inscribe the history of the city onto its wide pavements. The installations on Reichenbergerstraße in the district of Kreuzberg (see page 152), or more recently of Gunter Demnig's famous *Stolpersteine*, are a good example of this.

In front of Steinmetzstraße 22 in the Schöneberg district a section of grey paving has been replaced by a colourful mosaic of a friendly-looking spotted cow with a swollen udder. The mosaic is a reminder that until 1982 the inner courtyard of the building was home to the 31 cows of Milchhof Mendler, the last milk house in the "inner city" – Berliners call the part of Berlin inside the *Ringbahn* the *Innenstadt*, meaning "city centre".

The first courtyard was a shed that served as a point of sale from where more than 80,000 litres of milk were distributed every year. As for the cowshed, it was located in the second courtyard. To complete the menagerie, pigs, chickens and rabbits were raised in the cellars.

The farm was then relocated to Rudow; until 1996 it had 80 dairy cows, 300 breeding pigs, and 30 hectares of cultivated land. Today, the farm has been converted into a horse riding school with 65 hectares of land still dedicated to corn and pasture.

A unique example of urban biodiversity in Europe

With 2,500 public parks, 48 per cent green space, 53 mammal species, a bird sanctuary (180 bird species are represented in Berlin, more than in the whole of Brandenburg), and 20,000 plant species, Berlin is a unique example of urban biodiversity in Europe.

In 2018 the German capital, whose 1,900 hectares (19 square kilometres) of land are still farmed by 41 farmers, officially had more than 1,200 farm animals, despite the fact that farming activity now takes place exclusively on the outskirts of the city.

In 1928 there were about 25,000 dairy cows in Berlin, crowded into the inner courtyards of workers' housing areas in the heart of the capital. At the beginning of the 20th century, virtually every street in the "inner city" had at least one cowshed supplying the neighbourhood with butter, cheese, and fresh milk seven days a week. By the end of the 1920s, these barns alone covered about 17 per cent of the city's dairy needs ... with all the associated inconveniences: smell, noise, and unhygienic conditions.

Until the early 1980s, the incongruity of these urban milk houses in West Berlin was prolonged by the presence of the Wall; Berliners of Turkish origin were particularly pleased as it meant they were still able to find the fresh unpasteurised milk that allowed them to make delicious yoghurt.

FAÇADES OF KIRCHBACHSTRAßE 1 AND 2 ⑤

A spectacular contrast

Kirchbachstraße 1–2, 10783 Schöneberg
S1, 2, 25, 26 / U7 (Yorckstraße)

At numbers 1 and 2 of Kirchbachstraße in Schöneberg are two surprising twin buildings, each of which includes a multi-storey car park topped with apartments.

While the building at number 2 has remained unchanged since its construction, its twin was richly decorated by the street artist Phlegm in 2015.

With the two buildings being side by side, the contrast between the before and after is particularly spectacular.

Built between 1977 and 1979 according to the plans of Peter Henrichs and Joachim Wermund, the listed complex embodies the fundamental place occupied at the time by cars.

Back then, town halls were destroying entire districts to make way for motorways. Living above one's own car park, built not in the basement but on the first floors of the building, seemed to be the ultimate must.

On the façades, the sixteen vents of the car park's air ducts look just like portholes, giving the building a distinct factory look. It appears that this was also the impression left on Phlegm, an illustrator by profession, for whom the excesses of modern society are a recurring theme. Here, the artist emphasises the mechanical side of the building and interprets the large panels hiding the car park as the spaces of a comic strip.

In Phlegm's illustrations we find his favourite character: a skinny boy with his head stuck in an oversized hoodie.

Scaling the ever-growing mountain of gadgets, the boy strives to remain atop, until the mountain overwhelms him and reduces him to the status of consumer-servant, bending a little more under the weight of his purchases, the devices turning him into a pseudo-cyborg.

THE "RELOCATED" TOMB OF THE LANGENSCHEIDT FAMILY

6

Transferring the deceased

Alter Matthäus-Kirchhof
Großgörschenstraße 12-14, 10829 Berlin
efeu-ev.de
From 8 am in the summer and 9 am in the winter until sunset
S1, 2, 25, 26 / U7 (Yorckstraße)

At the entrance of the old St Matthew parish cemetery, on the left-hand side, on the wall of a more recent building, there is a stylised representation of a funerary monument bearing the inscription "Langenscheidt".

Langenscheidtstraße and the Langenscheidtbrücke (bridge) are close by. They were named after the Langenscheidt publishing house, founded in 1856 by Gustav Langenscheidt, the head office of which was situated in Crellestraße until 2005 (it is now in Munich).

Until 1938, the family burial vault of the founder of the famous publishing house was in Saint Matthew's parish cemetery. However, just like the Tiergarten district, the parish cemetery around Saint Matthew's church (where the Kulturforum now stands) had to give way to the construction of the north-south axis which was planned as part of the Germania project, the capital of the Reich (see page 192). In 1938, a third of the cemetery was therefore "deconsecrated" and the tombs were flattened. These measures transformed the whole of the northern part of this site which runs along Großgörschenstraße.

After 1938, Berliners were not the only people to have been affected by this initial construction work aimed at transforming the capital of the Reich: the deceased were also denied eternal rest. In addition to the old Saint Matthew's parish cemetery, the newer cemeteries of the parishes of the Twelve apostles and of Schöneberg I and IV (Priesterweg) were also to become the victims of Hitler's *folie des grandeurs*, either because the cemetery was in the zone that was planned for the north-south axis, or because it was in one that was planned for a new railway station, a large station for routes to the south to which a huge goods terminal was to be added. By 1940, some fifteen thousand tombs had thus been transferred to Stahnsdorf.

At that time, a dedicated plot (called "Alte Umbettung") was specially set aside to receive about 120 of them, some of which were luxurious family vaults.

The mausoleum of the Langenscheidt family was one of the privileged few that was well treated. The remains that were exhumed from 2,000 tombs and that were not identifiable, were put into a communal grave.

NEARBY

The children's cemetery

The south-eastern corner of the cemetery is particularly moving. The bodies of numerous children who were stillborn or who died prematurely lie in graves here. The graves are decorated with toys and other childhood objects.

VISITING THE SCHÖNEBERG COURT

7

A neo-Baroque building that survived the war

Grunewaldstraße 66–67, 10823 Berlin
Mon–Fri: 9am–1pm on presentation of an ID card
U7 (Eisenacher Straße), U4 (Bayerischer Platz)

Built between 1901 and 1906 according to the plans of Paul Thoemer and Rudolf Mönnich, the Schöneberg Court is one of the most interesting neo-Baroque buildings in Berlin.

It is also one of the few in the area to have survived the bombings of World War II, having suffered damage only in the west wing (on the corner of Martin-Luther-Straße), which was subsequently rebuilt and extended in the late 1950s.

Viewed from Grunewaldstraße, the monumental façade and characteristic entrance represent perfect examples of Berlin's early 20th-century architectural taste.

As in other buildings designed by Thoemer and Mönnich – the Kammergericht Schöneberg (see page 176) and the Amtsgericht Mitte (see page 60) – the sandstone central part of the building is set back from the rest of the façade. Its outwardly stretched columns, wide arched windows and carved ornaments are reminiscent of the elaborate forms often present in Baroque churches.

Above the main door, a high relief depicts Lady Justice blindfolded in the midst of a jumble of human bodies.

Adorning the high tympanum is a group of sculptures that includes St. George on horseback slaying the dragon with his spear.

In between the saint and the dragon is a female figure symbolising human law, while an eye in a radiating triangle (the "Eye of Providence") is superimposed on a thickly branched oak tree, itself often associated with the theme of justice.

The court can be visited during opening hours, after a few security controls. Inside, the bright colours of the ceiling, walls, and wrought iron railings contrast sharply with the austere exterior, while a spectacular circular atrium leads to three upper floors via wide side staircases. The stucco decorations are particularly beautiful, as are the large arched windows that give the room its remarkable lighting.

ORTE DES ERINNERNS MEMORIAL

⑧

A memorial for the neighbourhood

Streets around Bayerischer Platz, 10779 Berlin
stih-schnock.de/remembrance.html
U4, 7 (Bayerischer Platz)

Discreetly placed to the right of the entrance to Schöneberg Town Hall is a map pinpointing several locations around Bayerischer Platz, just a few minutes' walk away. These points highlight a series of 80 street signs that recall anti-Semitic laws of the 1930s. One side of each sign displays text and the date on which the corresponding law was enacted; on the other side is a pictogram related to the text. The signs are a spectacular symbol of remembrance.

In 1933 there were 16,000 Jews living in this district of Schöneberg, which was then called the Bayerisches Viertel ("Bavarian Quarter") because of the architecture of its bourgeois buildings. Among the residents were the physicist Albert Einstein, political scientist Hannah Arendt, writer Gertrud Kolmar, and photographer Helmut Newton. More than 6,000 Jews from this district were murdered by the Nazis after Hitler came to power.

Schöneberg was one of the first districts of Berlin to take the initiative to honour a duty of remembrance, ensuring that its lost inhabitants were

not forgotten. Designed by artists Renata Stih and Frieder Schnock, the Orte des Erinnerns ("Places of Memory") memorial was inaugurated in 1993.

In order to strengthen the link to the past, certain signs are sited in symbolic locations; for example, the sign declaring "Aryan and non-Aryan children are not allowed to play together" appears next to a playground (opposite Heilbronner Straße 14) once visited by families in the neighbourhood.

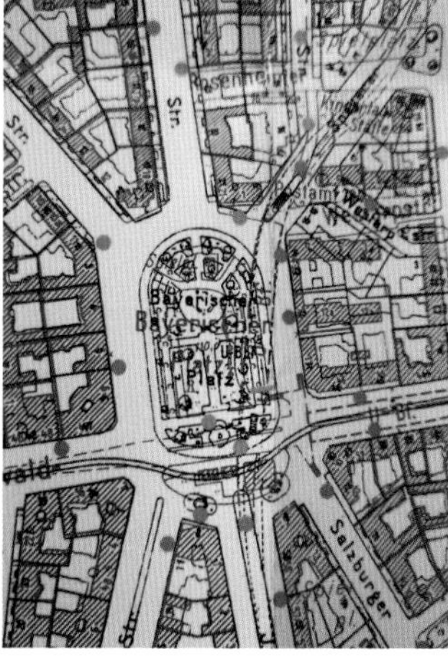

Two other maps showing the locations of the 80 signs are located at the south-east corner of Bayerischer Platz and on Münchener Straße, just south of the intersection with Hohenstaufenstraße.

Some examples of signs

Jews are not permitted to leave their apartments after 8pm (9pm during the summer). September 1, 1939

Costs for treatment by a Jewish doctor after April 1, 1933 will not be reimbursed by the City of Berlin's public health insurance company. March 31, 1933

Jews are no longer allowed to have household pets. February 15, 1942

The smartphone application "Orte des Erinnerns" is available to translate versions of the texts to visitors who do not speak German.

THE FRONT DOOR OF EISENACHER STRAßE 68

⑨

An Art Nouveau jewel

Eisenacher Straße 68, 10823 Berlin
U7 (Eisenacher Straße)

Built in 1901-1902 by the entrepreneurs Christoph Schilling and August Wiehe, following the design of the architect Paul Jatzow, the building at number 68 Eisenacher Straße possesses a remarkable Art Nouveau façade that goes unnoticed by many of the inhabitants in the neighbourhood.

With its floral-themed stuccoes, beloved of Art Nouveau, and its door which stands for the most part within an originally circular structure, it is, however, one of the most beautiful examples of this style of architecture to be seen in Berlin. This style sprang up everywhere in Europe at the beginning of the 20th century under different names: Art Nouveau in Francophone countries, *Jugendstil* in Germany, *Sezessionsstil* in Austria, *Modernismo* in Spain, *Modern style* in the Anglophone countries, and *Liberty style* in Italy.

Having been almost completely destroyed during the Second World War, the building was restored in 1947 and then renovated in 1976.

Jatzow was also one of the creators, some ten years later, of the remarkable Rüdesheimer Platz, possibly one of the most beautiful squares in Berlin, sadly unknown to those who do not live in the neighbourhood.

NEARBY

The Museum of Unheard-of Things ⑩

Crellerstraße 5-6, 10827 Berlin

Wed–Fri 3pm–7pm

Open three afternoons a week, the Museum of Unheard-of Things (*Museum der Unerhörten Dinge*) is a small museum displaying some thirty objects each bearing a written explanation. As its owner will tell you, the story linked to each object is possible ... but not necessarily true, even if he will not always say so. Each paper (translated into several languages) therefore becomes a fun exercise of style bordering on surrealism. If prompted, the person in charge of the place may show you the storeroom of objects, where tens of objects are hanging on the walls arranged in order of their weight: from 10 to 20 grams and from 20 to 50 grams, etc.

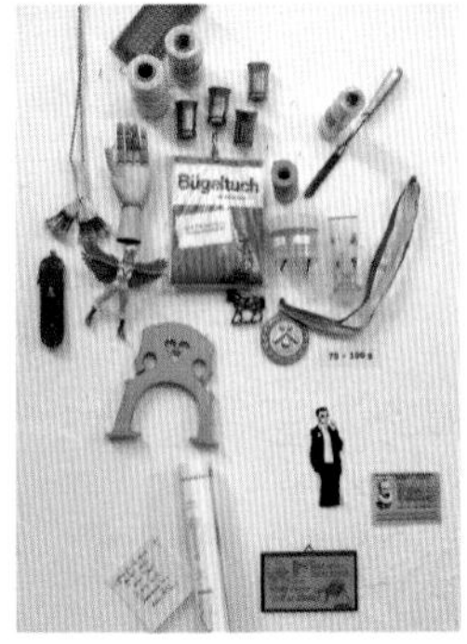

THE SCHWERBELASTUNGSKÖRPER

⑪

A huge concrete cylinder that measured subsidence for the Germania project

General-Pape-Straße 100, Tor 1, 12101 Berlin
schwerbelastungskoerper.de
Apr–Oct: Tue, Thur, Sat & Sun 2pm–6pm
S1, 26 (Julius-Leber-Brücke)

Hidden away from the street behind trees on General-Pape-Straße is an astonishing and spectacular secret place: the *Schwerbelastungskörper* (literally "heavy load structure") is a large concrete cylinder weighing 12,650 tonnes and measuring 21 metres in diameter by 14 metres high.

Hitler's monumental Arc de Triomphe – which was part of the Germania project (see next double page) – was supposed to be erected just a few metres away and last an eternity: the 170 metre-wide arch was called the "T structure" by the Nazis and stood 117 metres high, over twice the height and 20 times the weight of the Arc de Triomphe in Paris. The names of all the German soldiers who had fallen during the First World War were to be engraved on its façades – all 1.8 million of them.

Hitler hated Berlin and did not hesitate to destroy whole sections of it, but he feared that the city's ground – made of till, a mixture of rocky sediment and unstratified loose material left behind by glaciers – would collapse under the colossal weight of the arch. The *Schwerbelastungskörper* was used to test (down to a depth of 17 metres) the capacity of the ground to support the expected weight of the monumental arch. To do this, an optical device located inside the structure measured how fast the concrete cylinder was sinking into the till.

Designed in 1941 by Albert Speer, the building ultimately went unused. But unlike the many colossal constructions that were planned but never built by the Nazis, this concrete mastodon is undeniably real, and has been listed as a protected building since 1995.

In the two and half years following 1941, the Schwerblastungskörper sank 19.3 cm instead of the required 2 cm maximum limit.

Germania, Hitler and Albert Speer's crazy project for the "world capital"

After having failed the entrance exam to the Vienna Academy of Fine Arts twice, Adolf Hitler was convinced that he was an unrecognised artist. To earn a living, he sold watercolour sketches of Vienna. After having been temporarily blinded in the First World War, he decided to launch into politics after he was cured in 1920. At this time, he was already obsessed by the idea of a Great German Reich and was sure that even a thousand years after the fall of this empire, its greatness would be measured by what it would leave behind.

Hitler developed the idea of two flagship buildings in the architectural sketches he drew in 1925 – these buildings would be in the capital of his imaginary Great Reich that he called "Germania" and constituted a triumphal arch and a grand people's hall for assemblies. After his accession to power, Hitler's architectural ramblings began to take form during discussions with Albert Speer, a fervent Nazi and freshly qualified architect, whom the dictator promoted to the rank of Inspector General of Construction for the capital of the Reich. In 1937, after having received Hitler's approval, Speer's partly illustrated plans for Berlin/Germania were published in the press. On 4 October, the new law on the reconstruction of German towns constituted the legal basis that was to allow the grand scale demolition of existing districts to make way for new buildings situated in strategic areas of the city centre. The published plans made absolutely no reference to the "world capital Germania". Hitler simply referred to "Germania" or to the restructuration of the capital of the Reich. The prestigious buildings imagined by Hitler (the Great Dome/ Hall of the People and the Triumphal Arch) are only vaguely mentioned as mere outlines. However, in the plan of the new Berlin that was made public, it is possible to make out an east-west axis and a north-south axis. The latter was planned to go from the new North station to a new South station which would have replaced the S-Bahn Papestraße station near a new town (Südstadt), which would be home to hundreds of thousands of inhabitants. The western part of the east-west axis – including several new buildings – was finished in time to celebrate Hitler's 50th birthday in 1939: it ran from the Brandenburg gate to Adolf Hitler square (today named Theodor-Heuss-Platz) going through

the new Großer Stern roundabout to which the Victory Column had been moved. The preparatory work for the construction of the Great Dome and the Triumphal Arch, as well as for the entire north-south axis, included the demolition of the districts of Alsenviertel and Tiergarten, and the erection of the "heavy loads structure" of the German Society for Soil Mechanics (DeGeBo) to study the resistance of soils composed of non-stratified materials (see page 190). It also included the construction of railway tracks on a level with Priesterstraße and three tunnel segments for the road traffic where the two axes were planned to cross over. On the north-south axis Grazer Damm and the Tourist Office were created on the Place Ronde.

The new airport of Tempelhof is not specifically referred to in the project as plans for it had already been drawn up. It was practically finished when the war broke out and it would have been the central airport for the restructured capital of the Reich. Inaugurated for the 1936 Olympic Games, the stadium of the Reich, with all its annexes, would have been the heart Germania's sports installations. The embassies that were moved outside the district of Alsenviertel (see page 265) were supposed to form Germania's new district of embassies. The head offices of Krupp in the capital of the Reich and those of many other companies in addition to the State's administrative buildings (for example, on Fehrbelliner Platz) were finished. The barracks and buildings of the army's General Staff and the Reich's youth organisations were also built. The exceptional, new buildings referred to in the plans and which were completely or almost completely finished, included the construction of the Faculty of the Technology of Armaments of the future university city; the Ministry of Popular Education and Propaganda; Goering's Ministry of Aviation; the enlarged Reichsbank; the Mint of the Reich and Molkenmarkt, the new administrative district with the new Mühlendamm lock. The new Mühlendamm bridge was not completed.

A sample section of the fourth motorway bypass around Berlin was tarmacked in front of the Telefunkenwerk factory of Zehlendorf (which brought together 37 of Berlin's old Telefunken workshops, see page 422). On the edge of Spandau, a community of forced labourers, put there to build the Great Dome, was also created. After the declaration of war, only a few building sites commenced work. Speer, the Inspector General of Construction, put a stop to the demolition of old buildings for the north-south axis.

What buildings and traces has the Germania project left behind?

1. Charlottenburg tax centre (*Finanzamt*)
2. The central House of Assembly of German municipalities (*Deutscher Gemeindetag*)
3. Charlottenburg Bridge
4. Victory Column with its access routes and sculptures
5. Albert Speer's streetlamps along the east-west axis (to the west)
6. Segments of the road traffic tunnel on the north-south axis planned for the circulation of traffic without crossroads
7. Kerbstones of pavements on the proposed north-south axis on a level with the intersection of the east-west axis (see page 266)
8. Post Office N4
9. Ministry of Popular Education and Propaganda
10. Ministry of Aviation of the Reich
11. The extension of the Bank of the Reich
12. Ministry of the Interior of the Reich
13. District Employment Office (*Gauarbeitsamt*)
14. Municipal insurance Feuersozietät
15. Post Office SW 11
16. The Mint of the Reich
17. Schwerin Palace
18. Administrative buildings on the Molkenmarkt
19. The Mühlendammschleuse
20. Municipal administrative building C
21. The Embassy of Japan
22. The Embassy of Italy
23. The Embassy of Yugoslavia
24. The Embassy of Norway
25. The Feuersozietät der Provinz Brandenburg
26. Head Offices of Krupp in the capital of the Reich
27. The House of the German Labour Front (DAF)
28. The Nordstern life insurance bank
29. The Office of Cereals of the Reich
30. The administrative head offices of the German Labour Front (*Deutsche Arbeitsfront*)
31. Karstadt administrative building
32. Head Office of the construction of motorways of the Reich and Federation of the dairy industry
33. Tempelhof Central Airport
34. Grazer Damm buildings
35. Structure for heavy loads (*Schwerbelastungskörper*, see page 190)

36. Transfers from the Matthäuskirchhof parish cemetery (see page 186)
37. Clearance of the Tiergarten district
38. Pristerweg goods station
39. A trial section of the 4th motorway bypass (*Ring*, see page 422)
40. Telefunken plant in Zehlendorf
41. SS Central office of administration and the economy (WVHA) with the Fichtenstraße bunker
42. Command of the airborne division (*Luftgau*) III
43. Ruins of the Faculty of Amament Technology (buried under the rubble of the Teufelsberg)
44. Telephone tunnel of the GBI (Inspector General of Construction, Speer) in Postfenn
45. Intact original buildings from the "Sports field" of the Reich/1936 Olympic Park
46. Main hall of the Masurenallee exhibition centre
47. Messedamm glass gallery
48. "Große Halle workers' community"
49. Camaraderie SS living quarters of Krumme Lanke
50. Barracks of *Leibstandarte* Adolf Hitler's SS (personal guard) on Finckensteinstraße
51. General management of the Department of work of the Reich (RAD)
52. Youth centre for the Rehberge Hitler Youth
53. Association of Chemical Industry Professionals (*Berufsgenossenschaft*)
54. Reich school of air protection
55. Arno Breker's workshop
56. Command of the military district (*Wehrkreis*) III
57. General command of the 3rd corps of the land army
58. Allianz – und Stuttgarter insurance Lebensversicherungsbank on Mohrenstraße
59. Grain silo from the construction plan of the silos of the Reich in the west port
60. Philipp-Holzmann-AG's plant on the Heerstraße
61. General management of the Reich's youth
62. General Göring Barracks of the infantry regiment of the *Luftwaffe*
63. Arthur Vogt AG administrative building on Berliner Straße
64. Humboldthain Flak Tower (DCA)
65. Division of Prisoners of war of the High Command of the *Wehrmacht* (OKW)
66. House of Switzerland Friedrichstraße/Unter den Linden
67. Federation of the German beer industry in Badener Straße

HISTORICAL COLLECTION OF THE BERLIN POLICE

⑫

The capital of crime

Platz der Luftbrücke 6, 12101 Berlin
phs-berlin.de
Mon–Wed 9am–3pm
U6 (Platz der Luftbrücke)

In the right wing of the former Tempelhof Airport, where the Berlin Police has been headquartered since 1951, the Berlin Police Historical Collection is an interesting little museum that most Berliners don't know about.

Some of the objects on display are rather merciless. Who would expect to discover upon entering the museum a real medieval guillotine used by an executioner to decapitate an unknown number of convicts?

The brutality conveyed by these exhibits is all the more powerful given that they are seemingly displayed in no rational order. For example, paperweights or machine guns are displayed alongside homemade weapons, ranging from sticks sadistically garnished with sharp nails to copies of prehistoric axes. In another display case the skulls of unknown murder victims speak for themselves.

The exhibition is not sensationalist, nor does it try to be exhaustive. No attempt is made here to promote a strong and efficient police force (like in Hamburg). That said, nowhere else is there so much information about the Criminal Brigade founded in 1926 by the famous Ernst Gennat. Gennat's investigations into the murder of two Bülowplatz police officers implicated two communists (one of whom, Erich Mielke, was to become the head of the Stasi), and he was subsequently appointed director of the Berlin Criminal Police by Hermann Göring in the days of the brown shirts.

Of course, it is also possible to see objects related to some of the major cases that caused a buzz among Berliners: the case of the Sass brothers, who were safecrackers before the Second World War; or the blackmailing of Arno Funke, aka Dagobert, in several department stores. But those keen to know what happened to stolen objects like the Big Maple Leaf (a giant 100-kilogram gold coin) that was stolen from the Berlin Bodemuseum in 2017 will have to be patient; the investigation into that much-publicised theft, which involves an Arab clan from Neukölln, is still ongoing.

Berlin remains the capital of crime: in 2019 unknown individuals entered the police headquarters through a broken window and stole decorations, documents, and other collectors' items. The reaction of the Berlin police commissioner? "No comment."

THE PRISON OF GENERAL-PAPE-STRAßE

(13)

The very first concentration camp in the heart of Berlin

Werner-Voß-Damm 54a, 12101 Berlin
0 30 / 9 02 77 61 63
gedenkort-papestrasse.de
Tue–Thu & Sun 2–6 pm
Free entry: Free guided tours in German on request, booking by telephone
S1, 2, 41, 42 (Berlin Südkreuz)

It is commonly agreed that any place where deported people, prisoners of war, political prisoners, or individuals considered as enemies of the state are kept under surveillance by the police or the army is a concentration camp.

Bearing this definition in mind, the prison of General Pope Street (Gefängnis Papestraße), set up in mid-March 1933 at number 54a Werner-Voß-Damm (an outbuilding of the complex whose entrance used to be on the General-Pape-Straße), is considered today as having been Nazi Germany's very first concentration camp.

Since March 2013, (exactly 80 years after it was built), the old cells in the cellar have become a memorial, with archives and an exhibition giving details of the terrible events which took place there at the beginning of the Third Reich.

Since some prisoners had been allocated a number or registration date, research work to identify the prison's victims became possible and helped piece together a certain number of facts.

The first known prisoner was recorded on 15-16 March 1933 and was allocated the number 43. The last identified prisoner to date bore the number 1842, dated November 1933. It would seem, therefore, that in the basement of this former barracks attached to the railway division (Eisenbahntruppen) of the Prussian army, about 2,000 people were kept prisoner there during 1933. They were mainly communists and socialists from the KPD (The German Communist Party), the SDP (The German Socialist Party), trade unionists and prominent Jews. At least 30 of them were beaten and tortured to death. To date, about 500 prisoners have been identified.

There were other concetration camps in Berlin (see next pages).

© Harry Weber

The other concentration camps in Berlin

Some may find it surprising that concentration camps existed in the very heart of the German capital, only days after the elections of 5 March 1933 which enabled the Nazi Party to seize power. It is important to remember, however, that Hitler had been appointed chancellor as early as 30 January 1933, and a month later, on the very day after the Reichstag fire on 27-28 February 1933, he had already declared a state of emergency against the communist threat.

Freedom of expression, the right to gather and the majority of civic rights were suspended, and the hunt for communists and Jews was unleashed. In 1933 alone, the regime took an estimated 200,000 political prisoners.

The German prisons soon began to overflow, and it is likely that the first makeshift concentration camps were built, even before the elections at the beginning of March. This is how inter-war Berlin, which had been a bastion of communism and German socialism and had 170,000 Jewish residents, became rife with places of imprisonment and torture. According to current research, there were no fewer than 220 such places, of which 11 could be considered as having been organised concentration camps, generally in the city centre, visible to all, and aimed at terrorising the population and discouraging anyone who was thinking of resisting.

In addition to the Papestraße prison, two others were built in March 1933 and were amongst some of the first camps in Berlin.

- One was in the machine room of the Prenzlauer Berg water tower, a building measuring 100 square metres, dynamited in 1935, where a number of political prisoners and enemies of the regime were held and tortured between March and June 1933. A commemorative plaque and a sign placed in front of the water tower located at number 23 Knaackstraße commemorate the victims (see page 285).

- And another which was, by far, the capital's largest concentration camp was set up in the Columbiadamm former military prison in Kreuzberg, which stood on the south side of the avenue, on the corner of Golßener Straße (see page 130).

© Harry Weber

Der Gefangene .... geb. d. ....

eingeliefert d. .... 1933 .... Uhr hat die

Gefangenennummer ....

Berlin, d. ....

VISIT TO THE MALZFABRIK

⑭

Strange chimneys not for evacuating air but for sucking it in

Bessemerstraße 2–14, 12103 Berlin
reservix.de (Verlassene Orte – Schultheiss Fabrik)
"Malzreise" guided tours must be booked in advance
€17.50 per person
U6 (Alt-Tempelhof) / S2, 25, 26 (Priesterweg) / S41, 42, 45, 46 (Tempelhof)

Although the Malzfabrik in Schöneberg is not an unfamiliar sight to Berliners, very few have been inside and know what these intriguing chimneys were used for.

One large structure topped with four distinctive metallic extensions towers over other tall brick structures in the site on Bessemerstraße. These *Darrhauben*, each weighing 3.3 tonnes, are commonly known as "knights" (*Ritter* in German – which is cognate with *Reiter*, i.e. knight) as they seem to be straddling the roof.

These surprising features, which spin around separately, reacting to the slightest gust of wind, are not chimney caps: they were in fact designed to suck in the air and to carry it to the very heart of the building, where a constant stream of air was necessary for the production process.

The maltings belonged to the famous Schultheiss brewery, the main premises of which were located in Prenzlauer Berg (and which today is home to the Kulturbrauerei), but those premises in Pankow and Schöneberg were used exclusively for the production of malt.

During the guided tour of the partially conserved installations inside the Schöneberg site, visitors are taken on the *Malzreise* (the malt journey) showing the journey that the cereals (barley and wheat, for example) took before they were transformed into malt for the breweries in those days. It is a good way of getting to grips with brewer's jargon.

In the old *Tennenmälzerei* where the germination took place on a threshing floor, the grains were spread over a stone surface, sprayed with water and turned over with a fork or a rake by malters to air them. In the next phase in the Darren (drying kilns – the term comes from *dörren* – to dry/dehydrate), they were firstly aired to expel the water contained in the air coming from the "knights" before being dried with hot air (basic drying) then very hot air ("the blast").

At a later date, "pneumatic" malting was introduced: it was done in rectangular boxes with mechanical ventilation, then in rotating drums in which the grains could also be dried. These drums can be seen in the malthouse.

The pungent smell in the air and the sheer size of the place takes the visitor back in time to the atmosphere that must have once reigned there.

BLANKE HELLE SCULPTURE

A legendary backstory

Alboinplatz 8, 12105 Berlin
U6 (Kaiserin-Augusta-Straße)

In Alboinpark, at the northern end of Alboinstraße (on the corner of Burgermeisterstraße), a huge statue stands on a terrace with a view of a pond contained within a *Kettle* or *Soll*, i.e. a circular depression rather typical in Berlin. The sculpture was constructed in 1934-1936 as part of a job creation programme: sculptor Paul Mersmann Snr. (1903-1975) created this auroch (an extinct species of wild cattle) with the assistance of unemployed artists who were assigned to compulsory work. According to locals, the sculpture portrays "the biggest ochse in Berlin" (ochse can be translated into English as "ox", but also "oddball" or "saddled donkey"). Berliners gave it this nickname at the time of its construction.

The sculpture consists of small cubic paving stones from the Rüdersdorf limestone quarry arranged around a core of rubble from the Reich War Ministry (which had been destroyed to make room for Göring's Aviation Ministry). It appears as if the animal has stopped suddenly in its tracks, as often seen in bullfights.

While this sculpture is already quite astonishing in its construction technique, it also evokes the old legend of *Dame Holle* and the *Blanke Helle* glacial sinkhole. Legend has it that in pre-Christian times, Hel, the goddess of the underworld in Germanic mythology (from which the word *Hölle* or "hell" is derived, hence *Dame Holle*, or "Lady Hell"), helped a priest here by sending him powerful draft animals (notably bulls) every year to help him cultivate his field. In return, the priest was required to make offerings to Hel on a rock near the pond, which represented the entrance to the world of the dead.

The *Kettle* or *Soll* is a natural phenomenon that began after the last ice age at the end of the Pleistocene: when a large block separates from a glacier, little by little, the block is covered and pushed down under glacial sediments, which delays its melting. When it finally melts, it collapses and creates a hole that fills with water every year.

Alboin is the name of a Lombard king of the 6th century. The reason why his name was given to a square in the neighbourhood is unknown.

THE ORGAN OF THE MARTIN-LUTHER-GEDÄCHTNISKIRCHE

16

The organ of the Reich party congress

Riegerzeile 1a, 12105 Berlin
Information and bookings: 0 30 / 2 16 35 71
info@bfgg.de (Berliner Forum für Geschichte und Gegenwart)
U6 (Westphalweg)

The "Martin-Luther-Gedächtniskirche" (Martin Luther Memoria Church) was designed in a quasi-expressionist style by the architec Curt Steinberg (1880-1960). Inside there is a large chandelier in th shape of an Iron Cross, decorated with a garland of golden oak leaves Hindenburg, the president of the Reich (from 1925-1934), and Luthe face each other with an expressionless gaze, and a quote from Luther i written in Gothic lettering on the wall: "Our God is a fortress, a gooc sword and a weapon".

In the slightly sloping hall of the church, the Triumphal Arch stand out above the apse: 800 terracotta tiles laid side by side display symbol of Nazi ideology, alternating with those of Christianity. This is how for example, an eagle of the Reich, the Iron Cross, a head wearing th Wehrmacht's typical "bolt helmet" or the emblem of the NSV (th

National Socialist People's Welfare Service) to name a few, can be found side by side with Christ, the crown of thorns, the chalice, the dove of the Holy Spirit or the rose of Luther. The Triumphal Arch glorifies a muscular Christ on the cross, hardened by battle: the first soldier of the Aryan faith. There are other terracotta ornaments in the apse with no real political significance. The walls' sturdy pillars bear the heads of Christian reformers such as Martin Luther and Philipp Melanchthon, of the musicians Johann Sebastian Bach and Georg Friedrich Händel, and of the poets and hymnists Martin Rinckart and Paul Gerhardt. The founding fathers of the "Innere Mission", Johann Hinrich Wichern and Friedrich von Bodelschwingh, are also portrayed here. A closer look at the wooden sculptures of the pulpit will reveal an idealised Nazi family listening to a Sermon of Christ on the Mount: a soldier, a German mother and two children from the Hitler Youth. An unsettled SA (assault platoon) paramilitary, looking like Hitler, stands near the baptismal font.

Although the first stone was laid in October 1933, the Martin-Luther-Gedächtniskirche (which was supposed to celebrate the 450th anniversary of the reformer) was inaugurated in December 1935. At Hitler's request, the Walcker organ with its five manuals, 220 registers and 8,300 pipes had been inaugurated three months earlier at the Nuremberg Rally. It was played for the very first time in the Luitpoldhalle in front of 16,000 Nazis for the opening of their annual gathering. Backed up by 36 loudspeakers and a symphonic orchestra, the organ accompanied Göring's proclamation of the Nuremberg racial laws (on the citizenship of the Reich and the protection of German blood and German honour). It is to be noted that "Gott mit uns" (God with us) was written in an arch-shaped inscription on the buckle of the Wehrmacht's belt, a motto which was decorated with a half-crown of oak leaves. The central motif was an eagle with outstretched wings holding the swastika in its talons.

NATUR-PARK-SÜDGELÄNDE 17

A spectacular and unusual park

Prellerweg 47–49, 12157 Berlin
gruen-berlin.de/natur-park-suedgelaende
Daily 9am to dusk
No bikes allowed
S2, 25, 26 (Priesterweg)

Inaugurated in 1999, Natur-Park Südgelände remains a mystery to many Berliners, thanks in part to its three rather inconspicuous entrances. The main entrance, located to the south, is the easiest to find and can be reached via the tunnel of Priesterweg S-Bahn station.

The public park was built on the grounds of a former marshalling yard that housed repair and maintenance workshops. It is now an amazing 18 hectare-long nature reserve – a stunning environment where nature has regained its rights after years of neglect, and where hundreds of plant and animal species (60 of which are endangered) appear to be flourishing. Dotted here and there are strange artistic installations and interesting relics from the past, such as an impressive 50 metre-high water tower once used to fill the tanks of steam locomotives, a huge turntable that allowed the locomotives to change direction (see page 260), and a spectacular locomotive from the 1940s.

During the golden era of the railroad, the entire Prussian railway network was organised around the capital in a star shape. Berlin served as the transfer point between all the lines, and transit between various stations at the gates of the city was operated by means of the Ringbahn. However, freight trains sometimes included wagons that travelled through the capital before going on to different destinations. This heralded the invention of marshalling yards, where trains were reassembled according to the destination of the wagons.

North of Prellerweg, Tempelhof Station was created in 1889 right where the Anhalt and Dresden lines merged. It was expanded several times, and over the years it became one of Berlin's most important marshalling yards. After the Second World War and the construction of the Berlin Wall, the station gradually fell out of use. In the early 1980s, plans to redevelop the site were about to materialise, but nature had taken over the site to such an extent that a popular initiative easily demonstrated that dozens of endangered species had found refuge there, so the area was protected.

Today, hikers travel along a path made up of grids attached to metal pipes, which are themselves installed on the old rails. This is to allow the flora to grow unhampered, the fauna to move freely around the site, and the rainwater to flow naturally.

HOUSE AT NIEDSTRAßE 4

An incredible façade

Niedstraße 4, 12159 Berlin
S1 (Friedenau) / U9 (Friedrich-Wilhelm-Platz)

The *Drachenhaus* ("dragon house") at Niedstraße 4 is a spectacular building dating back to 1899. Its façade is decorated with a series of sculptures of characters apparently linked to the theme of enjoying life (note the vine, the beer mug, the monk and his belly) while being careful (the owl and his mirror) to avoid the harmful consequences (the dragon, the crow) of indulging too much. The sculptures, based on the drawings of an unknown artist, were produced by the Hermann Noak foundry, which was established two years earlier in Friedenau (now located in Charlottenburg), and to which Berlin owes the casting of many major works.

Supported by two gargoyle-shaped corbels, the oriel window is topped by a large winged dragon and shamrocks that appear under the windows of the second floor.

In the centre, a monk (with a rather prominent belly that demonstrates just what a *bon vivant* he is) emerges from a barrel marked with the year the building was inaugurated. Originally, he brandished a mug of beer in his outstretched left hand, but it has since disappeared. Two branches of vines are tied together around him with a ribbon, from which hang a large key and a pair of shoes.

On either side of the monk, two large birds are perched between vine leaves. On the left is a raven holding a spoon in its beak, perhaps a reference to painter Adolph Menzel's *Kinderalbum*, a book of illustrations for children that features a raven stealing a silver spoon. On the right, an owl holds up a mirror, probably referring to the acrobat *Eulenspiegel*, which literally translates as "the mirror of the owl".

Above the monk's head, a faun appears to be curled around a large hourglass and pointing at it; it is depicted with two wings and a halo decorated with 17 ears of wheat, a rare variation on the faun theme.

Finally, directly beneath the gable windows, surrounded by wings as cherubs often are, is the head of a 10-year-old child with a knot in her hair; she is strangely reminiscent of the characteristic face (particularly recognisable by her prominent chin) of Alice in Wonderland as she was imagined by Sir John Tenniel.

Niedstraße is commonly called the *Literaturmeile* ("Literary Mile") because of the many writers who lived here during the 20th century: the most famous were Erich Kästner (Niedstraße 5); Günter Grass (Niedstraße 13); and Uwe Johnson, who lived at Niedstraße 14, which is also where the legendary Kommune I was founded in 1967.

ENTRANCE GATES OF THE CECILIENGÄRTEN

(19)

An aesthetic celebration of work

Ceciliengärten 1–53, 12159 Berlin
S1 (Friedenau)

The Ceciliengärten district is a remarkable, little-known ensemble consisting of a pretty square, two beautiful statues (see below), beautiful entrance gates and interesting bas-reliefs on the theme of family and work.

Built by Heinrich Lassen between 1923 and 1927, and listed since 1995, the Ceciliengärten complex is first and foremost a social project.

Some of the medallions depict people farming the land or children playing, but most show various means of transport. They remind us that part of the complex was specifically made for the families of employees of the Berlin Public Transport Authority (BVG).

The complex is organised around the gardens (listed since 1977), which comprise an oblong public park surrounded by a promenade lined with chestnut trees. At the northern end is a large pool and at the southern end a pretty fountain topped by a fox.

Great care has been taken to highlight the two female statues by Georg Kolbe, which, although a good distance apart, face each other in the centre of the square. The arms of the first figure reach towards the sky; this is morning, stretching out her limbs after a good night's sleep. In contrast, the arms of the second one hang heavily; she represents the weariness of the evening and tiredness after a day's work.

Once again, these works highlight the purpose of these gardens: to celebrate the value of work from an aesthetic and architectural point of view.

An artist's studio in a tower

The tower overlooking the gate on the south side is crowned by an octagonal pavilion made of oxidised copper in the Secession style. A commemorative plaque to the left of the archway indicates that this workshop was designed to accommodate artists, including the painter Hans Baluschek, a socialist artist who was revered during the Weimar Republic and who lived here on an honorary basis from 1929 to 1933.

Copies of Georg Kolbe's sculptures in Barcelona

A copy of the sculpture entitled "Morning" by Georg Kolbe, one of the pioneers of modern architecture, can be found in the courtyard of Mies van der Rohe's famous Barcelona Pavilion (1929) in the Spanish city.

EISACK TUNNEL

(20)

Why is the U4 line so short?

Traegerstraße 5, 12159 Berlin
Guided tours by appointment once a month at weekends, in general at 9.30am and 3.30pm
Calendar on tunneltours.de/project/stillgelegt
Price: €22.50
S41, 42 / U4 (Innsbrucker Platz)

On the map of the Berlin metro network, the U4 line, shown in light yellow, catches the eye as it seems odd that it is so short: it runs for less than 3 kilometers through the Schöneberg neighbourhood from Innsbrucker Platz to Nollendorfplatz not far from the KaDeWe.

Inaugurated in 1910, before greater Berlin was founded in 1920, it was designed and constructed by the commune of Schöneberg (which was very wealthy at the time) strictly for the needs of the local population, which would explain why it only has five stations.

It was the first communal underground line in Germany and was run independently with no connecting lines to other stations, and therefore had its very own staff of mechanics and maintenance workshop.

Located on the site of what is now the Waldenburg-Oberschule, the workshop became redundant in 1926 when the U4 became part of the Berlin network. It closed several years later in 1932. Until this date, the trains of the U4 line were taken for repairs and maintenance through a tunnel of about 400 metres long starting from Innsbrucker Platz.

Today the group Tunnel Tours organises guided visits of this now-deserted tunnel which takes fans of Berlin 100 years back in time to tell the story of the U4 project and the technical achievement that it represented.

The tour, which lasts about two hours, starts on the platform of Innsbrucker Platz station before it leads down to the tunnel itself, a few minutes' walk away, thanks to a ladder which goes some ten metres down into the ground. Lamps are provided.

The Berlin underground network, comprising 26 lines and 475 km of metro and S-Bahn tracks, is one of the largest in the world after Seoul (940 km) and Beijing (690 km).

TOMB OF HEINRICH SACHS

21

Fulfill your duty

Schöneberg Cemetery III
Stubenrauchstraße 43–45, 12161 Berlin
Summer: 8am–6pm; Winter: 9am–5pm
S41, 42, 46 / U9 (Bundesplatz)

The charming Schöneberg Cemetery III at Stubenrauchstraße 43–45 – formerly the cemetery of the rural community of Friedenau – houses the graves of Marlene Dietrich and photographer Helmut Newton. Not far away (lot 12), the mysterious reliefs of the somewhat neglected tomb of Heinrich Sachs (1858-1922) are rather intriguing.

As the founder of a successful pharmaceutical company, Sachs was granted the title of Secret Commercial Adviser of Prussia (*königliche preussische Kommerziengeheimrat*) – an honorary title conferred to successful merchants in their field. The epitaph also indicates that he was made a knight of several orders, and it is in light of this information that one may understand the tomb made by artist Eberhard Encke, a friend of Sachs, whose reliefs evoke a Judeo-Christian theme that is dear to Freemasonry: spiritual rebirth.

Between the columns of a Greek temple whose pediment bears the French inscription *Accomplis ton devoir* ("fulfill your duty") are two reliefs. The first represents the destruction of the temple of Jerusalem,

to the right of which is a dead tree. The second shows the reconstructed temple surrounded by abundant trees, shining at the top of a hill immersed in the rays of a triangular sun that symbolises the divine Trinity.

In the Masonic tradition, the destruction of the temple symbolises the rupture between God and man. In this case, the artist interprets this with reference to an episode from the Gospels (Mark 11:12-25) in which Jesus curses a fig tree because it bears no fruit; as a result, the tree withers. The reliefs here suggest that God judges man according to his works and that we must symbolically rebuild the temple by fulfilling our duty through the exercise of our spirituality. The reliefs also suggest that Sachs was exemplary in this regard.

NEARBY

The Schöneberg Cemetery III columbarium

At the back of the cemetery, the two-storey columbarium (ground floor and basement, accessible via two staircases) was built between 1914 and 1916, probably according to the plans of Hans Altmann. Like the rest of the cemetery, it exudes a romantic atmosphere that is conducive to meditation. The ground floor is adorned with terracotta ornaments, such as flowers and salamanders. A symbol of persistent faith in adversity, the salamander has the reputation of surviving in the midst of flames.

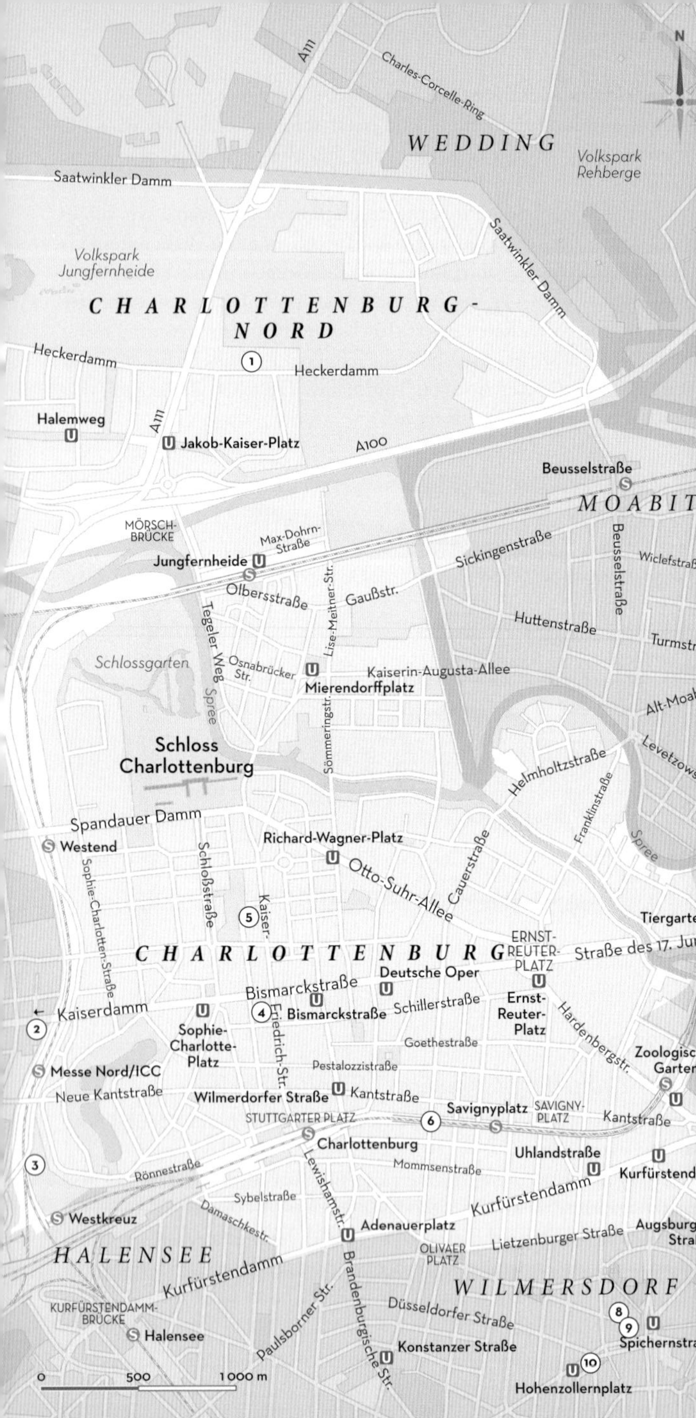

N
A111
Charles-Corcelle-Ring
WEDDING
Volkspark Rehberge
Saatwinkler Damm
Saatwinkler Damm
Volkspark Jungfernheide
CHARLOTTENBURG-NORD
Heckerdamm
1
Heckerdamm
Halemweg
A111
Jakob-Kaiser-Platz
A100
Beusselstraße
MOABIT
MÖRSCH-BRÜCKE
Max-Dohrn-Straße
Jungfernheide
Sickingenstraße
Beusselstraße
Wiclefstraß
Olbersstraße
Gaußstr.
Lise-Meitner-Str.
Huttenstraße
Turmstr
Tegeler Weg
Schlossgarten
Osnabrücker Str.
Mierendorffplatz
Kaiserin-Augusta-Allee
Spree
Sömmeringstr.
Alt-Moab
Schloss Charlottenburg
Helmholtzstraße
Levetzows
Franklinstraße
Spandauer Damm
Westend
Richard-Wagner-Platz
Spree
Schloßstraße
Otto-Suhr-Allee
Cauerstraße
Sophie-Charlotten-Straße
5
Kaiser-
Tiergarte
CHARLOTTENBURG
ERNST-REUTER-PLATZ
Straße des 17. Jun
Deutsche Oper
Bismarckstraße
Kaiserdamm
2
4
Bismarckstraße
Schillerstraße
Ernst-Reuter-Platz
Sophie-Charlotte-Platz
Friedrich-Str.
Hardenbergstr.
Goethestraße
Zoologisc Garten
Messe Nord/ICC
Pestalozzistraße
Neue Kantstraße
Wilmerdorfer Straße
Kantstraße
Savignyplatz
SAVIGNY-PLATZ
Kantstraße
STUTTGARTER PLATZ
6
Charlottenburg
Uhlandstraße
3
Mommsenstraße
Kurfürstend
Rönnestraße
Lewishamstr.
Kurfürstendamm
Sybelstraße
Damaschkestr.
Westkreuz
Adenauerplatz
Augsburg Stra
Lietzenburger Straße
OLIVAER PLATZ
HALENSEE
Kurfürstendamm
WILMERSDORF
Brandenburgische Str.
Paulsborner Str.
Düsseldorfer Straße
KURFÜRSTENDAMM-BRÜCKE
8
9
Halensee
Spichernstra
Konstanzer Straße
10
0
500
1000 m
Hohenzollernplatz

Charlottenburg - North Wilmersdorf

ALFRED HRDLICKA'S "DANSE MACABRE"

①

A murderous danse

Gedenkkirche der ev. Gemeinde
Heckerdamm 226, 13627 Berlin
Mon 10am–12noon; Thur 10am–12noon & 4–6pm
U7 (Jakob-Kaiser-Platz)

The *Plötzenseer Totentanz* of the Protestant church, Gedenkkirche, in the north of Charlottenburg, is the work of Alfred Hrdlicka (1928–2009). From 1965 to 1972, he drew with lead pencils, charcoal, chalk and sanguine on 16 wooden panels measuring 3.5 metres high by just 1 metre in width. It is easy to recognise the barracks of the Plötzensee prison, still standing, where the Nazis executed almost 2,900 people, some of whom had not even been sentenced. In one night, known as the "Bloody night of Plötzensee", under a constant stream of Allied bombs, 186 prisoners were hanged on butcher's hooks. Among them was the famous pianist Karl Robert Kreiten, who had been reported for making a joke against Hitler.

Even if the murders committed by the Nazis are not the unique

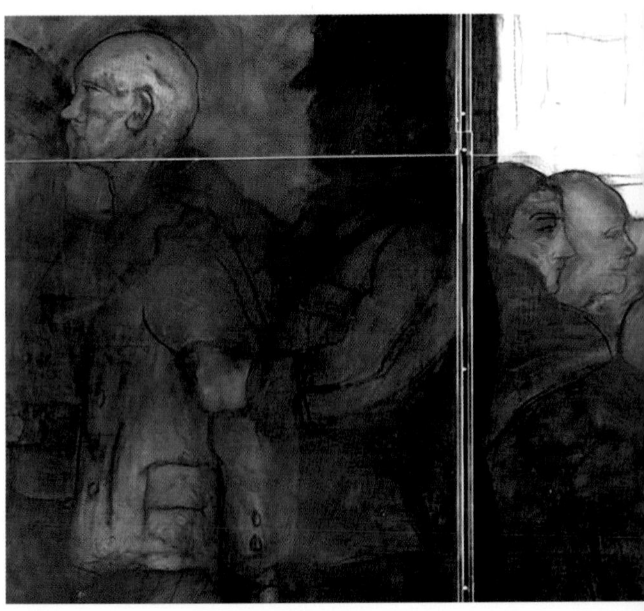

subject of the panels, the walls of the shooting squad are depicted in the background with their arched windows and butcher's hooks. The artist adopts here the theme of the *danses macabres* of the Middle Ages, the artistic representations which, since the 15th century, had invoked death, for the most part taking the form of a skeleton who led the characters into their last dance.

Hrdlicka uses this here to illustrate the violent deaths of the 20th century, representing, in addition to the bestial crimes of the Nazis, the death of a protester (Benno Ohnesorg) or that of a boxer in the ring (Sonny Banks).

In the process, the artist shakes up traditional representations: a recurrent motif in the danse macabre, the death of a young girl, taking the form of a dance of death with a prostitute, in which the latter takes the initiative by attempting to seduce the skeleton.

The layout of the pews in the church is also unusual: they are arranged around the altar, which is in the centre.

A 10-minute walk away, the former execution hall of Plötzensee is open to the public: gedenkstaette-ploetzensee.de

THE THREE GLOBES OF HEERSTRAßE

2

Freemasonry for all to see

Grand National Mother Lodge "The Three Globes"
Heerstraße 28, 14052 Berlin
0 30 / 3042806
U2 (Theodor-Heuss-Platz)

At number 28 Heerstraße, the golden spheres forming a triangle at the entrance of the house will certainly intrigue the more discerning passer-by. They indicate quite simply that the Freemasons' "Three Globes" Grand National Mother Lodge headquarters are housed here.

It was Frederick the Great (Frederick II) who brought freemasonry to Berlin. He first became a mason in Brunswick, in reaction to his misanthropic father, the "soldier king" Frederick William I of Prussia (who was hostile to any form of spirituality, despised everyone and often shot at his fellow countrymen with coarse salt). On the death of his father in 1740, Frederick II founded Berlin's first Freemasons' lodge in the heart of his newly formed court of Charlottenburg.

As he himself came from high nobility, he could not accept that some of the noble members of his court occupied the highest ranks in his very own lodge ("The First Lodge"). He let his advisor and friend, Charles Étienne Jordan, who was a civil servant and the Chief of Police of Berlin, found the city's lodge "The Three Globes" which brought together the bourgeois and aristocrats – and which still exists today in the form of the Grand National Mother Lodge. The symbolic meaning of the three globes comes from Frederick the Great: of deep philosophical erudition, he corresponded with renowned intellectuals, including Voltaire, Maupertuis and d'Alembert, whom he often invited to appear at his court. The sovereign saw in them three globes "a celestial globe, a terrestrial globe and an armillary sphere". To find out more about this topic, a visit can be arranged over the phone.

A museum of freemasonry

At the heart of the Grand National Mother Lodge, "The Three Globes" there is a small museum dedicated to freemasonry. Only guided tours are given, and they must be booked in advance. It is therefore a good opportunity to ask everything you have ever wanted to know about the freemasons.

MONUMENT TO THE GLORY OF MOTORCYCLE RACERS

③

A rare Futurist monument that survived the Nazis

Halenseestraße 40, 14055 Berlin
S3, 5, 7, 9, 41, 42, 46 (Westkreuz)

The only one of its kind in the world, this small monument stands alone on a traffic island, depicting two motorcycle racers in racing position, on their motorcycles. It was placed where the steep, old northern bend of the AVUS racing circuit used to be, and represents the racers Ernst Henne on a BMW and Ewald Kluge on a DKW. Heiner Fleischmann on his NSU is missing from the monument, even though he was drawn on the original plans.

Designed in 1938/39 by Max Esser (1885-1943), the sculpture, which could not be exhibited because of the war, is of real artistic interest: it is Berlin's only surviving Futurist sculpted group.

The Futurist movement was in fact one of the modernist artistic currents banned by the Nazis. The monument escaped the systematic vetoes of the official Aryan art diktats thanks only to the enthusiasm of the Germans for racing in the 1930s. Two of the three original sculptures, having survived in Noack's foundry workshop, were placed here in 1989.

The sculpture was mounted on a section of the original track surface of the famous sloping bend of the AVUS.

The granite column standing just next to the sculpture comes from the building at the entrance to the circuit.

There was a golden age for the AVUS motorcycle races (Automobil-Verkehrs-und Übungsstraße, literally "automobile training and driving street") between 1922 and 1939, even if they were later outshone by motor car racing. On 19 September 1929, Ernst Jakob Henne (1904-2005), the first of two motorcycle star racers immortalised by Esser, riding his BMW WR 750, became the fastest man in the world on two wheels, covering a mile at 216.75 km/h. Between 1929 and 1937, no fewer than seven world speed records were broken thanks to him, the last one on 28 November 1937 with 279.5 km/h on a BMW 500. This record, which was held for almost 14 years, was broken by Wilhelm Herz in April 1951. Henne retired after his last record.

With the war over, new races could take place from 1951 on the AVUS circuit. The motorcycling era came to an end for AVUS in 1966 (as did the motor car racing era in 1999).

ARCHAEOLOGY GALLERY OF SANITARY FACILITIES

④

Bathe at home!

Kaiser-Friedrich-Straße 35, 10627 Berlin
Guided tours for a maximum of 10 people
Booking at info@schwarzwaelder-gmbh.de
U2, 7 (Bismarckstraße)

A plumber's shop window displays a small but intriguing sign – "Archaeology Gallery of Sanitary Facilities". Current owner and grandson of the company founder Peter Schwarzwälder explains it with a laugh: "We don't do archaeological excavations, but we still find a lot of things worth preserving!"

The narrow rooms that make up the unique little museum are each the size of a bathroom.

The tour begins with hand basins, tiny wall-mounted water tanks with taps that date back to a time when there was no water supply system and water had to be fetched from fountains, pumps, streams or rivers.

The first portable baths could be rented to porters: taking a bath was an expensive luxury at the time.

The highlight of the collection is Dittmann's tilting bathtub: a comma-shaped bathtub, raised on one side and mounted on a wooden base. The bather could swing in the bath, as if in a rocking chair, to produce waves.

"Bathe at home!" was the slogan of the manufacturer of this whirlpool bath from 1894 until the 1930s, making it possible to enjoy the benefits of the waves at home without having to go to the beach!

An entire room is dedicated to engineer Hugo Junkers, who pioneered the development of water heaters and gas boilers for heating purposes. Junkers was also a pioneer in aircraft construction.

To conclude the one-hour tour, Schwarzwälder explains how the sauna in Kreuz works, as if he had tried the unbelievable machine himself.

After a visit, the humble bathroom and gas water heater will never seem the same again.

NEARBY

Building at number 17 Kaiser Friedrich Straße ⑤

17 Kaiser Friedrich Straße, 10627 Berlin
U7 (Richard-Wagner-Platz)

It is easy to walk past the building at number 17 Kaiser Friedrich Straße without noticing just how special it is. Its façade is in fact dotted with dozens of sculpted scenes within a square frame. Amongst other features, there are various characters: a woman with a lion, another woman playing the harp, various animals and cherubs, a curled-up snake, a key ... It is hard to find any kind of coherence to the whole, even if some figures refer to freemasonry and spiritual symbols: a bear holding a square and a compass, a handshake referring to the freemason greeting, a winged horse (symbolising a spiritual awakening) ...

HOLES IN THE PILLARS OF THE LEIBNIZSTRAßE BRIDGE ⑥

Like a knife through butter

Leibnizstraße 68, 10625 Berlin
S3, 5, 7, 9 (Savignyplatz)

It is easy to pass by the S-Bahn bridge in the Leibnizstraße without noticing anything particularly special. However, the pillars of the bridge on either side of the street include some interesting holes in the metal structure.

During the Battle of Berlin, in the last days of the Second World War when the Russian and Polish armies had practically surrounded the capital, American troops, inferior in number, were waiting on the Elbe River.

Berlin had long since been lost, but their oath to the Führer led the Wehrmacht soldiers and the unfortunate recruits of the "Volkssturm" (a last-minute makeshift militia) into desperate fights.

Hitler shot himself dead on 30 April while German troops attempted to escape captivity from the Soviet Union. Major-General Otto Sydow of the Luftwaffe (a recipient of the Knight's Cross of the Iron Cross of the Third Reich) was also Commander of the 1st Flak Division (anti-aircraft) of the Berlin Zoo bunker and air raid shelter.

At the time of the fight, he led what was left of the Müncheberg armoured division from the zoo to Spandau. They passed through Kantstraße along the tracks and using the underground tunnels. After fierce fighting to regain the famous bridge, they managed to break through on the Havel River on 3 May. The bullet holes in the Leibnizstraße bridge are evidence of this breakthrough.

The most powerful gun of the Flak Division was the 88mm Pak 43, and it is the calibre that corresponds to the most important hole in the bridge's structure.

The armour-piercing shells (APCR) fired by these guns were composite anti-armour ammunition: only their core was very hard and dense. Their muzzle velocity when exiting the gun barrel reached more than 1,000 metres per second. Like compressed air nail guns, they could perforate steel plates up to 23 centimetres thick. The closer the gunners were to their target, the greater the penetration capacity of these shells.

Somebody once wrote here "Never forget this!" as a reminder of the violence, but the inscription was covered when the bridge was renovated.

BINNINGER'S CLOCK

⑦

A clock of sets? Not at all, they are nothing more than additions

Budapester Straße 45, 10787 Berlin
U1, 2, 3 (Wittenbergplatz)

With its soft curves and bright colours, the astonishing clock on the corner of the Europa-Center, next to the zoo, is not some forgotten pop art icon or an instrument used for communicating with extra-terrestrials from the film *Close Encounters of the Third Kind*.

Clearly dating back to the 1970s, in keeping with the fashion that was then known in Germany as the *softline* design, this clock (for it is indeed

a clock) with its round lamp on the top which goes on and off every second, is intriguing in itself – not to mention the various rows of lights that lead up to it.

In order to tell the time with it, the lights must be added up in the following way: at the very top, in the first row, each zone of lights represents five hours that have gone by, whereas each zone in the second row counts for one hour. On the third row, the 11 bars each represent five minutes, and in turn, each rectangle in the last row at the bottom is worth a minute. Therefore, if, as in the photo, 2 / 3 // 8 / 3 zones are lit up, then the clock indicates 13 hours (2 x 5 + 3) and 43 minutes (8 x 5 + 3). The seconds flash at the top but are not recorded. If we are to believe the explanations provided, the clock runs according to the mathematical theory of sets. But the system hiding behind these calculations has, in reality, very little to do with this famous theory, which imagines a construction of all the mathematical tools (numbers, functions, relations, etc) founded on a primitive notion of belonging to a set. It is extremely tempting to link it to this as, on the first and third rows, the hours and minutes are grouped together (and form therefore, mathematically speaking, sets), but this reasoning all, very quickly, comes to a dead end: the only concept at work being additions, as this mysterious clock turns out to be really nothing more than a sort of abacus.

Initially, this installation was a publicity stunt by Dieter Binninger, a clockmaker in Eppertshausen in Hesse. It was aimed at attracting attention to and advertising a rather ordinary wristwatch that he was working on. Binninger gave his "Clock of Berlin" as a gift to Charlottenburg in1975. It remained in front of the Europa-Center opposite the church in memory of Kaiser-Wilhelm until 1995. As for Binninger's wristwatch, it was never put on the market, the development costs of the microprocessor were too high for him. On the other hand, a "tabletop" version of the clock was put on the market and is still on sale today. In the days of incandescent lamps, the great Clock of Berlin was an "electricity-guzzling" monster which cost a fortune. Every year, due to the vibrations caused by the traffic, the lightbulbs had to be changed by means of a hoisting platform, a system that was obviously not very cheap for Binninger. When he lost his life in a plane crash in 1991, the City of Berlin took over the maintenance until 1995. The clock was then dismantled to make savings, before being put back in 1996 thanks to entrepreneurs who continue to sponsor it today.

FAÇADE OF THE BUILDING AT PARISER STRAßE 61

8

Egyptian Jugendstil

Pariser Straße 61, 10719 Berlin
U2, 3, 9 (Sprichernstraße)

The magnificent Art Nouveau façade of the building at Pariser Straße 61 in Wilmersdorf (designed in 1904 by Gustav Bähr and Otto Jaegeler) stands out with its rich details themed on Egyptian mysticism.

The two Moorish-style entrance doors are presided over by an eagle with outstretched wings, echoing the winged sun, a symbol of divine power that appears above the doors of many Egyptian temples. Here though, the difference is that the eagle is looking down, as if to draw attention to the engraved inscription between the two doors – *SALVE* (salvation).

On the cornice of the portal stands Isis, Egyptian goddess of resurrection. In her left hand she carries the ankh, the symbol of eternal life. Modelled on the Pythia of Delphi, she draws inspiration from the aroma emanating from a tripod where smouldering sacred herbs bring her visions. On the opposite side is a bouquet of lotus flowers in a vase, a symbol of the sun and of renewed life, as they open every morning and close in the evening. Friezes of stylised lotus flowers are also visible on the balconies of the second floor, as well as on the capitals of certain columns.

Above the first-floor windows, two paintings depict children with typical Egyptian headdresses: on the left, two teenagers are accompanied by a wild beast that appears domesticated; on the right, two more children are bathing, while a woman lying on the bank holds a vase. One floor higher, four dance scenes can be seen. The oriels are crowned with capitals decorated with female faces, similar to those found on many Egyptian sarcophagi. Their thick hair is covered with headdresses that descend to chest level in long cylindrical braids.

The magnificent hall of the building (visible through the glazed entrance doors) is covered with blue laminated bricks decorated with hieroglyphs on a white background.

NEARBY

Golden magnolia tree at Pariser Straße 4 ⑨

Almost opposite at number 4 is one of the most beautiful façades in the capital; it features a large magnolia tree with golden flowers. Under the windows of the first floor, the oriels bear reliefs of four different species of fruit trees with different animals. A little higher up, they are adorned with vines intertwined around a floral coat of arms.

THE STAINED-GLASS WINDOWS OF THE CHURCH ON THE HOHENZOLLERNPLATZ

10

An exceptional choreography of dancing light

Nassauische Straße 66-67, 10717 Berlin
Tue & Thur 2pm–6pm, Wed & Fri 11am–1pm, Sat 1pm–3pm and for events and during services
A liturgy is sung every Saturday at midday
U2, 3 (Hohenzollernplatz)

Built between 1930 and 1933 from plans drawn by Ossip Klarwein, the assistant of the famous German architect Fritz Höger, the Kirche am Hohenzollernplatz (the church on Hohenzollernplatz) is no secret in itself with its 66-metre-high steeple. But who, apart from the parishioners, has ever visited its exceptional interiors? The church is effectively one of the most interesting examples of expressionist architecture in Berlin. A beautiful example of Backsteinexpressionismus (Brick Expressionism), an architectural style that is typical of Northern Germany and of which Höger is one of the main representatives, the church hides an interior (40 metres long and 20 metres high) with 13 lined-up, pointed arches, built in reinforced concrete, one of the emblematic materials of both Höger and German architectural expressionism.

The effect of the light coming through the stained glass windows on the sides and the huge stained glass window behind the altar is remarkable: shades of yellow, red and blue are reflected on the pale surface of the cement arches, adding to the mystical atmosphere of the place.

This extraordinary choreography of dancing light and shadows could not be seen when the church was first built in the 1930s. On 22 November 1943, the Kirche am Hohenzollernplatz was severely damaged during Allied bombing: the original organ, the frescos and the paintings were almost all destroyed during the fire which followed. The church was rebuilt after the war and has been a listed building since 1966. The marvellous stained-glass windows are the work of the German artist Achim Freyer, who made them as part of a vast renovation programme carried out in the years 1990-1991.

Every Saturday at midday, during *"NoonSong"*, a liturgy is sung by a professional choir.

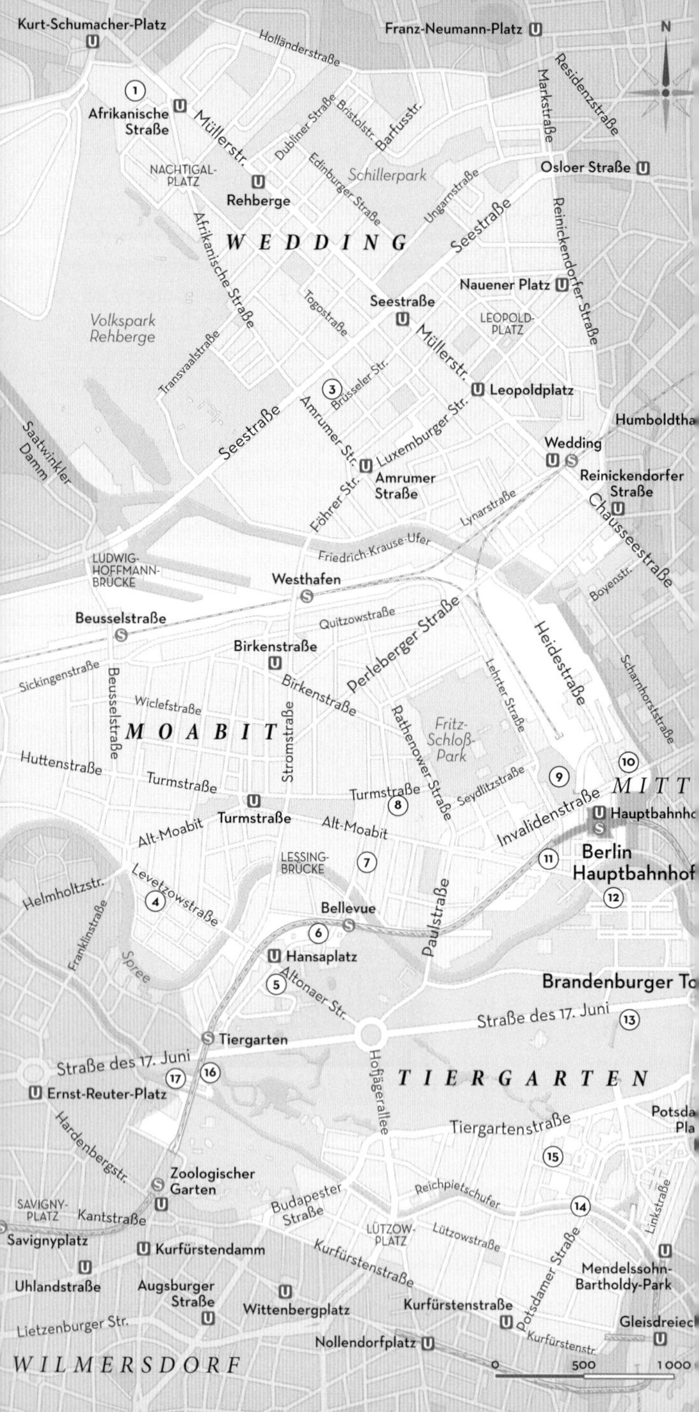
Kurt-Schumacher-Platz
Franz-Neumann-Platz
Holländerstraße
Residenzstraße
Markstraße
Afrikanische Straße
Müllerstr.
Dubliner Straße
Bristolstr.
Barfusstr.
NACHTIGAL-PLATZ
Rehberge
Edinburger Straße
Schillerpark
Ungarnstraße
Osloer Straße
Reinickendorfer Straße
Seestraße
WEDDING
Afrikanische Straße
Nauener Platz
Seestraße
Togostraße
LEOPOLD-PLATZ
Volkspark Rehberge
Transvaalstraße
Müllerstr.
Brüsseler Str.
Leopoldplatz
Amrumer Str.
Luxemburger Str.
Humboldtha
Saatwinkler Damm
Seestraße
Wedding
Amrumer Straße
Reinickendorfer Straße
Föhrer Str.
Lynarstraße
Chausseestraße
Friedrich-Krause-Ufer
LUDWIG-HOFFMANN-BRÜCKE
Westhafen
Boyenstr.
Beusselstraße
Quitzowstraße
Perleberger Straße
Heidestraße
Birkenstraße
Sickingenstraße
Beusselstraße
Birkenstraße
Lehrter Straße
Scharnhorststraße
Wiclefstraße
Rathenower Straße
Fritz-Schloß-Park
MOABIT
Stromstraße
Huttenstraße
Seydlitzstraße
Turmstraße
Turmstraße
Invalidenstraße
MITT
Hauptbahnho
Turmstraße
Alt-Moabit
Alt-Moabit
Berlin Hauptbahnhof
LESSING-BRÜCKE
Levetzowstraße
Helmholtzstr.
Paulstraße
Bellevue
Franklinstraße
Spree
Hansaplatz
Altonaer Str.
Brandenburger To
Straße des 17. Juni
Tiergarten
Straße des 17. Juni
Hofjägerallee
TIERGARTEN
Ernst-Reuter-Platz
Potsda Pla
Hardenbergstr.
Tiergartenstraße
Zoologischer Garten
Reichpietschufer
SAVIGNY-PLATZ
Kantstraße
Budapester Straße
Linkstraße
LÜTZOW-PLATZ
Lützowstraße
Savignyplatz
Kurfürstendamm
Kurfürstenstraße
Potsdamer Straße
Mendelssohn-Bartholdy-Park
Uhlandstraße
Augsburger Straße
Wittenbergplatz
Kurfürstenstraße
Gleisdreiec
Lietzenburger Str.
Nollendorfplatz
Kurfürstenstr.
WILMERSDORF
0
500
1000
N

Wedding - Moabit - Tiergarten

THE WEDDING SAND DUNE

①

A very secret sand dune

Scharnweberstraße 158, 13405 Berlin
Dune visible from the car park of the neighbouring DIY store, or by prior booking: bgmitte@nabu-berlin.de
U6 (Afrikanische Straße or Kurt-Schumacher-Platz)

On the SUZ (gardening school) site with its educational gardens, on the edge of the Rehberge park, there is an intriguing, secret sand dune that can be visited if booked in advance.

It was formed around the end of a glacial period called the Weichselian, or Vistulian, as it takes its name from the Vistulia river. When the last glaciers disappeared from this era around 12,000 years ago, they left behind large zones scattered with fallen rocks, moraines and sandbanks. The vegetation slowly began to take root, allowing the wind to blow the sand around freely, spreading much of it over the surrounding area and forming it into dunes.

Over the millennia, human intervention has caused vegetation to become denser with, for example, the planting of hedges to protect meadows and fields. In the 18th century, the systematic planting of dunes took place at the same time as the extraction of sand reduced the number of inland dunes.

Luckily, the plans for the Friedrich-Ebert-Siedlung workers' housing, which was supposed to be built here in 1929, were shelved. The Wedding dune therefore remained intact until it was partly integrated into the gardening school in 1950. In 1976, the area was registered as a protected natural site before a global conservation and development plan was drawn up at the end of the 1980s.

In 2002, the Wedding dune was given extra protection when the atypical vegetation of brambles and beeches was removed. Only the original types of dune vegetation, Scots pines and oaks, were left to flourish. The undying commitment of the German Federation for the Protection of Nature (NABU) in Berlin, has gradually given the dune its initial appearance back. Invasive plants are now systematically removed, and the layer of humus, which is 40 cm thick in some places, is also regularly reduced.

The dune can be partially seen from the car park of the neighbouring DIY store, but for a closer look at the oldest mound of sand from the glacial period in Berlin-Mitte, volunteers can join the NABU group of Berlin-Mitte to help maintain the dune.

THE SPA PAVILION BAS-RELIEF ②

A district named after the thermal baths

Badstraße 38–39, 13357 Berlin
U8 (Pankstraße)

On the corner of Badstraße and Travemünder Straße, on the last floor of the west-facing side of the house, there is a discreet bas-relief of a pavilion with a roof in the shape of a pagoda bearing the Latin inscription *"In fonte salus"* (health from the source).

This serves as a reminder that there was once a pavilion here which housed the old thermal fountain and gave its name to the surrounding neighbourhood. A walk through covered walkway number 39 will also take you to the old spa, which is now used as the local library. Although there are no particularly interesting remnants of its past to be seen inside, on the outside, the building's lovely frontages have been preserved.

This is where a mineral spring, possessing excellent medicinal properties according to studies carried out by the renowned Berlin chemist Andreas Sigismund Marggraf (1709–1782), was discovered in the middle of the 18th century. This chemist was also the inventor of beet sugar. King Frederick II was keen on thermal spa treatment (he went to take the waters in Pyrmont every year), and naturally gave his blessing to the project of a thermal spa in Berlin, having had the results of Marggraf's studies confirmed by the Obercollegium Medicum of Berlin.

This is how the court's apothecary, Heinrich Wilhelm Behm (1708–1780), obtained the right to build a thermal spa so that people could experience the remarkable benefits of this water by drinking it or bathing in it. Behm got to work quickly: the spring was enclosed with a pretty brick wall which was then covered by a beautiful pavilion, the copy of which on the library frontage is particularly realistic. Large gardens with spa buildings were created around the fountain. Amongst the visitors were people suffering mostly from rheumatism and eye disorders. In 1799, Luise, the young queen of Prussia, graced the spa with her presence. The baths were then renamed "Luisenbad" in her honour.

The thermal spa continued to be popular until the middle of the 19th century.

In the large spa resorts, there were many visitors who wanted just to enjoy themselves, and so inns, dance halls and casinos sprang up around Badstraße – all of this came to a sudden end in 1888 when the construction of a drain ruined the spring that had once offered multiple health benefits. All attempts to restore it were in vain.

The baths of Badstraße ("bad" means "bath") have given their name to the Gesundbrunnen (Fountain of health) district as well as to Brunnenstraße (Fountain Street).

THE ANTI-KRIEGS-MUSEUM AIR RAID SHELTER

(3)

Relive the bombings

Brüsseler Straße 21, 13353 Berlin
Every day 4pm–8pm
Free entry
U9 (Amrumer Straße)

Founded in 1925 by the pacifist anarchist Ernst Friedrich, the Anti-Kriegs-Museum (Anti-War Museum) was born from his need to denounce the horrors of armed conflict, in particular that of the First World War.

In 1933, the museum's collection, located at that time at 29 Parochialstraße, was entirely demolished by the assault divisions of the Nazi party. Friedrich was sentenced to seven months' imprisonment and was subsequently forced to leave Germany. It was opened again in 1982 by a group of teachers and Tommy Spree, the grandson of Ernst Friedrich, amongst others, and since 1998 the Anti-War Museum has been located in Wedding. Photographs, objects and documents showing the violence of the two world wars are on display here.

In the basement, there is an authentic air raid shelter dating back to the Second World War on display. In one corner of the shelter, two gas masks hang on a bunkbed together with a long leather jacket. On the top bunk there is an anti-gas cradle, which was used to protect babies during air raids.

A row of wooden chairs is lined up against the wall and there is a shelf holding various objects such as a lantern, a photo of women and children in an air raid shelter and two rusty helmets.

A radio which would sound the alarm for imminent bombings gives it all a final touch of realism.

The wooden door leaning against the wall is of particular interest: it used to belong to an air raid shelter in the Neukölln district.

A closer look will reveal that it is covered in dates written in pen. During the bombing in 1945, a Berliner used it to count the number of days spent hiding in his basement.

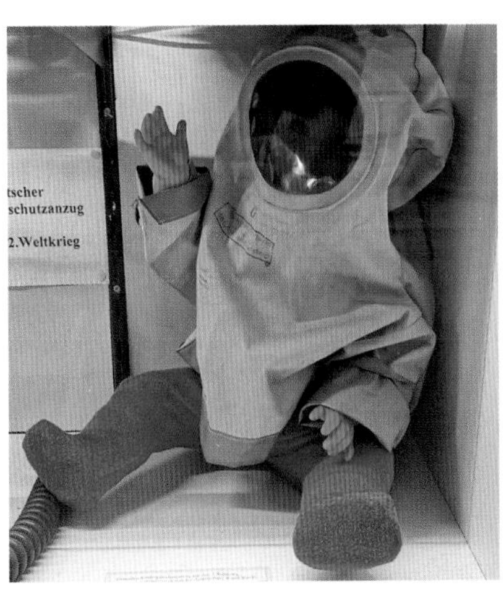

The very last date written is in fact 20 April 1945, the day on which the Red Army entered the German capital.

Another feature that is characteristic of this place is the *Luftschutz Apotheke* (air raid shelter pharmacy): a first aid cabinet hangs on the wall, containing medicine in addition to a first aid kit dating from the Second World War.

THE MEMORIAL FOR DEPORTED JEWS

4

A striking memorial site

Levetzowstraße 7-8, 10555 Berlin
U9 (Hansaplatz)

In Moabit, on Levetzowstraße, visitors will be intrigued by an imposing monument which takes up most of the pavement there: inside a goods wagon, blocks of sculpted stone show through its partially open door. On the access ramp leading up to it, there is a block of marble, which is also sculpted, with human figures huddled together, who seem to be going towards the wagon, and at the back there is a tall, iron stele with numbers and dates written on it.

It is the *Mahnmal Levetzowstraße*, a memorial erected in 1985 in memory of the most dramatic pages in the history of the district and of the entire city of Berlin.

This monument, the work of architects Jürgen Wenzel and Theseus Bappert and of the sculptor Peter Herbrich, recalls the deportations suffered by Berlin's Jewish community from October 1941 to April 1945. A more detailed look at the iron wall will reveal the departure dates of the convoys for the concentration and work camps, giving the names of the deported, in addition to their number. At the foot of the ramp, on the pavement, there is a series of square metal plaques: each of them presents a synagogue that was destroyed during the Nazi regime, with information on when it was built, its size and when it was destroyed.

The place where this memorial stands is highly symbolic: this was in fact the site of the liberal synagogue of Levetzowstraße, also known as the synagogue of Tiergarten.

Built in 1914, it was damaged in 1938 during the *Novemberpogrome* (The Night of Broken Glass), and in subsequent years was used as a collection point for deportations. Air raids during the Second World War caused further damage to the building, which was finally demolished in 1955.

Not far from the monument, on the corner of Levetzowstraße and Jagowstraße, a plaque relating the history of the synagogue was put up on a brick wall at the beginning of the 1960s, and can still be seen there today.

Since 1990, on the 9th of November every year, a memorial service has been held there to commemorate the pogroms of November 1938 and the tragic fate of the thousands of Jews setting out on a journey from which they would never return.

THE PAINTED CEILING OF ALVAR AALTO

5

A painting that was covered over by mistake

Alvar-Alto-Haus
Klopstockstraße 32, 10557 Berlin
U9 (Hansaplatz)

The history of the painting on the ground floor of the Alvar-Aalto-Haus is rather strange to say the least. This painting with its sinuous lines in shades of blue and white was created by the famous architect Alvar Aalto, who also designed the building which is named after him.

In 1957, Aalto suggested to those who had commissioned him that the Spanish painter Joan Miró paint the work, but the project, which was extremely costly, was rejected. Aalto therefore painted the ceiling himself a few days before the inauguration of the building, without even informing his clients. His assistant, Karl Feig, talks about this in the following terms: "[Aalto] found out who the decorator was, and I had to contact him urgently. Two hours later, the decorator, his apprentice, Aalto and I got together on the building site with pots of paint, brushes and step ladders. Aalto immediately started making sketches with charcoals attached to long rods [...] Two days later, just in time for the inauguration, the painting was ready."

Some years later, during renovation work on the building, the whole ceiling was covered with stucco and painted white, with no consideration for the value of the work that had been covered over. The painting remained hidden until 2007, when, during modernisation work on the ground floor, a request was made to inspect its condition. Unfortunately, the restorers found it impossible to recover all of Aalto's work, but they nevertheless managed to faithfully reproduce the forms and colours of the original using old photos to help them. Visitors can also admire the new, dark blue, wavy lines in the centre, which look as if they are diving into a surface of soft tones of white, and also the circles painted in a brighter tone of white around the lights which are equally round.

At the entrance of the building, a series of signs tell (in German) the astonishing history of the ceiling.

Between 1955 and 1957, the Alvar-Aalto-Haus was part of a project to reconstruct the old residential district of Hansaviertel, which stood on the north-west side of Tiergarten and which was almost totally destroyed by bombing in the Second World War. The building was presented during the Interbau 1957, a large architecture exhibition in which many internationally renowned architects such as Le Corbusier, Walter Gropius and Max Taut took part, submitting plans for a new complex of living quarters, which today is a conservation area.

MUSEUM OF LETTERS

⑥

An incredible museum of 3-D letters

Stadtbahnbogen 424, 10557 Berlin
0 177 4 20 15 87
buchstabenmuseum.de
Thur–Sun 1pm–5pm
S3, 5, 7, 9 (Bellevue)

Founded in 2005 by Viennese designer Barbara Dechant and art curator Anja Schulze, the Buchstabenmuseum is undoubtedly one of the most original museums in Berlin. The rooms of this incredible place showcase more than 2,000 three-dimensional letters and signage from various periods, the majority of them having been found in the German capital and the surrounding area.

The museum is the first in the world to collect letters that once belonged in public spaces and to present them as integral elements of urban history. Each piece on show has undergone thorough research to locate and document its origin, and sometimes even establish its date of production. Alongside the letters are fact sheets providing information on the typography used, dimensions, the date of the letters' discovery, and the materials used to create them.

Some rare finds – particularly the four large letters (H, A, U and P) that once formed the signage of the Berlin *Ostbahnhof* station, which used to be called the *Hauptbahnhof* – tell a story of 19th-century Berlin. The glitzy letters of the word *Zierfische* ("ornamental fish"), a historic shop that existed from 1957 until 2009 near the Frankfurter Tor, can be found on one wall; another room features the huge metal letters and integrated neon lights of the former headquarters of the daily newspaper *Tagesspiegel* on Potsdamer Straße.

The location of the museum is itself rather unusual. Since 2016, the exhibits gathered by Barbara Dechant and Anja Schulze have been kept in a Stadtbahnbogen, a viaduct under the rail tracks of the S-Bahn. Although this is not the only place of its kind in Berlin, its location near the Bellevue S-Bahn, away from the flow of tourists, and the amazing way in which the underground tunnels have been refurbished, make this a must-see place, located just a few steps from the equally interesting Hansa district.

THE FAÇADE OF THOMASIUSSTRAßE 5

⑦

Jugendstil metaphysics

Thomasiusstraße 5, 10557 Berlin
U9 (Turmstraße)

Number 5 Thomasiusstraße in Moabit has an extraordinary Jugendstil façade, created in 1902 by the architect Hans Landé and the sculptor Carl Caspary, with the enormous face of a bearded man, decorated with numerous elements cast in bronze.

With its open mouth, the face is undoubtedly that of God the creator, who created the world with his words. Duality, represented by two fauns of opposite sexes on either side of the pediment, spouts from his mouth: they are the two contradictory fundamental principles of the one reality, the Yin and the Yang, the conflict between them being illustrated by the fact that the female faun is playing unbearable music to the male faun, who is covering his ears so that he cannot hear it.

Just below this, on a level with the windows of the top floor, the roles change: on the right, the man seems disconcerted by his wife's annoyance, portrayed on the left.

Two floors further down, this conflict is associated with the double struggle taking place between a bull (without horns?) and a snake, an image of the antagonism between masculine and feminine energies.

Between these two scenes of combat, the columns separating the windows are covered with sunflowers. As it constantly follows the sun's course, the sunflower has, since ancient times, represented the search for truth in love. Here, the artist invites the onlooker to reflect on the nature of the divine which is at work in duality.

By placing a landscape representing Athens's Acropolis (on the left) and Cairo's Sphinx (on the right), above the main entrance, the architect suggests that the solution to the problem is to be found in the philosophy and wisdom of Ancient Egypt and Ancient Greece.

THE HALL OF THE MOABIT COURTHOUSE

8

A grand show

Turmstraße 91, 10559 Berlin
Mon–Fri from 8am to the end of the public hearings
Free entry (ID required)
U9 (Turmstraße)

Courthouses are not often considered as places which can be visited but they are, in fact, by definition public places which are open to the general public. The Kriminalgericht (criminal court) of Moabit is no exception. Built at the beginning of the 20th century, it provides a truly great show for visitors.

Behind the security checks, the huge entrance hall looks like the nave of a Gothic cathedral.

Incredibly modern-looking Art Deco lights hang from its keystones. KCG, which stands for *Kaiserliches Criminalgericht* (Imperial Courthouse), is written in stylised lettering on the terracotta floor tiles

and serves as a reminder that this is a construction dating back to Wilhelmian times. The hall, which is surrounded by galleries, has three floors connected by the crisscrossing flights of a magnificent staircase, just like something out of an etching by Piranesi. Three vaulted gates are surmounted by baroque allegorical sculptures: above the righthand gate, lies and truth; to the left, quarrels (*Streitsucht*) and leniency (*Friedfertigkeit*); and finally, at the back, forgiveness and justice bearing the sword of judgement, which will decide between guilt and innocence.

Attending a trial

It is possible to attend ongoing trials. Other than being an interesting experience, the architectural quality of some courtrooms make them worth a visit. Ask at reception which rooms are being used for hearings on the day you visit.

The largest courthouse in Europe

All the hearings concerning misdemeanours and crimes committed in Berlin are held here, up to 300 a day. The Kriminalgericht of Moabit is the largest courthouse in Europe with its 240 working judges, 80 court administrators and 300 prosecutors.
It is twinned with the remand prison, the (*Untersuchungsgefängnis)* of Moabit (Alt-Moabit 12a), situated a few yards away where an average of 1,300 people are held, awaiting trial.

Stunningly modern for its time

The building, inaugurated in 1906, was stunningly modern for its time. The courthouse was the first building in the capital to be entirely equipped with electricity, and was designed with its own electric power station, running water distribution network (including its own water tower), central heating, a telephone network and numerous lifts. Originally made up of 21 courtrooms, the building was repeatedly extended from the 1950s onwards, so much so that it is difficult today for visitors to find their way through the maze of corridors and staircases.

THE WALLS COMMEMORATING MOABIT PRISON

9

Berlin's former Guantanamo

Geschichtspark Moabit
Lehrter Straße 5B, 10557 Berlin
Opening times of the history park: summer 8am–9pm, winter 8am–6pm
S3, 5, 7, 9 (Hauptbahnhof)

It is hard to find words to describe the inhumane Prussian prison which stood in the park of Moabit from 1850 to 1905. A gigantic triangle of concrete walls stands as a reminder of the 20 prison yards, which were separated by high walls. The cells were arranged in a circle around them. The prison was designed to keep the prisoners, who were all political prisoners, from coming together. During yard times, they had to wear masks, and the prison warders made sure that they did not speak to each other. This inhumane treatment caused many prisoners to go mad. A lunatic asylum was added on to the prison, and in German the expression *"Im Dreieck zu springen"* (literally to jump into the triangle) is still used today. In the memorial park, a poem is written in large letters on the walls: "Out of all the suffering which fills this building, there remains, under the walls and the bars, a breath of life, a secret quiver." Written by the geographer Albrecht Georg Haushofer (1903-1945), an opponent of the Nazi regime who was put into pre-trial detention, these lines are the cry of a man who was trying to escape from encroaching madness. In April 1945, on the pretext that he would have to be transferred due to the Allied advances, he was shot dead in the back of the neck with 15 fellow inmates in the old ULAP park nearby (see page 262).

In 1847, this model prison had already played an important role in the treatment of political prisoners. 250 Poles, members of a free corps, rebelled against the Prussians in Poznań and were locked up in this unfinished building. Frederick-William IV, the King of Prussia, wanted to give them an exemplary punishment, and a kangaroo court was set up in Berlin to judge them. They were all sentenced and became the first prisoners in modern times to undergo long-term isolation. According to several sources, two of them – eight according to others – were sentenced to death. The others were given long prison sentences.

The Poles were, however, lucky: thanks to the March Revolution in 1848, the convicts were set free. The Berlin revolutionaries drove to the now-finished prison in a large carriage decked with garlands and freed the Polish fighters. They were then driven in triumph through the town on 22 March 1848 before being allowed to return to their home country.

AN OASIS OF GREENERY IN THE HAMBURGER BAHNHOF

(10)

A souvenir of the train station's turntable

Invalidenstraße 50–51, 10557 Berlin
S3, 5, 7, 75, 9 / U55 (Hauptbahnhof)

Opposite the famous Hamburger Bahnhof Museum of Contemporary Art, in the buildings of the eponymous former train station, is a forecourt composed of a circular garden surrounding an oasis of greenery, all perfectly contained within a boxwood hedge. The hedge echoes the turntable that used to be there until the closure of the station in 1884, and which made it possible for locomotives to turn and travel back in the opposite direction.

When railroads first appeared at the end of the 1830s, in order to limit noise and pollution, trains were not permitted to run through cities. Hence a station known as a terminus (see page 106) was built beyond the city boundaries, close to various points of access. The Hamburg terminus was originally near *Neues Tor* (New Door), which opened onto the current Robert-Koch-Platz on the city side.

However, the concept of a terminus raised a number of technical problems, not least how to get locomotives to go back the opposite way after reaching their destination.

The issue was solved by installing turntables on which the locomotives would rotate to face the required direction – hence the

need for a forecourt where a turntable, as well as enormous entrance archways (to allow locomotives to pass by before and after turning), could be installed.

The Hamburger Bahnhof perfectly illustrates this solution: after entering the station, the locomotive passed through the left archway, rotated on the platform – now indicated by the oasis of greenery – and exited in the opposite direction through the archway on the right.

As for the passengers, rather than use the central archway, they entered the station hall via more modest doors at the sides – following the subsequent construction of lateral wings, the doors are no longer visible.

It is possible to see two turntables in a near-original state at the Technik Museum. They correspond to the turntables of the Anhalter Bahnhof terminus.

THE STAIRS OF THE ULAP

11

Last minute barbarity

Opposite number 140 Alt-Moabit, 10117 Berlin
S3, 5, 7, 9 / U55 Hauptbahnhof

Opposite the recently inaugurated Federal Home Office in Moabit (2015), some very old, authentic stone steps have an unnatural slant to them. Skinny trees grow between the steps. In 1879, the first visitors climbed these stairs on their way to the Land's exhibition centre (ULAP) which had just been inaugurated. The first exhibition was on industry, the second on hygiene, and others followed until the mid-1920s. In 1936, the year of the Olympic games, the centre hosted Berlin's German aeronautic collection with the largest plane in the world, a German, civil flying boat: the Dornier Do X.

But to save this area from the speculation of real estate promoters, it would take more than the sole distinction of this historic centre and its exhibitions. In 1927, the building work carried out for the Stadtbahn uncovered 126 corpses, revealing that the site had been used as a graveyard; it harboured a considerable number of victims of political assassinations from the beginning of the Weimar Republic, and was also the scene of the cold-blooded executions perpetrated by the SS at the very end of the war in 1945. They were the remains of Spartacists who had been taken out of the prison cells in Lehrter Straße, the barracks of Moabit and the cells of Kriminalgericht of Moabit to be executed on the site of the exhibition centre. In March 1933, in a room located under the restaurant of the exhibition pavilion, the SA tortured the lawyer Günther Joachim to death. The bloody history of this place came to a climax with the murder of 16 political prisoners from the prison of Moabit on the Lehrter Straße on the night of 23 April 1945. Most of them were accused of being part of the plot on 20 July 1944, an attempted assassination of Adolf Hitler. At the very last minute, the SS made the prisoners go down these stairs, pretending that it was for a transfer due to enemy advances. They were forced to line up, and the SS shot them from behind. The sole survivor was a young communist called Herbert Kosney, as the bullet that was fired into the nape of his neck missed his spine.

Thanks to the information that he provided, the Soviet military police found the bodies a few days later. What became known as the "Sonnets of Moabit" were found in geographer Albrecht Haushofer's jacket pocket, and included the sonnet entitled *"Schuld"* (Guilt): "Early on I saw the whole tragedy coming - / I said it -- but not loudly or clearly enough!"

THE PAPER LEAVES OF THE SWISS EMBASSY

⑫

An unexpected work of art

Alsenviertel, Spreebogen
Otto-von-Bismarck-Allee 4A, 10557 Berlin
S3, 5, 7, 9 (Hauptbahnhof) / S1, 2, 25 (Brandenburger Tor)
U55 (Bundestag)

On the way into the (covered) entrance of the remarkable Embassy of Switzerland (see opposite), the ground is permanently littered with paper leaves. Do not take this for a lack of zeal on the part of the person in charge of cleaning the embassy: these (paper) leaves are part of an artist's work. Pipilotti Rist is the artist, as we learn from reading a small text on the right-hand wall. Once every twelve minutes, in the contemporary-style entrance hall designed in 2001 by the architects Diener&Diener, a paper leaf flutters down from the ceiling. The machine (if you look up you can see the hole that the leaves fall through) was built in Switzerland by Dimitri Westermann (Smokeball).

The paper leaves represent different types of tree leaves (maple, oak, ginkgo, lime and vine). On each leaf there is a photo of the leaf on one side and, on the other side, a short message such as: *Du bist ein Sonnenaufgang* ("you are a sunrise").

Written, in theory, in one of the four official languages of Switzerland (only messages written in German could be seen when we were there and the twelve-minute intervals were not always respected), the poetic texts are not linked to each other. This flutter of leaves littering the floor is a popular attraction as it is not the kind of artwork that you would normally expect to find in such an institution.

The artist sees these leaves "as a metaphor for democracy, they are the ambassadors of a universal message". For this reason, visitors are encouraged to take them away with them.

Originally planned to last for ten years, the work of art has been kept on by the embassy. Visits to see the machine which sends the leaves fluttering down must be booked in advance.

The last remnant of a district entirely destroyed by the Nazis

At the end of Spreebogen Park (a never-ending abandoned lot that is nothing like Berlin's other crowded parks) stands the peculiar Swiss Embassy.

The once affluent Alsen district (*Alsenviertel*) changed radically under the Nazis. Located at the tip of the north-south axis of Germania, the intended capital of the world (see page 192), Alsen is where they wanted to construct the largest building ever seen. Although plans for the new capital of the Reich (made public in 1938) focused on the magnitude of the project rather than the extensive demolition it required, it was clear that Alsen had to be razed in order to provide sufficient space for the construction of the Great Hall (also known as the People's Hall).

Located near Wilhelmstraße, Alsen had housed many embassies since 1890. From 1938, these embassies were relocated to a new district on the south side of Tiergarten Park. The stalling tactics of foreign diplomats were no match for the Nazis, and all the embassies (Argentina, Belgium, Chile, Denmark, Japan, Norway, Turkey, the Austro-Hungarian Empire, Romania, Siam and Uruguay) were forced to cede to their plans. By 1942, the only embassy remaining on the levelled plot of land was that of Switzerland. A bomb had obliterated the new building in the Tiergarten district and the lone cubic structure became the last remnant of the district destroyed by the Nazis.

At that time, the west side of the east-west axis of Germania was already under construction. It was actually completed in time to celebrate Hitler's 50th birthday in 1939. The Victory Column – which originally stood on *Königsplatz* (King's Square) and commemorated decisive Prussian victories secured against Denmark, Austria and France shortly before the proclamation of the German Empire – became out of place when Alsen was destroyed. It was relocated to the Großer Stern, a large intersection on the city axis, and true to their megalomaniacal vision, Hitler's so-called brown shirts had it augmented by a few extra metres.

Where does the name "Alsenviertel" come from?

The name *Alsenviertel* derives from the street of Als (*Alsenstraße*), which refers to the conquest of the island of Als during the Danish-Prussian War of 1864.

THE KERBS OF GERMANIA

Thankfully, there are limits

Straße des 17. Juni, 10117 Berlin
S1, 2, 25 / U55 (Brandenburger Tor)

Often hidden by tourist buses, two kerbs appear to have mysteriously sunk into the asphalt sidewalk of the Straße des 17. Juni. They can be seen clearly opposite the Soviet memorial on the sidewalk running along Tiergarten Park.

What appear to be markings left from construction works actually correspond to the first metre of the north-south axis of Germania, Hitler and Speer's intended new capital (see page 192), of which the current Straße des 17. Juni was the first part. To the west, the east-west axis had already been completed in time for Hitler's 50th birthday, 20 July 1939.

After the Soviet victory over Nazi Germany, the Soviets knowingly chose this site to erect their memorial. Indeed, as it blocks the access to what was intended to be the world's largest building, the Great Hall (Große Halle), and where the current German Chancellery currently stands, the memorial symbolises the crushing of Hitler's plans for world dominance

The huge forecourt of the Great Hall was intended to run alongside Hitler's giant palace and the Reichstag, which would have appeared very small in comparison.

By measuring the distance between the two preserved kerbs on the first metre of the north-south axis, it is possible to establish that the axis would have been 120 metres wide.

At 75 metres wide, the east-west axis located right behind is already Germany's widest street. Given that no traffic lights were planned for Hitler's Via Triumphalis in the southern direction, one would need to have been super human to cross the street successfully.

In order to ensure traffic safety at the crossroads of these two axes, huge tunnels were planned.

The first sections of these tunnels were constructed and are now preserved. Their ventilation shafts are located in the park, at the next intersection to the west of Bremer Weg.

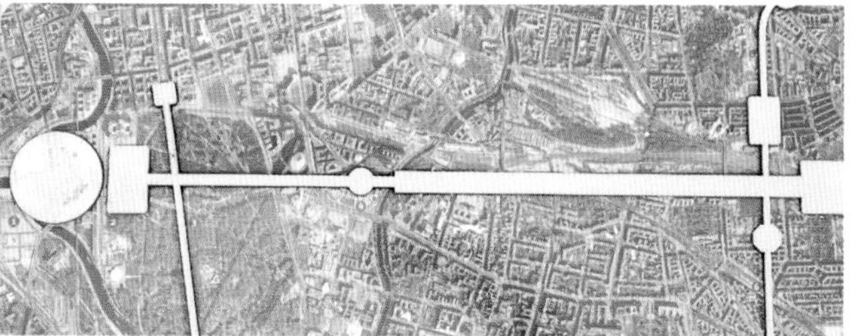

THE POTSDAMER BRÜCKE RING

(14)

A very discreet ring

Corner of Potsdamer Brücke and Schöneberger Ufer, 10785 Berlin
U2 (Mendelssohn-Bartholdy-Park)

You can cross over the bridge a hundred times and not even notice it: if you take the Potsdamer Brücke north towards the Kulturforum, at the very beginning of the bridge, on the left-hand side, there is very ordinary-looking ring, despite its size (58 centimetres in diameter and 10 centimetres thick) inserted in the railing of the bridge. It is impossible to remove it, even though it can be moved around the bar of the railings that it is fixed to.

The work of the artist Norbert Radermacher, the ring was designed in 1985 for the *Kunst in der Bundesrepublik* 1945-1985 ("Art in the FRG") exhibition, organised by the Neue Nationalgalerie.

After it was first placed there without permission, the ring disappeared. During renovation work on the bridge in 1997 and 1998, with the city's approval this time, a new bronze ring was cast and fitted shortly afterwards.

"The last house must remain standing!" 

If the Villa Parey (Sigismundstraße 4A) is so special, it is not so much thanks to the person who built it (Theodor Wilhelm Paul Parey, the most famous literary editor of his time, specialising in the fields of agriculture and forestry), but the fact that it is the only house of the former district of Tiergarten to remain standing today. Having inevitably suffered in the war, its front spattered with the bullets of machine gun fire gives it a desolated look which could have condemned it to destruction. But the surge of protests which came suddenly from the tenants of this building, belonging to the Stiftung Preußischer Kulturbesitz (Foundation for Prussian Cultural Heritage) blocked the construction project of the new Gemäldegalerie. For a long time, fortunately so for the disfigured villa, none of the plans presented by the architects were adopted, and the tenants' protest movement had plenty of time to take a political turn. In their tracts, the 23 residents summed up their demands as follows: "The last house must remain standing!"

The municipal councillors of the Tiergarten district finally decided in favour of the conservation of the building, as did the Housing Office of the Land which decreed that the building was basically in good condition. Even the director of the IBA 1987, the international exhibition of architecture the theme of which was "Die Innenstadt als Wohnort" (the town centre as a place for living), joined in the debate, declaring that the conservation of the villa Parey could be undertaken in a "very rational" way. The highest-ranking politician involved in construction in West Berlin was therefore caught in the crossfire. He was not so sure that the financial backers in Bonn, the capital at that time, would agree to modify the plans (which were costly and far from indispensable), and include this house which was not even registered as a listed building. The miracle happened. Only the coachman's house and the stables of the villa Parey had to be given up.

A house inspired by the Hartenfels Castle in Torgau, Saxony

An eclectic mixture of construction styles from the Gründerzeit at the end of the 19th century, it is thought that the Villa Parey was built on the model of the Hartenfels Castle in Torgau in Saxony. The windows that have been cut into the front of it are Gothic in style or framed with pilasters which – like its very ornate pediment – are reminiscent of the Italian First Renaissance.

THE GAS STREET LAMPS OF THE OPEN AIR MUSEUM

16

The most romantic museum in Berlin

Straße des 17. Juni, 10557 Berlin
Open 7/7, 24/24
S3, 5, 7, 9 (Tiergarten)

To get to the most romantic museum in Berlin, it is an easy ride from the S-Bahn Tiergarten station to the Zoo underground stop. The open air museum can be visited whilst walking through the park of the same name. It is free of charge and really worth seeing, especially at night when it is lit up, giving the visitor a feeling of being taken back in time.

The "open air museum" has the largest historic collection in the world of gas street lamps. GASAG, the oldest local gas distribution company, has sponsored the museum since 1978, when this lovely idea became reality. To this day, Berlin has remained the capital of gas street lamps: in 2009, there were still 44,000 in working order, more than anywhere else in the world.

The story of these street lamps in Berlin began with the Prussian Home Secretary who appointed the Imperial Continental Gas Association (ICGA) of London to set up the gas street lighting in Berlin. The first gas works (the Gas street lighting company) was built on the site of the open air swimming pool in Kreuzberg, and in September 1826 the first gas street lamps, powered by underground pipes, lit up Unter den Linden. By 1846, the ICGA had provided the town with a 100-km-long gas distribution network. After this date, the Berliners progressively took control of the production of gas for lighting, heating and cooking.

West Berlin continued to produce its own town gas until the 1980s, even if the rest of Western Germany used the natural gas supplied by the East. The town gas was actually produced in West Berlin, as was the electricity, from coal and petrol. Both had to be shipped by train from the West. With the easing of relations between the east and west, from 1983, West Berlin was also supplied by the Russian natural gas pipeline. However, the latter is partly converted into town gas and stored in large underground gas reserves ... Paranoia or mere precaution?

In Western Germany, gas street lighting rapidly disappeared in the 1970s and 80s. However, at the very same time these beautiful gas street lamps were to be given a new lease of life in the Tiergarten. To fight against vandalism, a poem by Erich Mühsam, an anarchist writer, was quoted on the public benches. It tells the story of a revolutionary who was a lamplighter by trade, and who protested when his companions tore down the street lamps to set up barricades. "I'm a lamplighter of this good lighting. I beg you to leave it alone. If we cut off this source of lighting, no one will be able to see anything".

A VISIT TO THE UT2

17

The world's largest cavitation testing station

Müller-Breslau-Straße 15, 10623 Berlin
dms.tu-berlin.de/menue/versuchseinrichtungen/umlauftank_ut2
Guided tours for groups during Heritage Days or by appointment
S3, 5, 7, 9 (Tiergarten)

Viewing the 35-metre-high UT2 building from afar (a hybrid of giant pink pipelines and stranded container ships), it's hard to imagine the interior. But inside, it's like a cargo vessel dedicated to scientific research.

UT2 stands for *Umlauf-und-Kavitations-Tank 2* ("Circulation and Cavitation Tank No. 2").

Cavitation is a phenomenon whereby the movement of a ship's propeller blades creates different kinds of bubbles underwater, whose energy, when they implode, has the potential to damage the propeller itself.

In extreme cases, these bubbles can have the same destructive effect as a hammer on metal.

UT2 simulates real-life conditions of stress on moving propellers; it is the world's largest testing station used to study these kinds of currents.

The main pipe, in which masses of water move during experiments, runs along the ground inside the building.

The surrounding walls are covered with open galleries, crowded with machines, control consoles, measuring equipment, and archive cabinets – not dissimilar to the hold of an oceanographic ship. This explains why researchers refer to different levels as "decks" rather than "floors".

The circulation of water through the looped pipe (120 metres long, 19 metres high, and 8 metres in diameter) is powered by two diesel boat engines capable of carrying 3,300 tonnes of water at a flow speed ranging from 4 to 10 metres per second.

Prenzlauer Berg

10
Jüdischer Friedhof Berlin-Weißensee
Weißenseer Weg
Ostseestraße
Volkspark Prenzlauer Berg
Weißenseer Weg
Kniprodestraße
Landsberger Allee
Storkower Straße
Paul-Junius-Str.
Greifswalder Straße
Storkower Straße
Karl-Lade-Straße
PRENZLAUER BERG
LICHTENBERG
Landsberger Allee
Conrad-Blenkle-Straße
Storkower Straße
Danziger Straße
Storkower Straße
ARNSWALDER PLATZ
Hausburgstraße
Danziger Straße
Kniprodestraße
Ebertystraße
Thaerstraße
Samariterstraße
Bötzowstraße
Petersburger Straße
Eldenaer Straße
Bänschstraße
Am Friedrichshain
Landsberger Allee
Richard-Sorge-Straße
Samariterstraße
Volkspark Friedrichshain
BERSARIN-PLATZ
Friedenstraße
Frankfurter Allee
Frankfurter Tor
Friedenstraße
Weidenweg
Karl-Marx-Allee
Weberwiese
FRIEDRICHSHAIN

REVERSE INSCRIPTION ON THE SENEFELDER MONUMENT

①

A tribute to lithography, Senefelder's invention

Schönhauser Allee, corner of Kollwitzstraße
U2 (Senefelderplatz)

At the corner of Schönhauser Allee and Kollwitzstraße in Prenzlauer Berg, near the southern exit of the Senefelderplatz U-Bahn station, is a monument dedicated to Alois Senefelder (1771-1834). It depicts Senefelder seated on a pedestal, at the foot of which are two children, one of whom is writing his name backwards. Far from being a sculptor's mistake, this act reminds us that Senefelder was the inventor of lithography (and colour printing) – in lithography, as in any printing technique, the motif to be printed must first be traced in reverse in order to appear correctly on the paper.

At the base of the sculpture, the second child is holding a mirror (not the original as it has been replaced twice, most notably after it was stolen in the late 1990s), which he uses to decipher the words written behind him.

Senefelder discovered lithography out of his need to develop a simple way of printing musical scores, which were particularly difficult to engrave in reverse without making mistakes.

Lithography is based on the principle of the natural repulsion between water and fat: an image is drawn with a soft pencil on a perfectly smooth limestone plate, which is then moistened.

Applied with a roller, the ink is repelled by the humidity of the stone towards the lines traced in pencil, the fatty content of which retains the ink. The advantage of lithography was that the pencil drawing could be done the right way round on special paper before being traced onto the stone plate.

Inaugurated in 1892 in the presence of Emperor Wilhelm II – a rare and distinguished honour – the monument, made of marble from Carrara (Italy), was created by Berlin sculptor Rudolf Pohle and was considered a masterpiece of new realism at the time.

It depicts Senefelder at work, carefully considering one of his famous plates. At his feet, rolls of cloth and instruments recall his contribution to the development of cloth printing techniques.

GDR TOY MUSEUM ②

A trip back in time to the childhood of Berliners

Choriner Straße 35–36, 10435 Berlin
0 30 / 4 49 04 91
onkel-philipp.de
Tue–Fri 9:30am–6:30pm; Sat 10am–5pm
U2 (Eberswalder Straße or Senefelderplatz)

Contrary to what its façade may suggest, *Onkel Philipp's Spielzeugwerkstatt* ("Uncle Philipp's Toy Workshop") harbours an extraordinary multitude of toys and souvenirs. This laboratory-boutique, opened in 1997 by Philipp Schünemann, showcases myriad true antiquities, some of which have been repaired by the owner and stored away on shelves where dolls, board games and electric cars can be seen piling up.

Setting off on a journey through the rooms of Uncle Philipp's store is like travelling through the childhood of several generations of Berliners. Many of the toys and the airplanes hanging from the ceiling date back to the GDR – all part of Uncle Philipp's twenty-year-old collection.

But the main attraction is in the basement. Opposite the cash register, from where the owner imparts advice to customers of all ages, is a mock gravestone bearing the inscription *R.I.P. Spielzeug der DDR 1949-1989* ("R.I.P. toys of the GDR 1949-1989"). This is in fact a small sliding door, through which customers can access a narrow winding staircase that leads to the lower floor. Here, customers can admire Uncle Philipp's rarest finds; it is a kind of museum of toys produced in the former East Germany.

Most of the dolls and stuffed toys in this little exhibition area are displayed in no specific order, forming a multicolour mountain of hair, arms, and eyes of various shapes and sizes. And not to be outdone, miniature cars and trucks with austere looks immortalise the various modes of transport used during the era of the GDR. A glass window protects them from wandering hands. As they now all constitute irreplaceable relics of the past, they are not for sale.

Unlike in a traditional museum, there are no signs or information panels here to guide visitors; they must simply enjoy looking at the toys and try to guess the period in which they were produced.

THE WELL IN THE JEWISH CEMETERY

③

A well where deserters hid in 1944

Jüdischer Friedhof Schönhauser Allee, Schönhauser Allee 23–25, 10435 Berlin
Mon–Thur 8am–4pm; Fri 7:30am–1pm
U2 (Senefelderplatz)

In the north-west sector of the Jewish Cemetery of Schönhauser Allee stands a little well protected by a guardrail. Above it, a plaque bears the inscription: *Den Tod anderer / nicht zu wollen / das war ihr Tod/ Hier verbargen sich am Ende des / Jahres 1944 Kriegsgegner / Sie wurden von der SS entdeckt / an den Bäumen erhängt / und hier verscharrt.* It means "They died not wanting others to die. This is where, at the end of 1944, war opponents hid. The SS found them, hanged them from trees and buried them here."

The plaque was installed after the war on the initiative of East Berlin municipal councillor Arnold Munter, an anti-Nazi resistance fighter who survived the Theresienstadt concentration camp.

This epitaph recalls a tragic event that occurred in the last few months before the end of the war. Several young deserters keen to escape the fighting hid in this cemetery. The group found refuge in an underground tank belonging to the brewery that was here at the beginning of the 19th century before the place was turned into a cemetery. Sadly, the deserters were discovered and hanged by the SS. After their summary execution, the bodies were buried on site in a mass grave. The identity and exact number of deserters is not known. The well leads to the hiding place where they were found.

The Jüdischer Friedhof Schönhauser Allee is the second oldest Jewish cemetery in the city. It was founded in 1827 to compensate for the closure of the old cemetery on Große Hamburger Straße, and was in turn replaced in 1880 by the cemetery at Weißensee, currently the largest Jewish cemetery in Europe.

Before entering the hushed atmosphere of the cemetery and wandering among the monumental tombs and headstones hidden among lush vegetation, a visit to the Lapidarium located at the entrance is recommended. This modern building with large bay windows houses more than 60 tombstones dating from the 19th and 20th centuries, and includes a number of explanatory signs on Jewish culture and funeral rituals.

Symbols on Jewish tombstones

Symbols have always played a fundamental role in Judaism. Each graphic sign was assigned a characteristic or quality and was intended to represent the link between humankind and God (unlike diabolism, which separates humankind from God) and to identify a family or a religious function.

Tombstones in Jewish cemeteries feature some common themes, notably the "priestly blessing", indicating the deceased person's priestly descent. It can be found on the tombstones of members of the Cohen (or Coen) family; in Hebrew *kohèn* means priest, i.e. a male descendent of Aaron, brother of Moses and first high priest of the Jewish community. The position of the hands, with spread fingers, is adopted during the blessing.

Another typical symbol is the pitcher pouring water. This symbol is a sign of belonging to the Israelite tribe of Levi (the Levi family), whose traditional duties were to assist priests during religious services by washing their hands before the blessing.

The oldest tombstones also bear another symbol prominent in Jewish funerary symbolism: the crown. This represents both the political authority and the dignitary role of the deceased and comes from a quote from *Pirkei Avot* (Ethics of Our Fathers), one of the founding texts of Judaism: "There are three crowns: the crown of Torah, the crown of priesthood and the crown of monarchy – but the crown of a good name outweighs them all."

From the 19th century, other symbols more in line with the trends

of the time began to appear. The clepsydra refers to the passage of time and the moment when life comes to an end. It sometimes bears wings, or can be associated with crossbones and a skull, making the connection to death even more evident. Similarly, the symbol of a torch turned upside down is used to represent mourning: the flame must be extinguished against the floor.

The ouroboros, the symbol of a serpent eating its own tail, recalls the notion of rebirth, while the crown of flowers can evoke the idea that the deceased acquired a reputation during his terrestrial life.

The butterfly, a symbol both ancient and common, refers to the soul departing the body and ascending into the sky.

The Star of David (*Magen David*) is perhaps the most famous symbol in Jewish culture. It was widely adopted throughout the 19th century and can be seen on many tombstones in cemeteries across the world.

Animal figures symbolise the name of the deceased: the lion, often seen next to a crown, not only indicates that the person is of royal descent and therefore belongs to David's lineage, it also refers to the name Leon (*Leo* in Italian, *Loeb* or *Loew* in Germany); the wolf is the emblem of Benjamin and is the representation of a very common surname in the Jewish community (*Wolf* in English and German, *Zeev* in Hebrew); and a deer, which represents descendants of the Naphtali tribe, refers to the surname *Hirsch* (in Yiddish and German), *Zvi* (in Hebrew) or *Naftali*.

WATER TANKS OF PRENZLAUER BERG

④

The remains of the city's old water supply network

Belforter Straße, 10405 Berlin
unter-berlin.de
Guided tours available only in German (see website for details)
U2 (Senefelderplatz)

Beneath the artificial hill of Park am Wasserturm lie the city's spectacular old water reservoirs, which can be visited by appointment. The narrow 20 metre-high tower on top of the hill was used to balance and measure water pressure, and was equipped with a safety valve. Built in several stages between 1852 and 1873 in a rural area once called *Windmühlenberg* ("Windmill Hill"), this complex, the first of its kind in Berlin, had two cisterns of different sizes.

The *Kleine Wasserspeicher* ("small water tank") was inaugurated in 1856 and has a diameter of 32 metres. It is divided by brick pillars connected by a series of arches. When in operation, it could hold up to 3,000 cubic metres of water, supplying the homes of more than 400,000 Berliners.

The *Große Wasserspeicher* ("large water reservoir") consists of five concentric circles divided into thirty-four sections topped by a vaulted ceiling. A spiral staircase in the centre of the structure leads directly to the octagonal tower visible on the hill.

In 1914, following the modernisation of Berlin's water system, the two cisterns were abandoned; since 1994 they have been used for classical music concerts, exhibitions, and other cultural events.

The guided tour also passes through the underground premises of the former *Brauerei Königstadt*, one of many breweries founded in Prenzlauer Berg in the 19th century. The tour retraces the history of the brewery, along with the history of the water network, and provides an insight into the interesting architectural features of both buildings.

At the north end of Park am Wasserturm, the *Wasserturm* is an imposing 30 metre-high water tower that was completed in 1877 and remained in use until 1952. The living quarters of the technicians who worked here were located inside, underneath a reservoir capable of holding up to 1,200 cubic metres of water. They have now been converted into private flats. In 1933, the engine room of the water tower was transformed into a concentration camp, where many members of the resistance were detained and shot. It was destroyed in 1935.

The *Wasserturm* complex currently houses a public library, a kindergarten, and a children's playground.

How does Berlin get its water?

Until the second half of the 19th century, the population was supplied with water from thousands of wells scattered throughout the city. The wells were often located a few metres from the septic tanks that contaminated them.

In 1856, water was pumped from the Spree and running water was installed: the first central water supply station was inaugurated in front of the Stralau Gate, one of the gates of the Customs Wall (see page 108), slightly east of the Oberbaumbrücke on the north bank of the Spree. Nothing is left of this gate. Water from the river was filtered with sand before being pumped into the town's water pipes. The system was supplemented by a water tower and a reservoir with a capacity of 3,000 m3 located on the Windmühlenberg (Windmill Hill) in what is now the Park am Wasserturm in Prenzlauer Berg (see page 294). Originally open-air, the reservoir, which was closed over by a vaulted ceiling in 1877, is no longer visible from the outside, but the tower, known as the Steigrohrturm, is still clearly visible (not to be confused with the much wider water tower that was built later overlooking Knaakstraße, which also served as a reservoir). The reservoir met the additional demand in times of high consumption and the tower was used to regulate the pressure in the pipes.

When the Stralau station reached its maximum capacity, it was first supplemented by a new station in Tegel in 1877, and finally abandoned in 1893 in favour of the Friedrichshagen station on the banks of the Müggelsee, which was then the largest and most modern distribution station in Europe. In addition, numerous water towers were built between 1877 and 1929 to meet the needs of hospitals and factories, or the new, rapidly expanding outlying districts.

Upon the instructions of the doctor and virologist Rudolf Virshow and the engineer James Hobrecht, the sanitary issues were tackled at the same time, and an underground sewage system was installed in the city to avoid polluting the Spree and the water tables with waste water, which formed an open sewer: this water contributed greatly to the cholera and typhus epidemics that devastated the city at that time.

The sewage network, which was more than 1,200 km in length, was built between 1873 and 1909. The city was divided into 12 so-called radial districts (*Radialbezirke*), because their sewage systems were arranged in a star shape around the lowest point of the district, leading the district's wastewater along a natural slope (see next double page). From there, it was pumped outside the city walls by means of powerful pumps, where it was used as fertilizer for land purchased for this purpose by the city (*Riesenfelder*): these vegetable crops in turn fed the Berliners.

These sewage networks, which are still in use today, continued using their original pumps for a very long time.

Following Germany's reunification, the Friedrichshagen waterworks were reorganised so that all the water was drawn exclusively from groundwater.

For this reason, part of the complex is no longer in operation: it houses the museum of Berlin's water management and its history.

This main station was supplemented by eight other stations, which have since been modernised many times: Kaulsdorf (1916), Wuhlheide (1914), Stolpe (Brandenburg) (1911), Tegel (1877), Spandau (1897), Tiefwerder (1914), Kladow (1932/1937) and Beelitzhof (1888/1894).

Today, through 8,000 km of pipes, these nine Berlin stations deliver almost 600,000 m^3 of drinking water every day, which they draw exclusively from the Berlin groundwater through 650 wells at a depth of 30 to 170 metres.

These stations therefore no longer pump water from the Spree.

On the other hand, 164 pumping stations (compared to the 12 historical pumping stations of the then much smaller city) pump waste water to six sewage treatment plants in Münchehofe, Schönerlinde, Wansdorf (Brandenburg), Ruhleben, Stahnsdorf and Waßmannsdorf, where it is treated before being discharged into Berlin's watercourses – the *Riesenfelder* concept is no longer used.

Berlin's 12 historic sewage pumping stations

Radialsystem I: Reichenberger Straße 66, in **Kreuzberg**, opened in 1879, demolished in 1977 despite strong waves of protest (a mosaic in Reichenberger Straße recalls the blasting operation, see page 155).

Radialsystem II: Gitschiner Straße 7-11 in **Kreuzberg**, inaugurated in 1879 and destroyed during the Second World War. Today replaced by modern facilities still in operation.

Radialsystem III: Schöneberger Straße 21 in **Kreuzberg**, opened in 1877 and decommissioned in 1979. Today it houses the offices of the collector Christian Boros (owner of the Boros Sammlung in Mitte).

Radialsystem IV: Scharnhorststraße 9/10 (from 1907 Scharnhorststraße 12) in **Mitte**, opened in 1879. It was taken out of service in 2011, then demolished.

Radialsystem V: Holzmarktstraße 31/32 in **Friedrichshain**, opened in 1880 and decommissioned in 1999. Since 2005, the modernised building has housed a private institution for cultural and business events.

Radialsystem VI: Urbanstraße 177 in **Kreuzberg**, opened in 1885. Destroyed after it was decommissioned in 1981. The gate of the original building has been preserved and is still visible at the same address.

Radialsystem VII: Lützowstraße 46-51 (**Tiergarten**), opened in 1885 and decommissioned in 1982. All the buildings still exist, including one of the original pumps. Since 1988, the complex has housed a youth centre, a youth hostel and a restaurant for private events.

Radialsystem VIII: Alt-Moabit 70 / Gotzkowsky Straße 22 (**Moabit**), opened in 1890 and decommissioned in 1989. The original buildings now house an auditorium and sports facilities.

Radialsystem IX: Seestraße 2 (**Wedding**), opened in 1886 and decommissioned in 1997. The buildings were demolished in 2000. Since 1997, a modern pumping station has replaced the old one.

Radialsystem X: Bellermannstraße 7 (**Gesundbrunnen**), opened in 1890.

Radialsystem XI: Erich-Weinert-Straße 131 (**Prenzlauer Berg**), opened in 1909 and decommissioned in 2002. Behind the magnificent period buildings there is now a modern pump that has replaced the original one.

Radialsystem XII: Rudolfstraße 15 (**Friedrichshain**), opened in 1893, the pump was modernised in the 1910s and 1930s and is still in operation today (it has been twinned with another modern pump station since 1999).

TOMB OF THE RIEDEL FAMILY ⑤

A spectacular representation of the resurrection

Cemetery I of the Saint George Parish Community, Leisepark,
Greifswalder Str. 229, 10405 Berlin
Dec & Jan 8am–4pm; Feb & Nov 8am–5pm; Mar & Oct 8am–6pm;
Apr & Sept 8am–7pm; May–Aug 8am–8pm
S3, 5, 7, 9 (Alexanderplatz), then Tram M4 (Am Friedrichshain)

In the *Georgen-Parochial-Friedhof I* cemetery, right by the gate on Heinrich-Roller-Straße, is the magnificent Riedel family tomb; it features one of the most moving allegories of the resurrection to be found in Berlin.

Presented in an extraordinarily dynamic manner, it is one of the masterpieces of renowned Berlin sculptor Rudolf Schweinitz and was created in the 1880s after a sketch by Johannes Länge.

Between the Doric columns of the ruins of a Greek temple, an angel lifts the heavy slab of a sarcophagus, revealing its empty interior, while the shroud that lay enigmatically on the lid falls to the ground.

A cherub is seated at the foot of the sarcophagus, turning towards the angel with a perplexed look. A flame is reborn at the tip of the torch he had extinguished as a sign of mourning.

To his right, a palm tree recalls Jesus' triumphant entry into Jerusalem, announcing his final victory over death, as well as his promise, written on the back wall of the tomb (John 17:24): *Father, I want those you have given me to be with me where I am.*

In the background, under a vaulted space that opens onto a fictitious exterior, a small, beautifully coloured mosaic depicts a subtle sunrise against a starry sky. A butterfly relief as the cornerstone symbolises the new life of glory that is promised after death.

The vault is topped by two palm leaves, a symbol of victory used since ancient times, and more specifically in the Christian context, over the ultimate enemy that is death.

TOMB OF THE PINTSCH FAMILY

⑥

An astonishing Greek temple to the glory of a family of geniuses

Cemetery I of the Saint George Parish Community, Leisepark, Greifswalder Str. 229, 10405 Berlin
Dec & Jan 8am–4pm; Feb & Nov 8am–5pm; Mar & Oct 8am–6pm; Apr & Sept 8am–7pm; May–Aug 8am–8pm
S3, 5, 7, 9 (Alexanderplatz), then Tram M4 (Am Friedrichshain)

Within the *Georgen-Parochial-Friedhof I* cemetery in Prenzlauer Berg, the imposing tomb of the Pintsch family appears like a ruined Greek temple.

Now somewhat forgotten, Julius Carl Friedrich Pintsch (1815-1884) and his descendants are among the most prolific and valued geniuses of the Industrial Revolution (see page 313).

Clearly inspired by the Parthenon in Athens, the Pintsch family tomb includes 12 columns, which either symbolise the twelve apostles of Christ or, given the family's obvious fondness for ancient history, the twelve signs of the Zodiac (the twelve months of the year) that give structure to time.

Open on three sides, the rear wall of the tomb lists in two rows the names of the deceased buried in the space within the colonnades. Between the two lists, another relief depicts a long laurel wreath, recalling the glory and the many achievements of the family, itself symbolised by the fruits overflowing from the jar above the wreath.

COVERED PASSAGEWAY OF THE BORNHOLMER STRAßE BORDER POST

(7)

The forgotten place where the division of Germany ended

Marienburger Straße 16, 10405 Berlin (access across the Winsstraße 57 or the Marienburger Straße 32A)
U2 (Senefelder Platz)

After heading a short way down Marienburger Straße from opposite Winnstraße 57, a right turn will reveal a yellowing plastic roof, under which a few cars are parked. It may not look like much at first, but this roof, with its barrelled ceilings and 1978 Svetlina lamp-post straight out of Bulgaria (upgraded with energy-saving lightbulbs), is an authentic historical curiosity. Out of a desire to make good use of the space after the reunification of Germany, an energy company that survived the GDR paid a bargain price for the lot through Treuhand (the body in charge of the privatisation of assets previously owned by the GDR). After the purchase, the company forgot about the plot of land.

Until 1989, this roof covered the Bornholmer Straße border post, the memorable checkpoint of Bösebrücke, which was the first to let crowds through to West Berlin. After 28 years on the eastern side of the Wall, the first 14,000 East Germans who wanted to have a look at "the other side" and go to West Berlin made their way, pushing and shoving, under this hideous roof and its terrible street lamps.

A little reminder: a new law was supposed to deal with the issue of travels abroad and curb the embarrassing number of citizens fleeing the failed GDR via third-party countries. It was intended to authorise (permanent) controlled departures for those who desired to leave East Berlin. During a press conference held on 9 November 1989, Günter Schabowski announced the new provisions but began to stutter when it came to confirming the date of their entry into force: "It shall be applicable, from what I understand, it's ... immediately!"

Nobody really cared that this law only had to apply to those wanting to leave the GDR permanently. The main goal was clear: leave. Just a few hours later, the commanding officer of the Bornholmer Straße border post, who had been given no advance notice, was faced with a crowd of people surging towards the border. As he had not received any orders, Harald Jäger (in charge of controlling passports for the Ministry of Security) took it upon himself to open the border crossing. It is under this now famous roof that the separation of Germany finally came to an end!

THE FISHERMAN OF WINSSTRAßE ⑧

A curious maritime monument

Winsstraße 34, 10405 Berlin
S8, 41, 42 (Greifswalder Straße)

On the corner of Winsstraße and Chodowieckistraße, the stucco bas-relief of a seaman with a white beard standing on a boat, pulling a rope to hoist his sail, runs along the front, on a level with the first floor. Under the colourful, stucco hull of the boat, which ploughs through the water and leans slightly towards the street, the golden colour of the lantern on it contrasts with the dark blue paint on the of the front of the building.

Built in 1906 from plans drawn up by Rudolf Krause, one of Berlin's relatively well-known architects at the time, the building was until 1980 home to the restaurant *Zum Anker* (The Anchor), the ground floor entrance of which was lit up at night by the lantern. Like the rest of the building, the place belonged to the Bötzow family, the owners of one of the city's biggest brasseries, the *Brauerei Bötzow*, from 1864 to 1945. At the very top of the building, there is a shield bearing the initials "GB" for Alfred Gilka-Bötzow, who inherited it and renovated it a short time before the fall of the Wall, converting it into a guesthouse with apartments for rent.

Even though Alfred Gilka-Bötzow closed down *Zum Anker* after receiving his inheritance, the fisherman of Winsstraße has remained where he was, even after the renovation work, in memory of the family's history: his grandfather, Alfred I Gilka, married a daughter of the Bötzow family in 1875, thus creating a new branch of the family, the Gilka-Bötzows. The Gilkas were brandy producers from Silesia and are still known today for their Gilka Kümmel, a flavoured liqueur made from caraway seeds. It is not clear why one of the first owners of the place wanted such a curious maritime decoration, but it is likely that the inspiration came from a holiday spent in a place on the coast.

COAT OF ARMS OF THE GRÜNE STADT GATE 9

A tribute to tradesmen

Greifswalder Straße 55–56, 10405 Berlin
S 8, 41, 42, 85 (Greifswalder Straße)

Between numbers 55 and 56 of Greifswalderstraße in Prenzlauer Berg is a large vaulted entrance flanked by two gates that leads to the inner courtyards of the Grüne Stadt (Green City). This former municipal social housing complex was built in 1938-39 by architect Werner Harding and later privatised in 2004. The dwellings were intended for the working-class population – the gate bears witness to this.

In contrast to the building's façades – a simple plaster coating exempt of decoration – the portal, with its red terracotta tiles, is bordered by a frieze etched in stucco, composed of interlace patterns and coats of arms. Painted in black and white on a red background, these coats of arms are a collection of emblems (in some cases dating back to the Middle Ages) representing traditionally manual trades, a tribute to the working-class populations who lived here.

Above the door on the left is the emblem of the rope makers; it comprises the heart, anchor, rake (used to guide the ropes while they are being braided), and hooks with hand cranks (operated in order to braid rope). Above the door on the right is the emblem of the brewers, which features a ladle, shovel, ears of wheat, and hops.

From left to right around the large vaulted entrance are the emblems of many more trades: locksmiths (keys and a cogwheel) engineers (compass, pickaxe and hammer); roofers (compass, hammer and pointed hammer); glaziers (glass-cutting diamond (horizontal), sledgehammer (vertical), hammer, and soldering iron); carpenters (compass, tri-square and rebate plane); tailors (needle, scissors and triangular protractor); house painters (imperial eagle and a shield marked with three small coats of arms); chimney sweepers (shovels and a small brush); stonecutters (a stonecutter's monogram – a signature with which the sculptors once marked every one of their stones); potters (potter's wheel flanked by flames and the letters T and O, probably for Töpfer-Orden – the Craft Potters Association)

carpenters (axe, tri-square and whipsaw – a saw with two handles, in this case attached to a pendulum); and woodworkers (scissors and a poorly drawn compass).

On the left inside the vaulted passage is the blacksmiths' emblem (a horseshoe), while on the right is the electricians' emblem, featuring a lightning bolt crossed by electrical wires and three disconnectors (a type of high-voltage switch).

From the courtyard above the left door is another depiction of the carpenters' emblem, while on the cornerstone is the masons' emblem, composed of compass, pickaxe, angle, and shovel.

Lastly, from the courtyard above the door on the right, is another rope makers' emblem.

THE TOMB OF THE LEWINSOHN AND NETTER FAMILIES ⑩

An exceptional tomb

Jewish cemetery of Berlin-Weißensee
Herbert-Baum-Straße 45, 13088 Berlin
Mon– Fri 7:30am–5pm (2:30pm on Fridays)
S8, 41, 42, 85 (Greifswalder Straße), then Tram M1, 4, 13 (Albertinenstraße)

In the heart of the magnificent Jewish cemetery of Berlin-Weißensee (perhaps one of the most beautiful cemeteries in Europe), it is easy to miss some of the beautiful graves and the quality of their features, as there are so many of them. The most beautiful one is a real gem that must not be missed. In order to find it, you should ask for a plan at the entrance and look for the plot at the junction of the paths IIA, IIB, IIG and IIH. Almost exactly at the junction of these four paths, the tomb of the Lewinsohn and Netter families is surrounded by a spectacular cast iron fence, decorated with dozens of golden flowers, entwined with green leaves and a burgundy red-coloured motif on the flower buds and on some of the leaves. Designed in 1893 by Fabian, the tomb houses four sarcophagi with plaques bearing the dates of birth and death of the deceased who passed away between 1893 and 1922. The tomb was restored between 2000 and 2002 with money from the historical monuments fund of the Land of Berlin.

Not to be missed either is the intersection of the paths IIK, IIJ, IIR and IIS: all the tombs in this little square are exceptional. Of particular interest are the tombs of the Adam, Friedlaender and Baszynski families, of Art Nouveau inspiration.

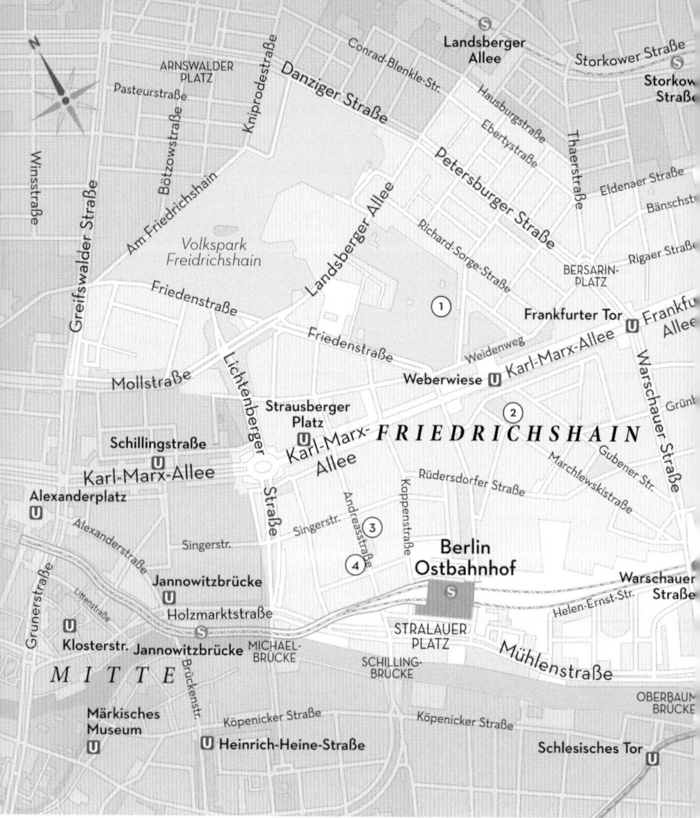

Friedrichshain - Rummelsburg

LICHTENBERG
Lichtenberg
Einbecker Straße
Möllendorffstraße
Magdalenenstraße
Frankfurter Allee
Buchberger Str.
Pettenkoferstraße
Bänschstr.
Margaretenstr.
Marie-Curie-Allee
Rigaer Straße
Frankfurter Allee
Schulze-Boysen-Straße
Weitlingstraße
Samariterstraße
Scharnweberstraße
Gürtelstraße
Münsterlandstr.
Nöldnerplatz
Lückstraße
Weserstraße
Kaskelstraße
Nöldnerstr.
RUMMELSBURG
Wühlischstraße
Marktstr.
Simplonstraße
Rummelsburg
Hauptstraße
Ostkreuz
Modersohnstraße
Hauptstraße
Markgrafendam
Kynaststraße
Rummelsburger see
Corinthstraße
Fischzug
Stralauer Allee
Alt-Stralau
Spree
ELSEN-BRÜCKE
Treptower Park
Treptower Park
0
500
1 000 m

CIRCULAR GARDEN OF THE GEORGEN-PAROCHIAL II CEMETERY 1

The ages of life

Georgen-Parochial-Friedhof II
Friedenstraße 80, 10249 Berlin
Dec & Jan 8am–4pm; Feb & Nov 8am–5pm; Mar & Oct 8am–6pm;
Apr & Sept 8am–7pm; May–Aug 8am–8pm
U5 (Weberwiese)

To the right of the chapel of the Georgen-Parochial II Cemetery is a small circular garden built around a simple fountain. Around the fountain are four intriguing statues representing the four ages of human life.

The first depicts an old man bent under the weight of a heavy necklace. His flabby, wrinkled flesh indicates advanced age, while his muscles are evidence of a full life. Sitting on a parched stump, his head is covered by a hood that veils his gaze, which is fixed on a skull he holds in his left hand.

To the old man's left, childhood appears to us in the form of a young boy, also seated on a stump. But this stump has sprouted new life: a branch bearing an abundance of flowers. The boy gazes towards the sky. With his right hand he touches an eagle perched on his shoulder – a symbol of his ambitions and the heights he dreams of reaching.

On the eastern side is the melancholic teenager, overwhelmed by his emotions. Presented as a broken-hearted poet, he thoughtfully strums the strings of a lyre adorned with a female face, while a crown of flowers lies at his feet.

Finally, the middle-aged man with a straight back and a hard face is the image of unshakeable will. Sitting on a stone pedestal, he raises a fist in determination. At his feet a small figure clutching his right hand appears to be climbing onto a head embedded in the pedestal. The head looks very similar to the teenager's, suggesting that male maturity comes from overcoming romantic sentimentalism.

According to some sources, the face of the mature man is a representation of David Francke, father of Ernst Carl Francke (1823-1895), a prosperous lumber merchant and the founder of the David Francke Söhne company, whose monumental family tomb is to the left of the cemetery chapel.

Also serving as a private chapel, the interior was originally furnished with seven statues by the sculptor Johann Michael Bossard: in addition to the ages of the circular garden, the three statues on display in the cemetery chapel were a Pietà and two angels serving as candelabras.

For further information: Katrin Lesser, Jörg Kuhn, Detelev Pietzsch. *Gartendenkmale in Berlin: Friedhöfe*. Edited by Jörg Haspel and Klaus von Krosigk, Petersberg 2008.

THE COLUMNS OF WEBERWIESE ②

Columns that come from Göring's mansion

Marchlewskistraße 25, 10243 Berlin
U5 (Weberwiese)

Built in just a year, between 1951 and 1952, by the architect Hermann Henselmann, the famous tower of Weberwiese was the first high-rise tower block to be built in post-war East Berlin. Very few Berliners, or even inhabitants of the tower block, are aware that the remains of an old, private Nazi mansion were used to build this neoclassical construction. The dark black-green columns of polished dolerite at the entrance of the building, in addition to the material used in the main entrance hall up to the foot of the stairs, do indeed come from Carinhall, Göring's country estate north-east of Berlin.

At the beginning of the 1940s, the columns were used to decorate the enlargement of Carinhall, which was the country retreat of Reichsmarschall Göring, built as a northern-style wooden house on the banks of the Wuckersee lake, in the forest of Schorfheide. This enormous new building was built to house Göring's looted private art collection. Göring (who also owned another chalet near Hitler's Berghof in the Bavarian Alps) had Carinhall demolished when the war was coming to an end as he was afraid that his property would fall into the hands of the Allies. Some of the confiscated and stolen paintings, which he wrongly considered to be worthless, were burnt. The ruins were removed at the time of the GDR, and today there is nothing left but a bunker full of random waste, which regularly attracts treasure hunters.

Built mainly with bricks found in the rubble after the bombings, the tower block was fitted with an outer cladding in Meißen ceramic (not porcelain!) – supplied by the long-established factory, founded by Carl Teicher in Meißen, which produced tiling for stoves and buildings.

Applying the principles of the training that he had received, Henselmann initially designed the building in the modern pre-war architectural style, but his initial design was rejected. This piece of socialist realism was therefore built instead, which, strangely enough, meant that Nazi neoclassicism was upheld in the east. This building was to inaugurate the national reconstruction plan for the entire newly-established GDR, and serve as a model for the planned Stalinallee. It proved to be so costly that the building alone was to embody the whole economic concept of the GDR, namely to take advantage of generous state subsidies to impress the crowds. Until 1989, an apartment in this building cost only a ninth of what would have been needed to cover the building and maintenance costs.

SIGN OF THE HORNS ON THE "CRAFTSMAN AND SON" STATUE

③

A discreet sign to ward off bad luck

Andreasstraße 21–22, 10243 Berlin
U5 (Strausberger Platz)
S3, 5, 7, 9, 75 (Ostbahnhof)

In the centre of a large green space in front of Andreasstraße 21-22 in Friedrichshain, a marble statue depicts a blacksmith and his young son. The seated man holds a hammer in his right hand, while the boy grasps the hammer's head and listens carefully to his father, who is explaining to him the rudiments of his future trade.

Less apparent to the casual observer is the blacksmith's left hand, with which he is making something reminding us of the sign of the horns (index – here, rather a thumb – and little finger stretched out in a fist).

Marble is notoriously difficult to carve and this has not appeared here by chance; this sign directed downwards with the left hand is traditionally a gesture aimed at warding off bad luck.

The child represents the future of the profession, which the superstitious father is trying to protect from evil.

Made in 1898, the sculpture was originally part of the Andreasplatz ensemble, which until the early 1960s was across the street.

The ensemble was organised around a fountain in the middle of a circular basin.

It consisted of three enormous polished granite benches interspersed with statues: Wilhelm Haverkamp's "Craftsman and Son" on one side, and Edmund Gomansky's "Mother and Child" duo on the other. The double duet embodying the ideal of the Wilhelmian family was consecrated by a bronze medallion set in the centre to represent Borussia, the allegorical female figure of Prussia.

This traditional family portrait was somewhat ironic, as it was set behind the Silesian railway station (now the Ostbahnhof) in an area where prostitution and crime were rampant.

Devastated during the Second World War, the district was rebuilt in the early 1960s. Located in East Berlin, Andreas Square gave way to the famous *Plattenbauten* (literally "building made of slabs", i.e. prefabricated parts) that can be found there today.

Since the feminist revolution had called many things into question, the two statues (which, taken together, celebrated the traditional division of labour within the family) were separated.

While "Craftsman and Son" remained nearby in memory of the industrial past of the district, "Mother and Child" found a new location in Virchowstraße, in the scented garden of the Volkspark Friedrichshain, not far from the playgrounds and the obstetrics department of the Landsberger Allee clinic.

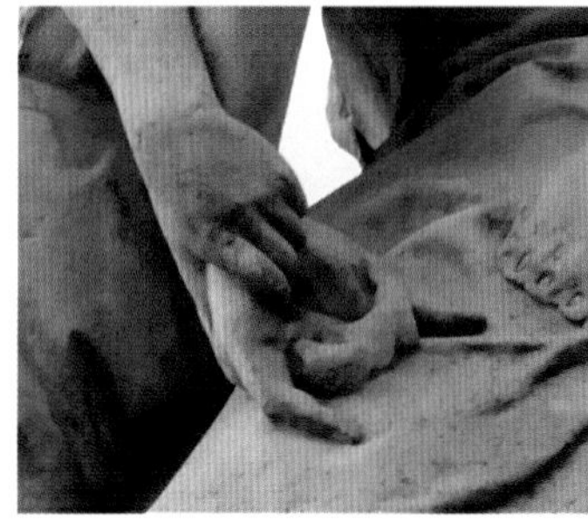

FORMER PINTSCH AG ADMINISTRATIVE HEADQUARTERS

④

A luminous genius

Andreasstraße 71–73, 10243 Berlin
S3, 5, 7, 75, 9 (Ostbahnhof)

Andreasstraße 71-73 is home to the impressive former administrative headquarters of Pintsch AG (later Pintsch BAMAG), behind which the entire factory complex once stood. The location of the building is closely linked to the company's success story.

In 1943 the young Julius Pintsch, a trained tinsmith, founded his own workshop in the basement of Stralauer Platz 4. Ambitious and persuasive, he quickly developed fruitful relations with his immediate neighbours – first with the gas industry (Stralauer Platz 33-34, today *Energieforum*) then with the railway companies.

The first customer for his new gas lighting system for trains and locomotives was the Niederschlesisch-Märkische Eisenbahn that operated the Silesian Station line (today's Ostbahnhof), which was inaugurated in 1842.

Given his strategic location, Pintsch had every reason to stay where he was. In 1848 he acquired number Stralauer Platz 6-7, and following further success he acquired Andreasstraße 71-73, where the current building was erected by Cremer and Wolfenstein in 1907-1908.

Above the portal with three entrances, four reliefs of male figures still bear witness to the original purpose of this colossal building. In the centre, two engineers are depicted in full reflection, while the fruit of their invention appears in the background: in the centre right the famous *Pintsch-Boje* or *Leuchttonne*, the light buoy invented by Pintsch to guide ships; in the centre left is what appears to be the globe of a lighthouse (*Leuchtfeuer*) (see next double page).

On either side of these intellectuals are two bare-chested workers, one of whom places a hammer on an anvil, while the second once held another tool, which is now missing. They recall the origins of the Pintsch company: the workshop of a simple tinsmith.

The façade is in the Berlin Secession style that was in vogue at the time. A few reliefs of laurel wreaths and garlands, symbols of glory and success, underline some of the windows. Just below the gable, the reliefs of four male faces perhaps represent the four sons of Julius Pintsch, who, when the building was inaugurated in 1908, had long since taken over the leadership of the company from their deceased father.

Julius Pintsch. Berlin.
1899

Julius Carl Friedrich Pintsch: an industrialist at the heart of many innovations

Our world today is shaped by Julius Carl Friedrich Pintsch (1815-1884) and his four sons Richard, Oskar, Julius and Albert.

Founded in 1843, Pintsch AG specialised in heating and lighting systems. The company made rapid progress in the 1850s when the city of Berlin began to break up the British monopoly of the gas industry. Julius Pintsch, then a tinsmith (*Klempner* in German), was regularly employed by the Berlin gas company.

As the development of the distribution network for private use required the installation of numerous meters, he saw an opportunity.

Pintsch made his fortune by inventing a gas meter that was much more reliable and accurate than the English instruments of the time. His meter, which he quickly distributed throughout Germany, even won him some international success.

Pintsch's subsequent contributions were innumerable and increasingly noteworthy; not far from the Silesian railway station (today's Ostbahnhof), he developed the first gas lighting systems for trains and locomotives.

Until then they had depended on oil or paraffin lamps, which were less safe and produced a duller light. Carriages were also heated using more efficient systems developed by Pintsch.

Pintsch also became the only European producer of incandescent sleeves (*Glühstrumpf*) – fabric wraps treated to generate intense light on contact with a flame, without which gas lighting would have been ineffective.

Later, Pintsch would become a worthy rival to Osram in the light bulb market. Marine signal towers were equipped with Pintsch lighthouses worldwide.

Finally, Pintsch invented the floating light signal. Probably his most memorable invention, the *Pintsch Buoy* (or Pintsch-Boje) allowed safe navigation at night; coasts of all the seas and waterways around the world (especially the Suez Canal) are now equipped with these buoys.

LEANING TOWER OF STRALAU CHURCH ⑤

A tower more inclined than the Tower of Pisa?

Tunnelstraße 5–11, 10245 Berlin
May–Aug Sun 1pm–4pm
S8, 9, 41, 42 (Treptower Park) / S3, 5, 7, 8, 9, 41, 42 (Ostkreuz), then Bus 347 (Stralau, Tunnelstraße)

Shortly before the tip of the charming Stralau peninsula is a small 15th-century church. Its white tower – a much later addition – is actually leaning more steeply than the Tower of Pisa. While its Italian counterpart slopes 3.9 degrees to the south, the Kirchturm Stralau is said to slope 5 degrees to the north-west. In this case, the church in Stralau would have one of the most steeply inclined towers in the world.

According to some sources, the tower is said to have buckled as a result of damage during the Second World War.

On 26 February 1945 the church was hit by a bomb that destroyed the entire nave vault. When the church was rebuilt at the end of the 1950s, it was said that the crater left by the bomb was badly filled in, which then led to subsidence of the ground and the inclination of the tower.

However, further research has shown that this inclination had been observed as early as 1934 – two windows of the nave of Stralau Church still have their original stained glass.

The cemetery located next to the church is a remarkable place to spend a quiet moment; the slope of the embankment overlooking the Spree is an ideal spot to rest and listen to the sound of water splashing along the bank.

SHOT TOWER

"Lead in the head"

Nöldnerstraße 16, 10317 Berlin
info@berlin-industriekultur.de
Guided tours on request and on Heritage Day (Day of the Open Monument)
S3, S5, S7, S8, S9, S42 (Ostkreuz)

The 38 metre-high red brick tower in the Rummelsburg neighbourhood of the Victoriastadt district (also known as "Kaskelkietz") is not just another industrial chimney. Built in 1908 by the Juhl & Fils company, this tower that stands almost as tall as the bell tower of the nearby *Erlöserkirche* (Church of the Redeemer) was used to produce lead shot.

A staircase of 200 original wooden steps leads to the top of the tower. In the wall, alongside a pipe 50 centimetres in diameter, is a series of glassless windows. A room on the upper level houses a furnace, its chimney rising up into the Berlin sky.

The chimney is actually rather small: lead melts at 327.5 degrees centigrade, a relatively low temperature compared to steel, for example, which melts at more than 1,100 degrees.

The ingenious system involved using a pulley to hoist lead ingots to the top of the tower where they would be melted down in the furnace. The liquid metal was then poured through a perforated sheet that acted as a sort of sieve.

The droplets of liquid lead hardened quickly as they fell, taking on a round shape, before cooling in a pool of water 30 metres below. Every day, four tonnes of lead fell through the pipe that protected the metal from the wind. As a result, perfect lead pellets were manufactured to satisfy the demands of hunting enthusiasts.

The tower was operational until 1939. During the GDR era the tower belonged to the VEB Druckguß und Formbau (die casting and moulding) company of Weißensee, whose workshop was located in Rummelsburg. As the only one of its kind in the metropolitan region of Berlin-Brandenbourg, the tower is now classified as industrial heritage.

The only neighbourhood in a German city named after an English Queen

The name Kaskelkietz refers to a lawyer and politician called Kaskel, while Victoriastadt is a tribute to the English Queen Victoria.

This is the only example of a neighbourhood in a German city that is named after a British Queen, and demonstrates the good relations between the German Empire and the British Royal House.

HARTUNG'S COLUMNS

⑦

Remains of a former railway bridge

Türrschmidtstraße, 10317 Berlin
S3, S5, S7, S9 (Nöldnerplatz)

The twelve cast-iron columns at the corner of Türrschmidtstraße/ Stadthausstraße are the last remnants of the piers of the nearby commuter train bridge.

In 2005, after 102 years of loyal service, the bridge was rebuilt in concrete and its original metal piers were left redundant.

A panel now details what makes these columns so special and why they typify the art of building Berlin's railway bridges from the 1880s onwards.

When the bridges of Berlin's railways had to be raised to allow double-decker buses to pass beneath, intermediate piers became necessary.

It was decided that not just any piers would do; a competition was held and "Model 2" by architect Hugo Hartung was chosen. Hartung's column could be made of cast iron, thereby reducing costs enormously.

To lessen the impact of the loads and vibrations produced by the circulation of trains on the cast iron (which is more brittle than traditional steel), Hartung added additional seals at the top and bottom of the columns and reinforced the middle.

THE "NICARAGUAN VILLAGE – MONIMBO 1978" FRESCO ⑧

A naïve painting of a bloodbath

Skandinavische Straße 26, 10317 Berlin
S5, S7, S9, S75 (Lichtenberg) / U5 (Lichtenberg)

On the wall of a house on Monimbó Platz in the district of Lichtenberg is an impressive painting covering a total area of 255 square metres. The painting features two white houses with tiled roofs, along with a dozen thatched-roof huts in a plain landscape at the foot of a mountain, on top of which stands a fortress. Children are playing among the huts while men and women work in the fields. Soldiers in green uniforms appear on the left, taking aim at the villagers. Helicopters and planes circle above, shooting at the people below, some of whom lie lifeless on the ground. A shrouded body is being carried on a cart. In the foreground, some characters take up stones as weapons. These resisters belong to the Sandinista National Liberation Front — the words FSLN appear several times on the walls of the two buildings.

The emotional shock elicited by this magnificent fresco arises from the staggering contrast between the cheerfulness of the colours (typical of this painting technique) and the subject represented.

The fresco was created in 1985 by Nicaraguan artist Manuel Garcia Moia. Born in 1936 in Monimbó, Nicaragua, the indigenous district of the city of Masaya, Garcia Moia spent the first few years of his life there. The fresco on Monimbó Platz depicts the 1978 killing in Monimbó, Nicaragua, of 343 villagers during an uprising against the third and last dictatorship of the Somoza family. The massacre was perpetrated by Somoza's mercenaries. A year later, Anastasio Somoza Debayle was thrown out of the country by the FSLN guerrilla group. The uprising failed because international concern for the problems that Nicaragua was facing developed too late and foreign aid did not reach the village in time. After the bloody repression of the Sandinista rebels, Monimbó became a national symbol.

The East German Socialist Unity Party (SED) supported the struggles of the Nicaraguan people against Somoza's dictatorship, so the municipality of East Berlin commissioned the painting. Manuel Garcia Moia also received help from East Berlin graphic designer Martin Hoffmann and the sculptor, painter and cartoonist Trakia Wendisch.

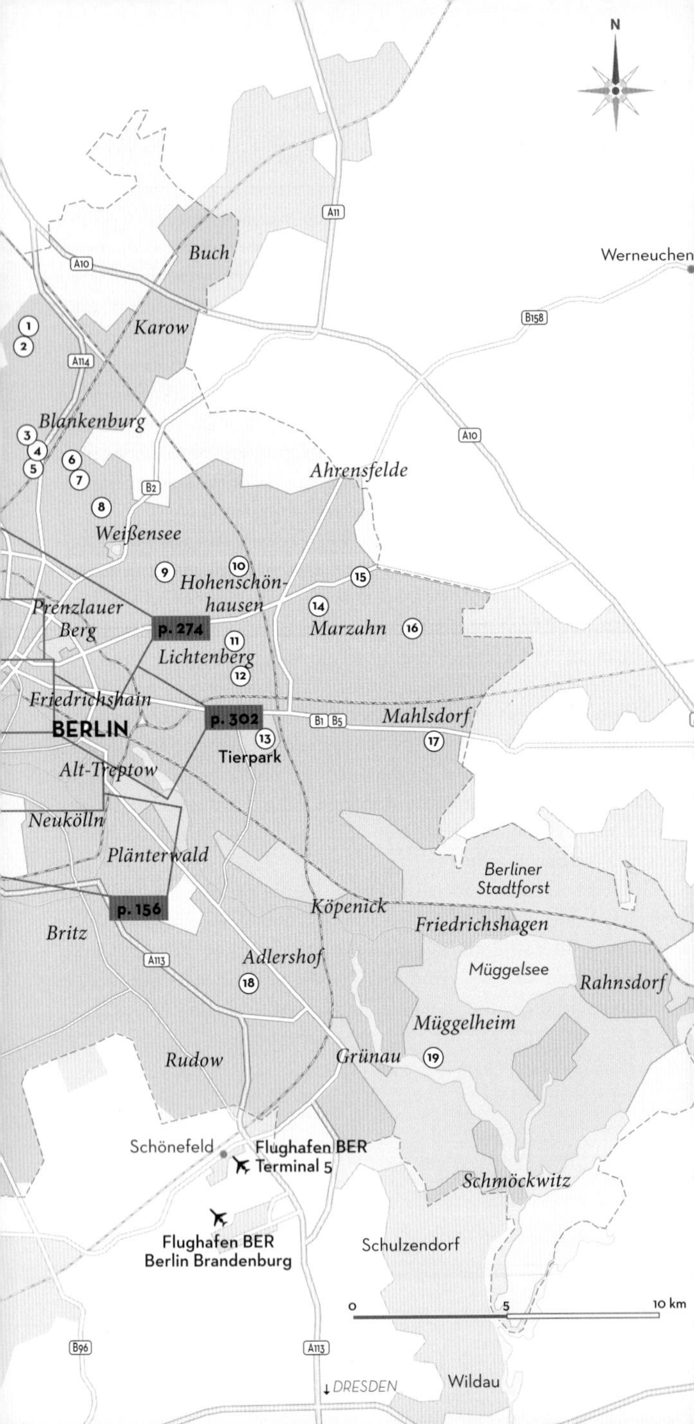

N
A11
A10
Buch
Werneuchen
Karow
B158
A114
Blankenburg
A10
Ahrensfelde
B2
Weißensee
Hohenschön-
hausen
Prenzlauer
Berg
p. 274
Marzahn
Lichtenberg
Friedrichshain
p. 302
B1
B5
Mahlsdorf
BERLIN
Tierpark
Alt-Treptow
Neukölln
Plänterwald
Berliner
Stadtforst
p. 156
Köpenick
Friedrichshagen
Britz
A113
Adlershof
Müggelsee
Rahnsdorf
Müggelheim
Rudow
Grünau
Schönefeld
Flughafen BER
Terminal 5
Schmöckwitz
Flughafen BER
Berlin Brandenburg
Schulzendorf
0
5
10 km
B96
A113
DRESDEN
Wildau

Pankow - Lichtenberg - Marzahn Hellersdorf - Treptow/Köpenick

REMAINS OF THE BLANKENFELDE ① RECEPTION CAMP

For prospective immigrants ... from the West

Blankenfelder Chaussee 7, 13159 Berlin
Bus 107 (Revierförsterei Blankenfelde)

The gate, the fences and the rusting barbed wire near the forester's house of the district of Pankow are a first reminder of the existence of the former Blankenfelde reception camp for West Germans travelling to the East. Behind the fence is a small concrete blockhouse with observation slits and embrasures under an RSL1 lamp-post of the GDR: this one-man blockhouse provided an unobstructed shooting range if ever anyone tried to scale the fence.

"The wooden barracks were demolished years ago," says the forest ranger. "The building that still stands today is the shooting range of the people's police in charge of the protection of buildings (*Betriebsschutz*). The border police, the Ministry of Security, and the criminal police were all here. The poor buggers who wanted to come to the GDR, whether it was for the first time or to return home, underwent a thorough investigation; all the precautions had to be taken to make sure

no enemy of the State would infiltrate the territory." The forest ranger sniggers, "The reception camp existed between 1957 and 1972. After that, the influx was too big to handle!" Seeing that the interlocutor has understood the joke, the forest ranger bursts out laughing.

During the pivotal year between 1989 and 1990, of the 20 reception camps (which between them could welcome a total of 1,500 people), the only camp left – with 117 beds – was the reception camp of Röntgental, opened in 1979.

Blankenfelde could welcome up to 300 prospective immigrants from the West. This is where, for a period of 38 days, assessments were made to determine what each candidate could bring to the GDR's economy, and what their true political convictions were. As for those who had fled to the West and decided to return home, they were required to provide a self-critical analysis in due form. Their confessions were published in the national newspaper *Neues Deutschland*. Between 1957 and 1988, some 800,000 people left Western Germany to settle in the GDR, and of this number, 400,000 were actually returning to the GDR having previously fled the State.

Shortly before the construction of the Wall, the number of migrants going from East to West compared to the number of migrants going in the other direction followed a different trend than what is commonly imagined. In 1957 there were 40,000 newcomers from the West, while 262,000 people fled the East. Two years later, 63,000 people arrived in East Germany from the West, while 144,000 people went the other way. It was only with the construction of the Wall in 1961 that the number of people arriving in the GDR's reception camps, as well as the number of people leaving the territory, fell rapidly. Nonetheless, in 1989 some 1,000 people arrived from the West requesting an entrance visa for the GDR.

GEOLOGICAL WALL ②

A major geological attraction

Botanischer Volkspark
Blankenfelder Chaussee 5, 13159 Berlin
geowand.gruen-berlin.de (interactive geological wall)
Mon–Sun, sunrise to sunset
Exhibition greenhouses: Tue–Thur 10am–2pm, Fri–Sun (and holidays) 11am–5pm
Bus 107 (Botanischer Volkspark)

With its many numbered stones scattered here and there, the long wall of natural stones at the farthest corner of the Botanischer Volkspark seems to have been erected by an overly enthusiastic landscape gardener. Built between 1891 and 1896, this wall is in fact a major geological attraction and a historical curiosity in the city of Berlin; it has recently been ranked 78th "national geotope".

Eduard Zache (1862-1929), a member of the German Geological Society and the Brandenburgia History Society, was the man behind this "geological wall". The wall was originally located in Humboldthain Park, which used to be a botanical and geological garden for educational purposes in memory of Alexander von Humboldt.

In 1909 the central pedagogical garden on the road to Blankenfelde (the current botanical park) was entrusted with this educational mission as part of a broader scientific aim. The geological wall of Dr. Zache (PhD and professor at Andreas High School on Koppenstraße) was therefore also transferred to this new site.

The 30 metre-long and 2.5 metre-high wall reproduced an ideal cross-section through the geological history of Central Europe. Divided into 20 parts, it is comprised of 123 types of stone, minerals, earth, and ore from Brandenberg, the Rhine region, Silesia, Saxony, and Thuringia.

Starting on the left, where the most recent sediments are located, and moving right, the layers date back in time. At the end are the oldest rocks of the crystalline basement. In reality, these strata are laid out vertically from top to bottom. However, to make the presentation of this structure easier, and the wall relatively small, Dr. Zache inserted faults between the layers (which should be imagined as vertical fractures) that constitute the canals along which magma travels to reach the surface, as well as fold formations that disrupt the chronological order of the strata. Minerals and fossils are incorporated in several places. Flying over the wall from left to right, a bird would cross 300 million years of our geological era in no time at all.

LUNA BUNKER

③

Diving into the dark years

Hermann-Hesse-Straße, at the intersection with Schützenstraße, 13156 Berlin
S1, S25, S26 (Schönholz)

A simple path unwinds between the brick walls of Schönholz Castle shooting club premises up to a little wood. On the left, protruding from between the trees, is a dark hill, like a very flat gabled roof on top of a large sunken barrack. This strange hill is in fact the concrete roof of a blockhouse that peeks out from the ground by about two metres.

Frost has cracked the surface of the blockhouse here and there to such an extent that the bare structure of the reinforced concrete is visible. A glance at the entrance reveals several connecting arched undergrounded passageways. Protruding from the ground near the wall facing the path is a large metal ring. Metal rings arranged in a circle were connected by steel wires to the top of a transmission tower: the bunker was a shelter for Wehrmacht connections during the Second World War.

The Schönholz concentration camp, built between June 1940 and April 1945, one of the largest forced-labour camps in Berlin, is located not too far from the bunker. By the end of 1942 there were 2,500 Polish, French, Belgian, Croatian, Serbian, and Eastern European workers from various regions of the USSR, all held prisoner in order to work for the armament factories of Spandau. The camp was called the "Lunapark Camp", like the eponymous amusement park that had closed a few years earlier in Halensee. On relocating the amusement park to Schönholz, a few fairground entertainers decided to give it new life by renaming it the "Land of Dreams" and installing an 18 metre-high rollercoaster – "The Himalaya".

The blockhouse later became known as the "Lunabunker" and served exclusively as a shelter for radio operators and communication equipment. Labourers were not allowed to enter the shelters. Prisoners who were held captive near the bunker hid petrified in simple ditches covered with planks during air raids. In fact, about a quarter of the victims of the bombings in Berlin were unprotected labourers. A few of the camp prisoners who fell victim to the bombings were buried next to Germans in a grove reserved for the dead not too far from the blockhouse.

THE OLDEST REMAINS OF THE BERLIN WALL

④

The Berlin Wall was not always made of concrete

Schützenstraße/Buddestraße, 13409 Berlin
S1, S25, S26 (Schönholz)

The little wooded area located in the triangular plot of land between the streets of Schützenstraße and Buddestraße and the suburban railroad was undoubtedly the wildest area in the district of Pankow.

Directly opposite the Schönholz S-Bahn station on the Buddestraße is a path that winds up to the railway line. Although well protected by foliage in summer, a fence can be seen around a construction site, along with an opening made by Berlin street artists looking for the best "spots". Some tags are very well executed, like the ruin of a Mayan temple that seems to come straight out of *The Jungle Book*. Disregard the few mouldy mattresses and the rubbish that litters the ground and it's easy to appreciate the romanticism of this part of the wall. Measuring 80 metres long and dating back to 1961, this is the oldest remnant of the Berlin Wall.

What is striking is that here the wall was built of bricks and not concrete: instead of adding a concrete layer to the wall (as was done later) to ensure it was not possible to climb it, this first wall ("Mauer 1") was equipped with an anti-personnel device. The device incorporated V-shaped angles to support electrified barbed wire and cables, which, at the slightest contact, triggered an alarm at the command post. A junction box for the cables is still embedded in the wall.

In the rush to complete the first border closure around West Berlin, some of the residential buildings in Schützenstraße that had been partly destroyed by the war were put to use. Entrances to the cellars of the houses were hastily closed up, and holes and sharp angles in the walls were filled with stones and other random materials, including stones from the "Lunapark Camp" (see opposite) and "Traumland" amusement parks.

When the more modern outer wall was built, the original was largely forgotten.

THE CHERUBS OF PANKOW

Each angel represents a type of human temperament

Breite Straße 45, 13187 Berlin
Tram 50 (Pankow Kirche)

A few metres from the tram tracks at Breite Strasse 45, four small stone angels stand on stelae. These four sculptures are copies of the originals (part of the sculpture collections of the Berlin State Museums since 1962, where they are protected from pollution) by the famous sculptor Gottfried Knöffler (1715-1779). They represent the four types of human temperament as described by Hippocrates:

The choleric character, angry and enraged, even though his more troubling problem is being in the mouth of a fire-breathing dragon.

Beside the angel (his symbol), the spirited and fiery sanguine character makes overly ambitious plans from atop his cumulus.

Leaning on his spade as if it were a pilgrim's staff, his hands tied, the phlegmatic character will not waste an ounce of energy on unnecessary labour.

The melancholic character casts a dubious glance at a book (perhaps the Bible) without reading it. He spends his life worrying, ends up feeling sorry for himself, and withdraws from the world.

Built in 1770, this single-storey building, called Kavalierhaus (the equivalent of a castle's communal area), was in fact just a simple country house. It never belonged to any member of the court, but to merchants such as Carl Philipp Möring (1753-1837), who in 1814 had one of Germany's first steam boilers installed in the orangery; and Charles Duvinage (1804-1871), who established the Hohenzollern library.

From 1866 to 1939 the house was owned by the family of the chocolate manufacturer Richard Hildebrand. From 1947 onwards the building was used by the Great Berlin Social Welfare Office, before it became a school day care centre in 1953.

In 1998 the Caritas-Krankenhilfe Berlin e.V. acquired the building and renovated it in accordance with the regulations for the preservation of historical monuments.

ART INSTALLATIONS IN GUSTAV-ADOLF-STRAßE

6

Pop art at death's door

Gustav-Adolf-Straße 92–103/Obersteiner Weg 45–49,
13086 Berlin
S8, S9, S42 (Prenzlauer Allee), then Bus 156 (Gustav-Adolf-Str./Amalienstr.)

In stark contrast to the Segensfriedhof just opposite, the five buildings in the housing complex at 92-103 Gustav-Adolf-Straße in Weißensee form a colourful ensemble studded with animal figures (several of

which are missing, having unfortunately peeled off over the years).

Each building displays a single colour and a single animal, except for the fifth building, which is a combination of the first four: fish swim in the blue façade of one building; the pink building is a morning sky with fluttering birds; hares hop across the daisy-studded grass of the green façade; and butterflies twirl in the orange glow of a summer day.

On the sides of the first four twin buildings, polyester sculptures of the creatures – which are illuminated at night – are hung in such a way as to suggest that the animals pass through the buildings, entering from one side and exiting the other.

The garden is also laid out to suggest a close correlation between science and life in harmony with nature: visitors enter through a pair of organically shaped posts topped by a geometric form.

The shape of the posts (echoed in the canopies above each door) represents nature, while the geometric forms represent the mathematical laws governing nature, which we must understand in order to live in harmony with it.

A little further on, another organic sculpture depicts the Greek letter pi – the mathematical symbol of the infinite number, which for ancient Greeks had a fundamental and sacred purpose in the cosmic order.

Finally, the giant red rose in the garden, a leitmotif in the work of Berlin pop artist Sergej Alexander Dott (there are others in Dreigleiseck), has been a symbol of resurrection and fulfilment through work or sacrifice since time immemorial.

The symbol is omnipresent in Freemasonic imagery, and probably refers in this case to the renovation and modernisation of the complex, suggesting that the artist could be part of a Masonic lodge.

These installations, created in 2007 by Dott, are an initiative of the real estate company Sparkling, which had acquired the complex a year earlier.

Dating from the 1930s, the complex was in very poor condition at the time – half of the apartments were uninhabitable.

The developer undertook a thorough renovation of the premises, converting them into low-energy buildings and transforming the complex into an artistic project evoking nature and life.

THE DUTCH DISTRICT OF WEIßENSEE

7

Brick in the spotlight

Woelckpromenade 25-35
S8, S9, S41, S42 (Greifswalder Straße), then Tram M1, M4 (Antonplatz)

The housing complex at Woelckpromenade 25-35, known as the Dutch Quarter because of its wide stepped gables reminiscent of Potsdam's Dutch Quarter, is a remarkable architectural ensemble that could be easily overlooked. It was built by Joseph Tiedemann between 1925 and 1929 in the spirit of the social housing policy of the inter-war years. Unlike the rabbit hutches of the industrial revolution (the famous "rental barracks"), it guaranteed a degree of satisfaction of basic needs while providing affordable accommodation.

Composed of standardised dwellings that each include a balcony overlooking the large, airy, bright and quiet inner courtyard, the complex's pretty gardens are divided by hedges that form geometric patterns.

The choice was made to create this complex with exposed brick out of a desire to make it a continuation of the magnificent project completed a few years earlier around the Kreuzpfuhl, located just a few steps away.

At the beginning of the 20th century, Weißensee was a growing rural community where workers from the saturated capital flocked. The councillor at the time, Carl Woelck, tried in vain to raise it to the status of a town by endowing it with the usual institutions, which he organised around the beautiful Kreuzpfuhl. Built between 1908 and 1919, this *Gemeindeforum* or *Munizipalviertel* was designed by Carl James Bühring in the style of the *Reformarchitektur*, which put an end to the imitation of styles that had been in vogue until then, returning to a more traditional and practical way of building. Regional building materials, in this case brick, were showcased. Buildings were designed according to local weather conditions. Ornaments were no longer added; instead, the buildings promoted an interplay of the elements that constituted the building itself. The natural needs of humans are respected, notably the need for air, light, space, nature, harmony with the landscape, and sport and cultural activities.

Bricks in response to swampy soil

During the Industrial Revolution, Brandenburg produced an average of one billion bricks a year for Berlin, whose marshy soil had no effect on stone.

Nevertheless, the presence of bricks remains hidden in Berlin's residential architecture, whose masonry is mostly covered by stucco or plaster.

THE PAINTER OF THE MOTORWERK

8

A discreet tribute to an "industrial painter"

An der Industriebahn 12, 13088 Berlin
S8, S41, S42 (Greifswalder Straße) then Bus 225 (Roelckestraße/Nüßlerstraße)

In the industrial wasteland that once incorporated the Weißensee railway junction, to the left of the entrance to the former long production hall of Ziehl-Abegg, stands a rather surprising work of art: an enigmatic bespectacled dwarf poses with his arms behind his back next to what was once the company's flagship product — an electric motor with an external rotor.

Anyone with an interest in Berlin's 19th-century art history will immediately recognise the caricatured man; the white beard covering chin and cheeks, the silhouette and oversized head barely poking out above the motor, and the look of eternal grumpiness all belong to Adolph von Menzel (1815-1905), a Prussian historian and the first "industrial painter". His best known painting, *Das Eisenwalzwerk* (The Iron Rolling Mill), completed between 1872-75, is hanging in the Alte Nationalgalerie.

Emil Ziehl (1873-1939), the founder of the Ziehl-Abegg company, was a gifted artist, and even wanted to become a painter for a while. His fascination for engineering gradually took over, but he continued to draw for pleasure. So when the time came to think about a work of art for his new factory, he made a whimsical sketch in homage to the first Berlin painter who had drawn inspiration from industry. The drawing is symbolic of modernism catching up and taking over the "spirit" of fin-de-siècle.

On the same wall, an advertisement also shows Ziehl's caricature of old Menzel standing in front of the Ziehl-Abegg external rotor electric motor. After Bruno Buch and Karl Herrmann built the production hall for the Ziehl-Abegg electricity company at the beginning of the 1920s, the Motorwerk site became a venue for events.

VILLA LEMKE

A "simple little house" by a great architect

Mies van der Rohe-Haus, Oberseestraße 60, 13053 Berlin
Tue–Sun 11:00am–5:00pm
Free entry
Tram 27 / M13 (Am Faulen See)

Karl and Martha Lemke wanted a "simple little house" that would "stretch out into the garden when the weather was nice". And in 1932 Ludwig Mies van der Rohe envisioned precisely that. The Lemke's country house, with its notable minimalist style, was completed in 1933; it was the last house built by the Bauhaus master before he immigrated to the United States. It occasionally hosts exhibitions, and from its garden it offers a charming view of Lake Obersee below.

Karl Lemke owned a graphic arts establishment with a printing house in Mühlenstraße in Friedrichshain. He was also a passionate art collector. After the Red Army requisitioned the villa, his collections (of paintings and watches) and the Mies van der Rohe furniture found their way to the Berlin museums.

Original furniture of the Villa Lemke

Now on display at the Kunstgewerbemuseum in Berlin, the original furniture for the office and bedroom of the Villa Lemke was designed by Mies van der Rohe and Lilly Reich, his partner at the time. The furniture in the living room belonged to Karl and Martha Lemke.

Contrary to the promotional photography of the Thonet company in 1933, which suggested that Lilly and Mies appointed the villa with steel items, they opted for exclusively wooden furniture – one type of wood per room: lemon tree for the bedroom, Makassar ebony for the study. Yellow pigskin parchment was used for the double bed, the office chair, the club chair and the stool.

DAIMON MUSEUM 

Greatness and decadence

Hohenschönhausen Castle
Hauptstraße 44 D, 13055 Berlin
schlosshsh.de/daimon-museum.html
Mon–Fri 10am–4pm
Free entry
Bus 256, 294 / Tram 27, M5 (Haupstraße/Rhinstraße)

On the first floor of Hohenschönhausen castle, the Daimon museum is dedicated to Paul Schmidt (1868-1948), founder of the Schmidt electrotechnical factory and creator of the DAIMON brand, a world leader in these markets for many years. In addition to the torches, bicycle lamps, dynamos, light bulbs, batteries and the advertising that goes with them, there are other, lesser-known, products from the brand on display (such as car headlights, lights for boats, ventilators, microphones and radios) as well as documents on Paul Schmidt and Daimon.

The permanent exhibition is called *"Die helle Freude"* (Bright joy) just like the old slogan of the brand, which evokes both light and happiness.

In 1882, Schmidt set up his own electricity business in Wedding where he sold and repaired electrical appliances – more and more frequently of his own making. In 1896, he managed to make an improved version of the so-called "dry" or "saline" electric battery.

In 1905, he applied for a patent for his "electric pocket lamp" which he produced in the 1920s in Arnstadt, Danzig, Děčín and Cologne-Rodenkirchen and sold throughout the world.

However, in 1927, Paul Schmidt lost control of Daimon due to debts owed to the British Eveready Export Company (BEREC) which were no longer refundable. In 1948, he died, a ruined man, in Wedding.

The Daimon brand fell into many different hands (Duracell's and Gillette's, to name a few) and no longer exists today, except in rudimentary form within Procter & Gamble.

Paul Schmidt lived in the castle, which he owned, from 1910 to 1921.

THE HERZBERGE BOILER ROOM ⑪

Hitler's heating

KEH Hospital Haus 29
Herzbergstraße 79, 10365 Berlin
museumkesselhaus.de
Tue & Thu 2pm–6pm
S7 (Springpfuhl)

Covered in a thin layer of rust, these metal giants look as if they are dozing. The objects on display are familiar yet outdated: brass manometers with a needle to indicate the level of pressure, zinc-encased thermometers, steel handwheels, electric meters from 1900, and old registers.

A member of the Association of Friends of the Kesselhaus Herzberge e.V. museum volunteered to be our guide for this private visit, giving us an insight into what this small, sleepy place has to offer. 100 years of industrial history can be seen through three generations of boilers used to heat a renowned clinic. It was, in fact, a municipal lunatic asylum built by Hermann Blankenstein and inaugurated in 1893. We are standing under a double-fired tube boiler made by a company called Borsig. Dating from 1892, it is one of the ten enormous metal zeppelins that turned this hall into an incubator at the time. In those days, coke had to be shovelled into them, as it would later be on the Titanic, so that the large tubes transferred the heat to the water for the hot water supply and the heating.

The old boiler room is now a rather romantic and peaceful side wing of the vast, bustling site of the current KEH (evangelisches Krankenhaus Königin Elisabeth Herzberge – named after Elisabeth of Bavaria, queen of Prussia), which replaced the general hospital that had opened here in 1942. Four additional giant boilers were brought to the hospital (to the boiler room, to be more precise), coinciding with the arrival of the casualties of the Soviet army after the end of the Second World War. They were "inclined tube boilers" and that's not all! They came from Hitler's New Reich Chancellery – the only building that Albert Speer finished for the government. Before the inauguration of that pompous building on the Voßstraße, the coke-guzzling foursome of boilers – three of which are intact today – had already been pushed to maximum capacity to speed up the drying out of the Neue Reichskanzlei which had been built in record time. In 1945, realising just how much these machines were worth, the Soviets recovered them, and they were used to fulfil a humanitarian mission in the first central hospital for Soviet troops in Berlin.

MEMORIAL TO THE REVOLUTION ⑫

Memorial to the only monument erected by Mies van der Rohe

Zentralfriedhof Friedrichsfelde
Friedhofstraße, 13053 Berlin
Every day from 8am until nightfall
S5, 7, 75 (Friedrichsfelde Ost) – 25 minutes' walk from the station

At the back of the central cemetery of Friedrichsfelde (Zentralfriedhof Friedrichsfelde) (it is advisable to come by bicycle), the memorial to the German Revolution of 1918-1919 was the only monument that was ever designed by the famous Bauhaus architect Ludwig Mies van der Rohe. Demolished by the Nazis, it

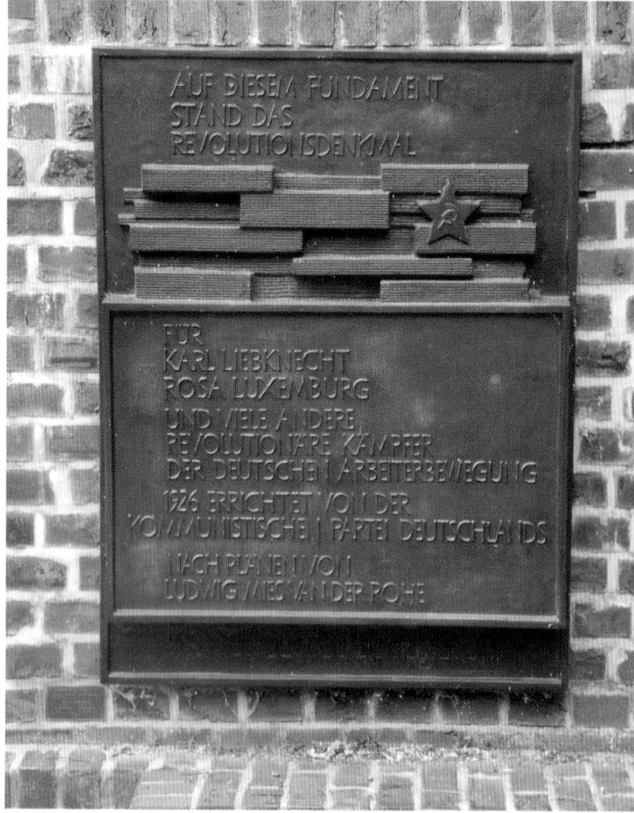

has been replaced by a small metal plaque in relief which refers to the original monument. Signs around this site give the visitor a better idea of its history and of what the former monument looked like.

The monument was a tribute to Rosa Luxemburg, Karl Liebknecht and the 19 other victims, members of the USPD (a splinter group of the SPD) and the German Communist party.

Why did the GDR never rebuild this memorial? No one really knows and it is all the more surprising as the first revolts which broke out after the First World War against the state run by the last German emperor were often commemorated. In the cemetery of the victims of the 1848 German Revolution (which the Germans call The March Revolution), the memory of the fighters is also celebrated.

The monument was the clever design of the young architect Ludwig Mies van der Rohe, from both a political and architectural standpoint. It was practically the first time that he had put his Cubist ideas to the test (ideas that he would develop throughout his life). The monumental wall represented the wall of a firing squad. The traditional bricks, which symbolised the smallest units of mass, were there to show that the wall of barbarism could be broken. At the same time, by merging into the larger entities, also made of brick, but recessed or jutting outwards from each other, they showed that nothing made them form a monolithic block. The Nazis clearly understood the message. In 1935, just before the Olympic Games in 1936, they dismantled the monument of their communist opponents brick by brick, and tore down the commemorative plaques and tombstones.

The employees of the cemetery nevertheless managed to hide the original stones dedicated to Karl and Rosa.

FOUR BRONZE LIONS OF THE TIERPARK

(13)

One of the rare remains of the William I National Monument

Am Tierpark 125, 10319 Berlin
U5 (Tierpark)

Four gigantic bronze lions stand guard in front of the felines' enclosure in Berlin's Tierpark (the former East Berlin Zoo). Together with the imperial eagle in the Märkisches Museum and the original pedestal (see page 84), these sculptures are among the few remains of the Wilhelm I National Monument, which stood on the banks of the River Spree in front of Berlin Castle until 1950.

During his reign, William I managed to politically unify the Germanic countries around the Hohenzollern dynasty, raising Germany to the status of an almost invincible power. Inaugurated in 1897, some

ten years after his death, the William I National Monument celebrated what would soon become Europe's nightmare. Four lions, figures of nobility and domination, stood at the corners of the memorial facing the four cardinal points.

Seeing it as a symbol of Prussian militarism, the East German regime had the monument dismantled and liquidated together with Hohenzollern Castle in 1950, a few months after the founding of the GDR. Deprived of the Zoological Gardens, East Berlin decided to buy a zoo, and the lions that had been stored in the Museum of the History of the Old Arsenal (at Unter den Linden 2) were brought out.

How was it then that the GDR looked favourably upon these lions (along with the eagle in the Märkisches Museum)? They had in fact been modelled by internationally renowned animal sculptor August Gaul, who had joined the Berlin Secession, a movement that revolved around painter Max Liebermann and gallery owner and publisher Paul Cassirer, both intellectuals who played a decisive role in the development of modern art in Germany, which was abhorred by the Nazis.

THE MARZAHN TOWER MILL

⑭

A visit which is anything but 'run of the mill'

Alt-Marzahn 63, 12685 Berlin
Visits and guided tours subject to prior booking
marzahner-muehle.de
Apr–Jun & Sep–Oct: every second Sunday in the month 3–5 pm
S7 (Berlin Marzahn) S7 (Berlin Marzahn), then Bus 192, 195 (Hinter der Mühle), Tram M6 (Freizeitforum Marzahn)

From the top of its hill, the windmill overlooks the old village of Marzahn, surrounded by blocks of flats and busy roads. The hill is in fact manmade, and the mill is a fully working replica of the last of the old tower mills of Marzahn.

Visitors to this site will come across numerous fans of mills – members of "Mühlenaktiv", a very active association in Marzahn – which would explain the perfect working order of their little treasure and its main features, like the "chair" (*Bock* in German), an enormous piece of French oak timber holding the rotating cap of the mill. This chair alone weighs seven tonnes and the beams holding it together are certainly some of the largest you will ever see. As for the body of the mill, made of larch wood and Douglas pine with its long, single-piece posts, it weighs 37 tonnes. With its "central tree" (*Hausbaum*) which runs into and pivots the chair, it is protected from the wind and rain by the cedarwood cladding boards surrounding it. The four sails of the mill are arranged in a cross, and each sail is fitted with adjustable slats like those found in louvred shutters and is 10 metres long. On the hill, the wind has blown so strongly in the past that the sails have previously been ripped off in a storm.

Visitors can enter the mill by climbing up the steep wooden stairs, running along the "tail" (*Steerts*) which almost touches the ground and is used to rotate the body of the mill to face into the wind. There are also anchoring ties and the hoist which is used to drive the tail.

At the top, where the grain is ground, the miller Jürgen Wolf, welcomes you with a typical "Glück zu!". Above the visitors, the huge wooden gear wheels and noisy drive shafts are impressive. These are what transfer the wind power to a pair of millstones with a diameter of 1.4 metres that grind against each other. The flour from the mill of Marzahn is used not only to make the products in the building's shop, but also to make the bread in certain select bakeries. In keeping with the spirit of the Triller family – a dynasty of millers based for many years in Marzahn, and who used Germany's first wind-driven power station here in the 1940s – in addition to the flour, the mill now produces about 150 days' worth of electricity a year.

THE HOUSE OF FRICK

Silent witness of the liberation

Landsberger Allee 563, 12679 Berlin
S 7 Berlin Marzahn then Bus 197 Brodowiner Ring

The house at number 563 on Landsberger Allee stands out in stark contrast to the rather depressing nearby high-rise blocks. It is now a listed building and stands as a silent witness to the arrival of the Red Army troops in Berlin shortly after the fall of Nazi Germany.

Above an engraved stone plaque, "Victory!" and "To Berlin!" are written in Cyrillic lettering on the dark red wall with the date in large characters “21 April 1945”.

There is a five-pointed red star with a fine white border above this date. The plaque reads : “On the road to the liberation of Berlin from Hitler’s fascism, the Soviet soldiers hoisted the red flag of victory in Berlin Marzahn”.

The memorial is the work of Otto Schack, an artist born in 1937. At the time of the GDR he created numerous murals in the Brandenburg region for political reasons, but they rarely functioned as propaganda. He always used a limited palette of colours, preferring mainly black, white and red, and worked in the tradition of the Bauhaus movement: “The shape fits the function”: there should be no aesthetic expression or artist’s signature, and rather than some beautiful artwork, it was to be an artisanal masterpiece.

The sgraffito technique is used on the wall: The line of the drawing is scratched into two layers of different coloured underglaze. The white lime coating was applied before the red underglaze set. The two coatings then dried and hardened together. A thick layer was applied so that the date stood out clearly.

There was no real reason why the house of market gardener Gustav Frick, located as it was outside the town on the outskirts of Berlin, (and which is thought to have been used around 1900 by the Falkenberg estate as a frontline stronghold), should have been the first one that the Soviet army reached on 21 April 1945 when it was marching on Berlin. However, it was not on this “house of the liberation” that the occupiers’ flag was flying, but on the bell tower of the parish church of Marzahn, about one kilometre away to the south-west.

WBS 70 MUSEUM APARTMENT

⑯

No better way to relativise certain conceptions of what chic is

Hellersdorfer Str. 179, 12627 Berlin
01 51 / 16 11 44 47
stadtundland.de/Unternehmen/Museumswohnung.php
Sun 2pm–4pm (closed on public holidays)
Free entry
U5 (Cottbusser Platz)

In the blocks of flats in Hellersdorf, in one of the buildings which were made with preformed concrete slabs in just 18 hours, it is very cramped, much like it would be at a family reunion. In the three largest rooms (the sitting room, the master bedroom and the children's bedroom), all the seats are taken. Visitors can touch the furnishings and the decorations, which are all originals, in this reconstructed interior from the days of the GDR: books, dolls, cups, vases, boxes and toys. A couple are trying out the marital bed. A group of visitors are "testing" the huge sofa in mossy green velvet. In the tiny kitchen (big enough for just five people), you must bend your knees under the table. The bath is not designed for outstretched legs. But on the balcony, at least, you can stretch your legs by putting your feet on the parapet.

This type of apartment, which became available from the end of the 1970s, was very popular with families with one or two children, or couples without children who needed a study. It was costly to furnish: one RTF Staßfurt colour television cost 4,200 East German marks (DDM); the unit, made by the VEB Möbelwerke of Schleiz, which covered the whole wall was 4,000 DDM. A worker in the GDR earning a monthly wage of 1,000 DDM would have had to invest 10,000 DDM in total if they had wanted to buy the inventory of furnishings and fittings in the flat in the museum. The rents in the GDR, however, had been frozen at 1936 prices. Until reunification, the monthly rent of an apartment like the one which can be seen in the museum was 109 DDM. "Ostalgia" is the romantic version of the GDR way of living, often a longing for it to come back. However, many young "ostalgics" only know about the GDR from what they have read. In this 61 square-metre show flat built by the communal real estate company STADT UND LAND, they are faced with the harsh reality of that time. They can at last experience a very ordinary apartment in a block of flats from the 1980s, and all this in one of the last and newest housing estates of the GDR. There is no better way to relativise certain conceptions of chic.

But the real "Ossies" are moved by the experience: "To be honest, it's a bit like if I was rummaging through my "old" life. At a time when I felt happy as Larry inside my four walls, like here. ...". This is what one of the first visitors wrote in 2004 in the brand new visitors' book for the show flat in the museum that had just been inaugurated. When planning the entire restoration of the Grabenviertel district with 1,850 apartments, STADT UND LAND decided to perpetuate the GDR way of living, and not only for nostalgics.

THE "GRÜNDERZEIT" MUSEUM ⑰

The last bistro and its hotel room used by prostitutes

Hultschiner Damm 333, 12623 Berlin
gruenderzeitmuseum-mahlsdorf.de
Wed & Sun 10am–6pm (guided tours only)
S5 (Berlin Mahlsdorf)

From the outside with its tidy little garden, the neoclassical villa at number 333 on Hultschiner Damm has an air of provincial nobility about it. But once inside, a remarkable collection of furniture, decorative and everyday objects awaits the visitor in the 17 rooms which have been arranged in what is known as the "Gründerzeit" style.

This was at a time when the bourgeoisie was enjoying an unprecedented economic boom in Germany. Between 1871 and 1890, businesses, joint stock companies and banks sprung up all over the country. Lucky speculators, the nouveaux riches and smart engineers took over from the nobility to form a new upper class that was wealthy and influential.

The style of the architecture and furniture from this period was "Neo-Renaissance". For the decorative arts, both the freedom of tone of the 15th century Florentine New Renaissance (Quattrocento) and the 16th century Italian High Renaissance (Cinquecento) were fashionable. At the

dawn of the 20th century, this new elite who had become rich thanks to their entrepreneurial spirit, thus laid claim to be the successors of the high-ranking nobles of the patrician bourgeoisie of the Old Regime. In the Gründerzeit museum of Charlotte von Mahlsdorf, visitors can admire madam's red and green drawing room where coffee and cakes were served for friends; the master's smoking room with its emblematic piano or pianola, ash trays and billiard table; a rather surprising Neo-Gothic style dining room; a room with mechanical musical instruments – and, in the cellar, a well-equipped bourgeoise kitchen, a laundry and a bar with an adjoining bedroom used by prostitutes (in some ways, the typically proletarian antithesis and conclusion of the Gründerzeit period that was to end with the world economic crisis).

Charlotte von Mahlsdorf, famous for her role in promoting a transgender society (well before the reunification), began establishing the museum's collection from the age of 18. In the 1960s, she squatted in the old manor of Mahlsdorf which had been falling into ruin, and she managed to save the entire interior of the Mulackritze, to some extent recreating some of its atmosphere from the days when it was the most famous bistro in the popular district of Scheunenviertel where Marlene Dietrich and Gustav Gründgens were regulars.

The room at the back was used for the prostitutes, and with its special collection of sado-masochistic regalia for prostitutes from the 1920s, it is, without a doubt, one of the highlights of the visit.

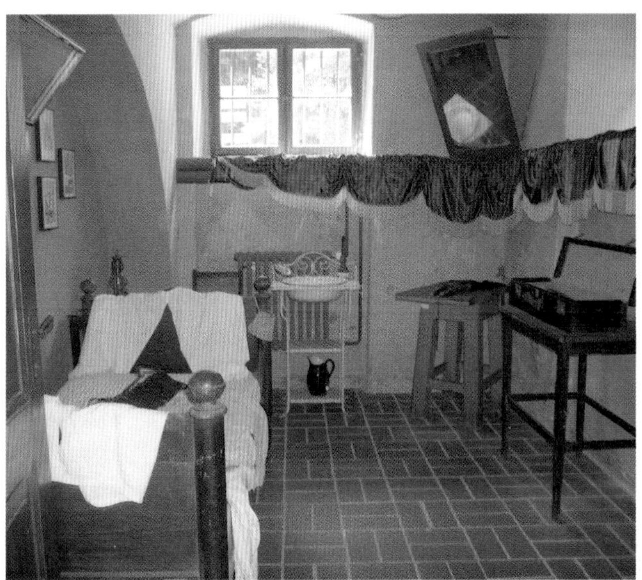

TRUDELTURM VERTICAL WIND TUNNEL

(18)

A concrete egg to study spinning

Adlershof Aerodynamic Park, Brook-Taylor-Straße 2, 12489 Berlin
Visits possible during Heritage Days in September
Tram 60, 61, 63 (Karl-Ziegler-Straße)

Though far from the city centre, the Adlershof aerodynamic park – located on the site of the Deutsches Zentrums für Luft und Raumfahrt ("German Aerospace Centre") – should be on every architecture enthusiast's list of places to visit.

Surrounded by the district's modern university buildings, the centre comprises three exceptional buildings from the 1930s, the era of pioneering aeronautical research.

Among the three is the large wind tunnel where the aerodynamics of the world's largest fighter aircraft, the Messerschmitt ME 262, were apparently optimised. It still seems to be operational and has been used several times as a location for science fiction films; the former aircraft engine test bench, with its large chimneys in the shape of exhaust pipes, has been converted into a cafeteria; and the enigmatic Trudelturm, the wind tunnel tower for spinning tests.

Evoking a high-rise dwelling on the planet Mars, the Trudelturm resembles a giant concrete pear with a single door almost halfway up, which is accessed by an external staircase that follows the building's curvature.

Once inside, the impression of being in a turbine is striking. A large concrete ring runs around the wall above visitors' heads; this is where simulations were carried out using model aircrafts to study the dreaded spin phenomenon, which was still relatively unknown in 1936.

The wind generator built into the ground projected a powerful upward flow of air. From these experiments, techniques were developed that helped enable pilots to prevent spins when an aircraft stalled and tilted, or to quickly and safely stop a flat or steep spin, regardless of the direction of rotation.

It is possible to view online a film that was made back in the day for the DVL (*Deutsche Versuchsanstalt für Luftfahrt* – the "German Aeronautical Research Centre") showing a simulation in the vertical wind tunnel. The film is entitled *Maßnahmen zum Beenden des Abkippens und Trudelns* (1941), which translates as "Recommendations for recovering from a stall and a spin".

Located nearby, the former Berlin-Johannisthal airfield has become an astonishing and beautiful protected natural area. It would be a pity not to visit it after the aeronautical park.

THE SCHMETTERLINGSHORST BUTTERFLY COLLECTION

(19)

Butterfly hunting in the Köpenick forest

Zum Schmetterlingshorst 2, 12559 Berlin
schmetterlingshorst.de
Apr–Sept: Mon–Fri 10am–6pm & Sat–Sun 10am–7pm; Oct–Mar: Tue–Fri 11am–4pm & Sat–Sun 11am–5pm
Tram 62 (Wendenschloss)

Opposite Grünau beach, on the north bank of the Langer See, the "Schmetterlingshorst" (also a base for the Treptow-Köpenick District Sports Association) offers a pleasant terrace for a quiet drink, though few guests believe that the name of the place (*Schmetterling* in German means "butterfly") still has any significance.

However, the central building houses a remarkable collection of butterflies and insects, some of which are rather frightening. In total there are 3,150 butterflies spanning 1,250 varieties, along with 870 other insects, some of which are rare specimens of species that have already disappeared.

This world-class collection (the largest of its kind in Germany and the second largest in Europe) originated in the early 20th century. Johann Bittner, a master glass engraver originating from Bohemia, had set up his small refreshment bar here.

The honourable "Circle of Lepidopterists* Orion" (founded on 1 August 1890) soon made the bar its official inn and a starting point for excursions through the Köpenick Forest. The hostel rapidly grew in popularity and was the natural choice to host the collection that Herbert Jacobs, one of the members of the Orion association, had built up between 1902 and 1952.

* *Butterfly collectors*

N
HAMBURG
A10
A111
Henningsdorf
Frohnau
B96
Wittenau
Spandauer Forst
Tegel
Wilhelmsru
Hakenfelde
p. 238
Wedding
Gesundbru
Spandau
p. 12
B5
Moabit
p. 46
Wilhelmstadt
Westend
Charlottenburg
B2
Tiergarten
BERLIN
Halensee
Kreuz
p. 220
p. 98
Grunewald
Schöneberg
A115
Friedenau
Tempelh
Dahlem
Steglitz
p. 170
Wannsee
Marien
Zehlendorf
Lankwitz
Wannsee
B101
Marienfelde
Teltow
Potsdam
Lichten
Stahnsdorf
L40
L76
0
5
10 km
1
2
3
4
5
6
7
8
9
10
11
12
13
14
15
16
17
18
19
20
21
22
23
24
25
26
27
28
29
30
31
32
33
34
35
36
37
38

Reinickendorf - Spandau - Grunewald Wilmersdorf - Steglitz/Zehlendorf

THE CORINTHIAN CAPITAL IN BRIX-GENZMER-PARK

1

The forgotten remains of the old Dom of Berlin

Brix-Genzmer-Park
13465 Edelhofdamm
S1 (Frohnau)

At the western end of Brix-Genzmer-Park, just in front of the remarkable Buddhistische Haus, there is an old Corinthian capital which seems a little out of place here.

A small, unassuming sign, a few metres away, tells us that the capital comes from the old Dom (cathedral) of Berlin, which Frederick II commissioned the architect Johann Boumann to build from 1747 to 1750 next to Lustgarten, opposite Berlin castle.

In 1817, during the celebrations for the 300th anniversary of the Protestant Reformation and the union of the Lutheran and the Reformed churches, the cathedral underwent a major overhaul: for the jubilee (which also celebrated the victory over Napoleon), King Frederick William III commissioned the architect Karl Friedrich Schinkel to add a more majestic tower to this building, which was too sober for his taste. It is for this reason that, during the conversion work, a barrel vault and new columns with capitals were added.

When the building was knocked down in 1893, it would seem that two professors, Josef Brix (architect and urban planner) and Felix Genzmer (architect), had the capital brought here to protect it from destruction, show it to their students and also to enrich the public park.

At that time the two professors were lecturing at the Royal technical college of Charlottenburg (today TU Berlin), which caused the demolition of the old Lutheran church at the end of the 19th century.

THE WATER TOWER IN THE CEMETERY OF HERMSDORF

②

Max Beckmann's water tower

Cemetery of Hermsdorf, Rohnauer Str. 112-122, 13465 Berlin
Mon–Thur: 7am–3pm, Fri: 7am–1pm
S1 (Frohnau), then Bus 125 (Friedhof Hermsdorf)

In the centre of the cemetery of Hermsdorf, it would be easy to miss the water tower which stands on the steeply sloping hill near Frohnauer Straße: hidden as it is amongst the trees, many local residents do not even know that it exists despite the fact that it was often portrayed in some of the artist Max Beckmann's important works.

Built from 1908 to 1909 by the architect Carl Francke on naturally high ground, it supplied water to Hermsdorf, Frohnau, Waidmannslust and Lübars at a time when the villages were not yet connected up to Berlin's drinking water network. Standing at a height of 24.5 metres, there is a cylindrical metal tank with a capacity of up to 500,000 litres housed in the tower's cantilevered highest and widest part. In 1929, the water tower fell into disuse when the pipes were connected up to Berlin's network. After a significant amount of renovation work, it is now being used as a transmission mast for mobile phones.

Not far from this water tower, the artist Max Beckmann (1884-1950), spent his summers from 1906 to 1914 with his first wife, Minna Tube-Beckmann, at number 17 Ringstraße in Hermsdorf in a studio that she had designed. This is where he immortalised the water tower twice on canvas during its construction.

In the first painting dating from 1909, the truncated tower, surrounded by wooden scaffolding, stands majestically tall on a hill on which, at that time, there was no cemetery. With its dominant – clear and Impressionist – sandy tones, Beckmann's painting is characteristic of his desire, at that time, to give a distinctive, modern dimension to his work. The artist was influenced by those whom he saw as an example – in particular Max Liebermann, an immensely successful painter from Berlin – and who, for the most part, refrained from taking the liberties that were so common among the Impressionists.

Hanging in the Stadtmuseum of Berlin, the second painting dating from 1913, is "freer" from an artistic point of view. The tower, which was in fact already finished, looks slightly different and is portrayed during its construction. We can see here the beginnings of the decisive strokes that were to become so typical of Beckmann's work. The plasticity of the mud on the building site on the hill is such that it makes us want to squelch around in it in wellington boots.

Reproductions of these two paintings are on display in the museum of Reinickensdorf

TEGEL RUSSIAN ORTHODOX CEMETERY

③

A bit of Russia in Berlin

Wittestraße 37, 13509 Berlin
pogost-tegel.info
Chapel and cemetery: Mon–Sat 10am–4pm, Sun 9am–5pm
U6 (Holzhauser Straße)

The chapel of the charming Russian Orthodox Cemetery in Tegel (also the church of the Russian Orthodox parish of Saints Constantine and Helena) is a stylised miniature version of Saint Basil's Cathedral in Moscow, and probably the most beautiful chapel in all of Berlin's cemeteries. Since it was founded in 1892, the cemetery remains the only Russian Orthodox civil cemetery in Berlin. Many famous Russian exiles are buried here, as are the fathers of two famous artists: architect Mikhail Ossipovich Eisenstein (father of film director Sergei Mikhailovich Eisenstein) and Vladimir Dmitrievich Nabokov (father of writer Vladimir Nabokov). Mikhail Glinka, a composer who died in Berlin but was buried in St. Petersburg, is also commemorated here.

The cemetery was created by the Brotherhood of Saint Prince Vladimir, a charitable organisation. After the upheavals of the two World Wars and the division of Germany, the brotherhood resumed its activities, although its former building that was erected on the cemetery site (with library, printing house and meeting room) no longer exists.

The small but charming chapel consists of only one room with a beautiful iconostasis.

Symbolism of the three bars of Orthodox crosses

The three bars of the Russian Orthodox funeral crosses recall the crucifixion of Christ. The shortest at the top represents Pontius Pilate's *titulus* (the sign on the cross bearing the inscription INRI for *Iesus Nazarenus Rex Iudaeorum*, "Jesus of Nazareth, King of the Jews" in Latin). The middle bar, the longest, is where Jesus' arms were fixed. The lower bar, inclined in Russian iconography, evokes the *suppedaneum* (the wooden board onto which the feet are nailed and on which they rest).

THE BOEING 707 D-ABOC "BERLIN"

4

A real-fake historic plane

West of Tegel Airport
Adlerweg, 13405 Berlin
Bus 123 (Mäckeritzwiesen)

A small path at the corner of Adlerweg and An der Mäckeritzbrücke leads north into the forest. It quickly turns left along Tegel Airport then right after about five minutes by bike. There, abandoned at the edge of the runway behind the fences, stands a Boeing 707.

A closer look at the plane reveals several details: firstly, beside the front footbridge is the Berlin coat of arms; secondly, it's still possible to see the original colours of the Lufthansa fleet (for a long time, the Lufthansa logo was visible on the tail assembly until it was painted over); and the aircraft registration, D-ABOC, is also original.

In 1960 this aircraft was the first Boeing 707 to be put into service by the airline Deutsche Luftdienst, then Condor. It was named "Berlin"

by the mayor of the city Willy Brandt in Tempelhof. The plane heralded the era of jetliners and flew until 1977, before being sold. After several stopovers, it landed at Bournemouth Airport in 1983 (with the registration EL-AJC – the code for Liberia, Africa); it was de-registered, used until 1985 for firefighting exercises, and finally scrapped.

Oddly enough, in 1986, on the occasion of the delivery of the 200th aircraft to Tegel, Boeing presented a very special gift to Lufthansa: the Boeing 707 400 D-ABOC Berlin. The gift was initially parked in a prominent place on the terminal's parking lot. Then in 1991 it was moved to the left roundabout next to the traffic lane/taxiway SM.

In 1998 the 707 was moved to the edge of the forest. In the meantime, specialists had discovered that it was actually an Israeli aircraft (the 1961 707-458) and that it had never been flown by Lufthansa. In addition, it had been hijacked on 6 September 1970 by the Palestine Liberation Front (PLF) during Swissair's Zurich-New York flight.

Given that the original had already been scrapped, a similar aircraft was repainted to look like the historic Boeing, i.e. the 400 D-ABOC "Berlin". Needless to say the gift was not particularly appreciated, and to this day, the plane is still used for firefighter training exercises.

PLAQUE MARKING JOHN RABE'S LAST KNOWN ADDRESS

5

The Nazi who saved the lives of 250,000 Chinese

Harriesstraße 3, 13629 Berlin
U7 (Rohrdamm) then Bus 123 (Harriesstraße)

Within the Siemens workers' housing estate in Siemensstadt, a metal plaque at Harriesstraße 3 reminds us that this was the last home of John Rabe, a Nazi who saved the lives of 250,000 Chinese people.

John Rabe was a manager at Siemens and had been sent by the company to Nanking to defend its good reputation in the country. At the beginning of the Sino-Japanese War, as Japanese planes flew low-level bombing raids over Nanking, Rabe hoisted a huge swastika flag near his house. From then on, his property (about 500 square metres) was no longer a target; Germany and Japan were then allies, having both signed the anti-Komintern pact in 1936, which was aimed at fighting communism. Some 650 Chinese people took refuge in his house; many of them slept at night under the Nazi flag.

During the sacking of Nanking and the appalling massacres that followed in 1937, John Rabe assumed the presidency of the International Committee for the Nanking Safety Zone. About 250,000 Chinese found refuge in this zone as they fled the Japanese who raped and killed en masse throughout the city. Murdered children were even nailed to walls by raging Japanese soldiers. A total of 300,000 Chinese are estimated to have died.

Repatriated in 1938, Rabe was censured by Nazi Germany when he reported what he had seen. He even wrote directly to Hitler, asking that Chinese civilians be better protected from Tokyo, a partner in the military axis, and that Germany intercede with the Japanese.

After the war and the country's denazification, John Rabe ended his career as a translator for Siemens. With the publication of his diary *The Good Man of Nanking: The Diaries of John Rabe* in 1996 in New York, Rabe finally got the recognition he deserved. His house in Nanking became the Rabe Research Centre for Peace and Conflict Resolution.

The *John Rabe Kommunika-tionszentrum* ("John Rabe Communication Centre") in Heidelberg is also trying to get China and Japan to consider the idea of twinning the cities of Nanking and Hiroshima. The film *John Rabe*, the tomb of honour (*Ehrengrab*) erected for him in Berlin, and the fact that he holds second place in China's "Top Ten International Friends" voted by 56 million listeners of Radio China International, all further evidence his incredible impact.

BIBERTEICH

A street closed to traffic at night to protect beavers

Rhenaniastraße, 13599 Berlin
U7 (Haselhorst) then Bus 136 (Haselhorst Stadium)

Close to the corner of Rhenaniastraße and Bootshausweg there is a crystal-clear sign: beneath an illustration of a beaver is the inscription "Slow down - Thank You", reminding drivers that Rhenaniastraße (which forms a kind of dyke between the Rohrbruchwiesen marsh and meadows and the Rohrbruch pond) is a protected area for beavers. Officially, the street is even closed to traffic at night to protect the large semiaquatic rodents.

Observing the wildlife of the Rohrbruchwiesen banks through binoculars or a camera zoom lens from the roadside is an absolute must; in winter it is easy to spot gnawed or chewed trees. Beavers are able to cut down a trunk in just a few hours thanks to their oversized, curved, hard, and extremely sharp incisors.

However, they are quite short-sighted creatures, given that from a very early age they concentrate almost exclusively on what is right in front of their noses. This makes it difficult for them to judge whether they will succeed in bringing down their chosen tree. A trunk that they gnaw to the core from opposite sides – forming an hourglass shape – will often remain standing for some time, before simply tilting to one side or the other, held back by the surrounding branches or previously felled trees.

Beavers primarily cut down trees to build dams that will raise the level of running water; the entrance to their lodge must always be submerged. But here at Rohrbruch they only cut down trees to gain access to the tender foliage and branches of alders, willows and poplars. They also feed on the bark.

Coming from the Oranienburg/Hennigsdorf area, the first beavers settled in Berlin at the beginning of the 1990s after following the course of the River Havel. Today in Spandau, Reinickendorf and Treptow-Köpenick half a dozen beaver colonies comprise some 100-150 rodents in 20-30 family lodges. Unfortunately, in open areas, such as the crossing of Rhenaniastraße, they are easy targets for motorists, who tend not to pay too much attention to the animals. Every year in Spandau alone, about ten of them end up being run over.

THE MUSEUM FLAT IN THE HASELHORST EXPERIMENTAL DISTRICT ⑦

An eagle's nest in the experimental district

Lüdenscheider Weg 4/Burscheider Weg 6e
Dates and times of visits to the show flat in the museum: www.gewobag.de
gewobag.de/soziales-engagement/stadtteilinfos/spandau/haselhorst/museumswohnung
Groups of 15 to 25 people: €150–250 (contact Michael Bienert : haselhorst@text-der-stadt.de)
U7 (Paulsternstraße) then Bus 139 (Lüdenscheider Weg)

At the beginning (to the east) of Lüdenscheider Weg, look for the sign indicating "Lüdenscheider Weg 2, 2a, 2b and Lüdenscheider Weg 4-4d, 6-6d" and go into the small lane there that leads into the block of houses. About 100 metres away on the left in a playground, there is a bronze eagle with its huge, outspread wings, protecting its three chicks that are not yet ready to leave the nest.

This sculpture was erected in 1935 as a way of symbolising the arrival of the Nazis in the newly-built experimental district of Haselhorst, a working class district which was built during the Systemzeit, a derogatory term used in Nazi jargon to refer to the period of the Weimar Republic.

During the world economic crisis, Walter Gropius set up an experimental project which was a radical attempt to mass produce affordable lodgings for the workers and staff of the nearby Siemens factories. For this to be successful, it required both a strict rationalisation of the construction process and an ingenious reinterpretation of bourgeois housing.

At 6E on Burscheider Weg, in a museum flat that has been refurbished and furnished in the original 1930s style, Michael Bienert (who wrote a very comprehensive book about the district) shows which innovations made the rent more affordable.

There are two large rooms and a tiny one: 42 m2 in all. The electricity is only used for the lights on the ceiling, and there are no sockets for electrical appliances, as all the appliances, such as coffee grinders and meat mincers, in this new concept of a kitchen-livingroom (a small kitchen area opening out onto the living room) were manually operated. The "cooking machine", as it was then called, ran on wood and coal.

Ingeniously, a tiled stove was built into the living room wall to heat both the living room and the adjacent bedroom. The minute bathroom with its tiny bathtub, its wood-fired stove, toilet and clothes line gives you some idea of what claustrophobics must feel like. There was, however, already (cold) running water from the tap.

MONUMENT TO HOMING PIGEONS

(8)

A tribute to the homing pigeon soldiers

Falkenseer Damm 17, corner of Flankenschanze, 13585 Berlin
U7 / S3, S9 (Rathaus Spandau) / Bus 137 (Flankenschanze)

At the corner of the Falkenseer Damm and the Flankenschanze, a large granite boulder is adorned with a flock of bronze pigeons. The monument has stood here since 1939, although the 25 original birds were melted down in 1942 because the metal was needed for the German war effort.

The new bronze that replaced it in 1963, with only 10 pigeons, is the work of sculptor Paul Brandenburg. It evokes the memory of the homing pigeons that were in service during the First World War.

The original 1939 inscription ("To our homing pigeons 1914-1918") was not replaced in 1963.

Today, Kameradschaft 248 of the German Security Unit (a German military police troop that was responsible for the protection of British military installations in Berlin) is responsible for the protection of the pigeon memorial, among other things.

This responsibility has a symbolic character because the Germans and the British fought an intense intelligence war with pigeons during both world wars. Since there were still no secure radio links and the lines of communication were constantly disrupted in the chaos of war, these birds, whose instincts unerringly lead them back to their pigeon loft, were by far the best messengers: in wartime, a message sent by homing pigeon had a 95% chance of reaching its destination. Unfortunately, both sides shot enemy birds and even used trained falcons to chase the enemy's pigeons.

The exceptional capacities of homing pigeons

Whether they are released 500 metres or 100 km away from their home, or in some cases even further than 1,000 km, the homing pigeon has this fantastic ability to always know how to get home. Even if the reason for these exceptional capacities is still unknown, some would attribute this gift to the presence of small crystals in their brains. This characteristic was detected a long time ago, in particular by Julius Caesar who, during the conquest of Gaul, used homing pigeons to send messages to Rome and to inform his followers about the progress of the campaign.

On the other hand, let there be no mistake: what we sometimes see in the cinema, i.e. a pigeon that is released and asked to go and deliver a message and then come back, does not exist. The pigeon is only (so to speak) able to return home. That is why, in order to send a message to several places, you had to take along pigeons that had each been bred at the place where the message had to be sent. In order to send several successive messages to the same place, a substantial number of pigeons had to be taken along... When the recipient of a message was on the move, however, there was no miracle solution. Unless the message went from dovecote to dovecote, it was difficult to receive messages.

The restaurant building in front of the monument was once a shed belonging to the Pigeon Institute of the German Empire, where a picture of the terrible military dovecot can be seen.

SCULPTURE OF A BULL

A mistaken homage to the oldest surviving drainage system in Berlin

Egelpfuhlstraße, 13581 Berlin, next to the bridge over the Bullengraben
S3, 9 / U7 (Rathaus Spandau) then Bus M32 (Egelpfuhlstraße)

Although the stream of Bullengraben is 6 kilometres long, it is so narrow at times that it is easy to lose track of it. It is more like a small brook that carries water to the Havel from the plain at the foot of the Hahneberg. But this ditch is not as ordinary as it might at first seem: it is actually the oldest surviving drainage system in Berlin.

Archaeologists and researchers have traced it back to the seventh century. According to some of the more audacious theorists, it could even be part of the network of canals dating back to the bronze Age which were dug around the Havel – between the Havel and the Elbe, into which it flows. As early as the seventh century, Slavic tribes settled on the plain stretching from the area around the Havel to the Elbe. In those days, newcomers who had moved the furthest to the west were called "Slavs of the Elbe," as opposed to "Heveller" who had settled in the area around the Havel. Originally, Spandau was a Slavic village founded where the Havel meets the Spree. A fortified site grew out of this cluster of habitations by the end of the 10th century, but unfortunately its name is unknown.

The name for this system of ditches which was dug between 600 and 700 AD to drain the wetlands, and enable people to then cut the grass and hang it on wooden posts to dry and make hay, comes from the Slavic word for "ball of hay": *Bollen*. Over time, on land registry records, *Bollen* has become *Bullen* (*Bulle* means "bull" in German) and the ditch has become a drinking trough for so-called bulls. It is a shame that this commonly believed, yet mistaken interpretation was chosen when the sculptor Sebastian Kuhlisch was given a commission, resulting in a steel bull standing tall next to the bridge over the Bullengraben, on a level with Egelpfuhlstraße. A huge steel ball of hay would have had a greater impact, or would have at least been nearer to the truth.

STAAKENS'S OLD CONTROL TOWER ⑩

A forgotten witness of the heyday of zeppelins in Staaken

Am Zeppelinpark 27, 13591 Berlin
S3, 9 / U7 (Rathaus Spandau), then Bus M32 (Am Zeppelinpark)

At the end of Brunsbütteler Damm in Staaken, on Berlin's north west border, in a bland industrial zone, the old tarmac of Staaken's airfield (1915-1953) is now covered with rows of solar panels.

Even the locals have forgotten that, up to 1918, 12 airships were built in Staaken and some parts of the production hangar are still standing today. However, everything that remains is either hidden or in ruins (or both), and there are no signs telling the history of the place.

The most visible remains are those of the old brick control tower from the 1920s, a time when Staaken was a playground for many of Berlin's well-known characters who had obtained their pilot's licence, like Wernher von Braun, Heinz Rühmann (the actor in the propoganda comedy *Quax, der Bruchpilot*), Elli Beinhorn (the future wife of the racing driver Bernd Rosemeyer), Hanna Reitsch (the woman who conducted test flights of the V1 for Hitler) and the ill-fated Marga von Etzdorf from Spandau who, in spite of her successes at international flying competitions, committed suicide in 1933 after making two emergency crash landings.

It was in front of this rather ordinary control tower that Hitler admitted in public that he had not respected the Treaty of Versailles: by stationing all the airships at this place – Arodo Ar 65 biplanes – from the Richthofen fighter squadron, he admitted that the German Reich was building an air force.

It was also in front of this very same control tower that the first German transatlantic passenger airship was to take off: an Fw 200 V1 made by the aeronautics manufacturer Focke-Wulf – Lufthansa's D-ACON- registered Condor which flew, non-stop, to New York in a little over 24 hours, thanks to its reserve tanks.

Even faster on the return flight, it covered a distance of 6,392 kilometres in 19 hours and 55 minutes, which corresponded to an average speed of 321 km/h.

On the control tower, there is an inscription in Cyrillic characters testifying to the airport's last phase of use. The Russians moved out in 1953, leaving the airfield to its fate and closure in 1959.

THE FIELDS OF KAROLINENHÖHE ⑪

A magnificent relic of the history of the drains of Berlin

At the junction of Gatower Straße and Straße 270
15 min by bicycle from the station S3/S5/S9 Pichelsberg

To the west of the tower of Beringer (see next double page), level with the right angle formed by the border between Berlin and Brandenburg, a surprising and immense area of countryside begins. By bicycle, this particularly pleasant ride takes you, for example, from the fort of Hahneberg to the Havel. The dirt tracks, installed on a sort of dyke between the fields, feel almost like ancient rice fields. These fields, called Karolinenhöhe, are actually a magnificent relic of the so-called drainage fields (*Rieselfelder*) which were used in Berlin for more than a century to deal with the problem of sewage. Originally belonging to the autonomous town of Charlottenburg, the *Rieselfelder Karolinenhöhe* were made into a protected green area covering 220 hectares in 1987. The sewage treatment plants are relatively recent: in Berlin they have only really been in use since the end of the 1960s. Before then, sewage from the capital was taken to different pumping stations, which evacuated them out of the town using underground pressure pipes to some twenty so-called drainage fields (*Rieselfelder*) covering up to 10,000 hectares of land (Karolinenhöhe, Wansdorf, Schönerlinde, Blankenfelde, Buch, Hobrechtsfelde, Malchow, Falkenberg, Hellersdorf, Münchehofe, Deutsch Wusterhausen, Kleinziethen, Großziethen, Boddinsfelde, Tasdorf, Mühlenbeck, Waßmanndorf, Osdorf, Großbeeren, Sputendorf).

Filtered naturally, the sediments were used for market gardening to feed the city of Berlin. The history of these fields goes back to the advent of running water around the end of the 19th century: before it was installed, dry toilets could be found in interior courtyards. Once full, the septic tanks were emptied at night by the "Eimer-Weiber" (bucket women), who carried the contents, by cart, outside the city. As for the sewage, it was thrown into the gutters *(Rinnsteine)*. Placed between the pavement and the road, they formed a small rut, the width of a paving stone, filled with repulsive trickles of matter which flowed into the Spree.

With the arrival of running water, which also supplied enough water to rinse out the gutters, the dirty waters became mixed with the excrement from the toilets and also flowed into the gutters which lined the pavements, forming an open sewer throughout the city streets, the repulsive streams of which not only polluted the Spree but also soaked into the ground and down to the water table. The underground drainage network, with its pumping stations (see page 286) and the system of the *Rieselfelfer*, helped to solve this problem.

TOWER OF BERINGER

⑫

A memorial to delusions of grandeur

Gatower Str. 201, 13595 Berlin
S3, S9 / U7 (Rathaus Spandau), then Bus 134 (Zur Haveldüne)

Near the road to Gatow, just after the last houses in the Wilhelmstadt district of Spandau, there is a small stone tower in the forest with an intriguing coat of arms above its door. It shows an oblique representation of a bear crossing the arch of a bridge (or a wall?). This small coat of arms is that of the principality of Anhalt (of the House of Ascania) dating back to the 16th century, according to the blogger Uwe Gerber of Spandau, a local historian who has a good knowledge of coats of arms.

More precisely, the coat of arms could be that of the Beringer line, which it is thought, was entirely "invented" by the princes of Anhalt at that time to help them widen their influence and give weight to their titles. So what is a coat of arms doing on this tiny tower with a door that makes up half its height?

On the side, there are two large stones engraved with a scene depicting a chase and a Latin inscription referring to the legend of Jaczo which is very popular in Berlin. "Has per fauces, Jaczo, princeps Slavorum, / ab Albero Urso pulsus, ad habelam evasit. / Anno Domini MCLVII." ("Albert the Bear chased Jaczo, the Prince of the Slavs, as far as the Havel in the year 1157". On the opposite riverbank of the Havel at Charlottenburg, on the Schildhorn peninsula, a column was erected as a reminder that, thanks to divine intervention, Jaczo von Köpenick was saved from drowning before converting to Christianity. The little tower on this side of the river was baptized "Jaczo's tower" because of the inscriptions and the coat of arms, but according to the historian Uwe Gerber, this is rather misleading for those who are interested in its history.

In his opinion, the tower is not really about the Slav Prince Jaczo von Köpenick, but rather Albert the Ascanian Bear and the claim of the Beringer line, as this construction was built by the industrialist Emil Beringer. Judging by the markings on some of the bricks used in its construction, the tower was probably built between 1909 and 1914. It was part of a Romantic-style garden (with a waterfall) belonging to the Beringer family. By awarding himself the coat of arms of the fictitious Beringer line of the House of Ascania, it would seem that Emil Beringer was indeed revelling in delusions of grandeur in his garden.

THE SCHILDHORN MONUMENT ⑬

A monument erected in memory of an event which never, in fact, took place

Straße am Schildhorn 7, 14193 Berlin
S3, 9 (Pichelsberg)

A tall stone medieval-style column dating, in reality, back to the middle of the 19th century, in other words to the period of late German Romanticism, the Schildhorn monument offers a stunning view over the Jürgenlanke. It is topped by a circle that has been cut into four. It is all too clean and precise for it to date back several centuries. The shield (Schild) presumably having belonged to a warrior in olden times, is fixed to the column.

The column is unusual on two counts: firstly, because it was designed by a Prussian king, Frederick William IV and secondly, because it is a monument that was erected in memory of an event that never, in fact, took place. The latter is part of a Berlin legend, the legend of Jaxa, which is intimately linked to the myth of the foundation of Mark Brandenburg. In other words, we are faced with the fruits of the imagination of a Prussian king who was inspired by an old tale to erect something in a hitherto quiet place to encourage crowds of Berliners to go there.

The king sketched his idea on a piece of paper and gave it to August Stüler, his favourite architect who corrected the proportions somewhat (he raised the column) and it was all built. This is how the fluctuating history of an imaginary battle was invented from scratch. It was supposed to have taken place in 1157 between Albert the Bear and Jaxa (Jaczo) von Köpenick, a Slav prince who had effectively seized part of Mark Brandenburg, at the time when conflict was ongoing between Albert the Bear and the Slavs of the Elbe.

The legend goes that whilst fleeing from Albert the Bear, Jaczo von Köpenick almost drowned when his exhausted horse was carried away by the current of the Havel. As he did not know how to swim, Jaxa clung on to his wooden shield. But it was not until he had implored the Christian God that he did not believe in, that he was saved. Once back on the riverbank, he hung his shield (*Schild*) on an oak tree and swore that he would convert to Christianity.

"From falsehood anything follows"

The tower situated on the other bank of the Havel in Spandau (see previous double page) is also associated with the legend of Jaxa, and is due to the imagination of a certain Mr Beringer who considered himself to be a descendant of Albert the Bear *Ex falso sequitur quodlibet*: "From falsehood anything follows".

THE CEMETERY OF THE FOREST OF GRUNEWALD ⑭

The most mysterious, moving and poetic of cemeteries in Berlin

Schildhornweg 33, 14193 Berlin
Summer: 7am–8pm; Winter: 8am–4pm
S3, 9 (Pichelsberg)

Of all the cemeteries in Berlin, the rarely visited cemetery of the forest of Grunewald is probably the most mysterious, moving and poetic.

Its unusual location is due to its history: it was originally reserved for those who could not be given a burial in the parish cemeteries of the town. This was either because they had committed suicide or because they had been found on the shores of the Jürgenlanke, a small, nearby bay, and they had to be buried quickly. In 1920, when the management of the cemetery was handed over to the town, those who had committed suicide were given the right to a Christian burial.

Although, in the cemetery, there are two Russian Orthodox crosses dating back to the First World War (two forced labourers who committed suicide), a significant number of graves belonging to soldiers from the Second World War, some crosses for unnamed graves, and many very "ordinary" tombstones, three of the graves stand out from the rest. The first one belongs to Willi Wohlberedt, an author who had carried out research on cemeteries which were represented on the cover of his most important work: *The tombstones of Greater Berlin, Potsdam and its surroundings*. The tombstone of Willi Schulz, former inspector of the forest of Grunewald, is made up of three wooden planks standing side by side to form a tombstone. They are covered by small, pointed copper caps which come together to form the letter W for Willi in an Expressionist-style zigzag. On the right-hand and left-hand planks, a large cross has been carved into the wood; his name and title are engraved on the one in the middle, the largest of the three. Above the epitaph a deer's antlers have been fixed as a hunting trophy. Below the epitaph the sarcastic comment, "End of the hunting season!" has been added.

The most surprising tombstone belongs to Margarethe Päffgen and her daughter Christa Päffgen, alias Nico – a former experimental rock singer with the group Velvet Underground, Andy Warhol's ex-muse, fashionista, and former mistress of Alain Delon, killed in a bicycle accident. Judging by the large number of regularly renewed objects that have been placed around her tombstone (flowers, wine, cigarettes, cassettes), she continues to attract admirers of both sexes.

THE PARABOLIC MIRRORS OF THE "ERSCHIESSUNGSSTÄTTE V" ⑮

A peculiarly reflective memorial to a former Nazi execution site

Glockenturmstraße 3, 14053 Berlin
S3, 9 (Pichelsberg)

Between the ice rink and the Waldbühne, on the pavement on Glockenturmstraße, there is a strange traffic mirror. As it is tilted to face passers-by, it is apparently not being used for the safety of vehicles arriving at the ice rink. A short text inscribed directly onto the mirror tells us that the forest track that branches off from this point leads to the "Erschießungsstätte V" (execution site V) in Murellenberge.

This is actually where deserters, conscientious objectors, those who had refused to obey orders and, more generally, all the "subversive elements undermining the war effort" were executed. The names of 252 victims are known, but their number could be much greater.

Other mirrors have been placed along the track leading to the place where the execution posts are thought to have been, increasing in number as we walk down the track, forming small groups at the end of it in the middle of the forest. The texts that are engraved on 15 of the 104 mirrors relate the military past of this zone. At the end, there are extracts from witness accounts: "I vaguely heard parts of an execution sentence being read out: Obergefreiter (chief corporal) [...] aged [...] for desertion [...] to death [...], the Maat (second-master) [...] aged [...] sentenced [...] for cowardice before the enemy [...] to be shot [...]".

This unusual and remarkable memorial walk was devised by Patricia Pisani, an Argentinian artist living in Berlin and winner of the competition organised to design the memorial. The mirrors metaphorically reflect "what happens at intersections when there is no visibility: a risk or potentially imminent danger that cannot yet be seen. They show something that is out of sight from the place where we are standing at the turning point, in the past, in the future."

The death sentences pronounced by the Nazi court martial, condemning the deserters and "saboteurs of the fighting forces" were considered, for many years, as being legitimate, and it was only in 1998 that those who had been convicted were exonerated.

The forest of Murellenberge was used by the military as early as 1840: The Royal Infantry's shooting school in Ruhleben had set up many shooting ranges and *schanzen* (detached entrenchments of the fortifications). This is why the zone is called Schanzenwald. A surviving example of a *schanze* can be seen on the tennis court at the corner of Havelchaussee and Elsgrabenweg. In 2007, the 38-hectare plot of land that had been used for military training was cleared of its ammunition and buildings before being given back to the general public.

THE OLYMPIA SIGNAL BOX

16

The right end of the stick

U-Bahnmuseum (Metro Museum)
Rossitter Weg 1, 14053 Berlin
Open every second Saturday in the month 10:30am–3pm
U2 (Olympiastadion)

Every second Saturday in the month, on the lowest level of the Olympiastadion station, visitors can gain access to more than just the tracks of the U2 metro line: U-Bahnmuseum of Berlin, housed in the old signal box of the Olympiastadion station (Olympia-Stellwerk), is also accessible here. At the end of a little corridor, you are given a "ticket" to go to a sort of viewpoint overlooking the tracks in front of the Grunewald depot, the current command and regional control post which replaced the old signal box of the Olympia-Stellwerk in 1983.

The highlight of the visit is a technical gem, which has remained intact, and for the most part, is still in working order: the level actuators of the electromechanical signal box, type VES 1913. It started operating in 1931 and was the largest signal box of its kind in Europe. Imagine a 14-metre long keyboard, on which each note was produced by operating a lever. The partition looked like an immense optical control panel, placed just opposite, showing all the tracks of the Grunewald depot. Each engine and each signal is represented by a small light, the colour of which indicates their position at any given time.

On the wooden console, the switch operating levers are as large as those of an emergency handbrake on a vehicle, and are topped with large, blue buttons. These levers controlled 103 trains and 99 signals by managing 616 different train movement configurations. All the movements of tracks from the Grunewald depot and the metro station Olympiastadion were managed from this nerve centre, possessing the best possible view of all the rolling stock. All train movements as well as the positions of the signals and the tracks were displayed, thanks to 1,239 light bulbs, on a control panel that was six metres long and two metres high. During visits, the association AG Berliner U-Bahn, which brings together former employees of the metro, can still put on a demonstration of how this unique, electromechanical signal box was used. In an adjoining room, there is a giant relay station from which the commands from the signal box were transmitted by electrical impulses to the equipment on the tracks and the signals.

THE DIMENSIONS OF THE CORBUSIERHAUS

⑰

When Le Courbusier's first project was not respected ...

Flatowallee 16, 14055 Berlin
Guided tours: info@corbusierhaus-berlin.org (€40 for 1 to 4 people)
S3, 9 (Olympiastadion)

Although the Corbusierhaus in Berlin is obviously no secret to anyone, with its 530 apartments (see the enormous board in the entrance hall crammed full with all the doorbells and names of its occupants), it is easy to forget that the Berlin project of the famous Le Courbusier has a unique feature: it quite simply does not respect the dimensions planned by the architect.

There is a concrete relief at the entrance to the building reminding us how Le Corbusier, in accordance with his theory of harmony and proportions, devised his own system of measurements for the designs of his apartments, named "Modulor" (book entitled *Toward an Architecture* published in 1923). However, the strictly-applied regulations for construction in Berlin thwarted his plans which had been based on these ideals: the minimum ceiling height in Berlin was then 2.50 metres and the 2.26 metres originally planned by Le Corbusier had to be abandoned.

The proportion of the rooms could only therefore be respected by widening the apartments, from 3.66 metres to 4.06 metres. As for the system of duplexes which appeared on the original plans, it was removed to gain living space and allow for this modification. The shopping street that should have been created halfway up the building was also abandoned. Only a laundrette and a supermarket remained on the plans: the "small town in itself" that the Berlin building was meant to be had lost all its substance.

This is why Le Corbusier distanced himself from this altered version of his dream and disparagingly referred to it as the "bottle rack". In spite of the distortions applied to the Modulor system, the inhabitants of this complex have always been happy with it. Today, even the supermarket has disappeared, as everyone can go and do their shopping elsewhere, and some of the apartments are now used as holiday homes.

The dimensions of Modulor

Presented in 1923 in his work *Toward an Architecture*, Le Corbusier's theory of the harmony of proportions serves as a basis for his famous Modulor system. His objective, inspired by the classic architectural culture studied during his travels, was to update the system of measurements based on parts of the body like the cubit and the foot. For this universal measuring tool based on human stature, he used the measurements of an average-sized man (height from the navel, 113 cm: top of the head, 183 cm) as a reference combining it with Fibonacci's mathematical theory, according to which a value can be found by adding together the two previous values. The metrical values 226, 183, 113, 70, 43 and 27 cm (four of which are written on the front of the Corbusierhaus where the Modulor is represented) are the result of this.

This system is also used to calculate the dimensions of Le Corbusier's furniture (height at the seat of the stool, 27cm: height at the seat of the chair, 43 cm: table top, 70 cm: work surface, 113 cm) ... and the height of the ceiling, 226 cm.

THE RESURRECTION OF CHRIST CATHEDRAL

18

The mystique of Orthodox Russia

Hohenzollerndamm 166, 10713 Berlin
0 30 / 8 73 16 14
Timetable details by phone or on the online calendar rokmp.de/de/churches/hohenzollerndamm-166-10713-berlin
S41, 42, 46 (Hohenzollerndamm)

Consecrated on 13 May 1938, the Russian Orthodox Resurrection of Christ Cathedral (*Christi-Auferstehungs-Kathedrale*) comes to life during prayer times, especially during Saturday Mass: in an atmosphere of true devotion, and in a darkness that reinforces the mysticism of the place, crowds of the faithful light candles, burn incense and embrace the icons.

The three-nave church follows the same traditional layout as the first Russian Orthodox churches of the 11th and 12th centuries. This construction was approved by the Nazis because they considered the Russian Orthodox Church to be a form of protection against Bolshevism. The old iconostasis comes from a garrison church in Mínsk Mazzowiecki near Warsaw.

The proximity to the headquarters of the Nazi administration on Fehrbelliner Platz is noteworthy. Indeed, the diocese of Berlin once expressed its thanks for the right of residence it had been granted in an enthusiastic letter to the "most pious Führer and Chancellor of the Reich Adolf Hitler".

The parish used to have 5,000 members. Today they are 190,000.

What does Orthodox iconostasis represent?

"Iconostasis is the boundary between the visible world and the invisible world," writes priest Pawel Florenski. "Iconostasis is a sign of the presence of saints and angels ... of the presence of heavenly witnesses, and above all of the mother of God and of Christ himself."
The iconostasis communicates to the members of the parish the sacredness of the liturgy, which takes place out of sight in the sanctuary. The images of the iconostasis show what becomes of man when he binds himself to God; they demonstrate the level of devotion expressed by the faithful who come here to seek God's mercy, those who approach these consecrated paintings, often veiled, to come face to face with the divine world.
Dating back to Byzantine origins, the importance of the paintings is emphasised by the amount of gold applied to the chalk background, symbolising the richness of the world after death, when Jesus Christ, by his resurrection and ascension to heaven, preceded all believers.

A104 MOTORWAY TUNNEL BUILDING

19

A motorway running through a building

Schlangenbader Straße 18, 10585 Berlin
U3 (Rüdesheimer-Platz)

In the district of Wilmersdorf, the "Schlange" (snake) in the street name Schlangenbader Straße refers to the largest housing estate in Europe. At 600 metres long, with a maximum height of 45 metres, it accommodates 3,500 tenants across 1,215 apartments. Including

accessory constructions, there are actually 1,700 accommodations.

But its most unique feature becomes apparent when seen from above; the entire building straddles a stretch of motorway, the A104 (*Abzweig Steglitz*), which connects the A100 motorway with Hohenzollerndamm in the north and the B1 (via Schildhornstraße) in the south.

At the point where Wiesbadener Straße intersects the building, roughly in the middle, the motorway tunnel can be seen embedded in a concrete box, connecting the two halves of the residential complex like a bridge. To protect the accommodations from vibrations, the motorway box does not touch the walls of the superstructure; it rests on rubber pads, which in turn rest on enormous pillars anchored in the ground.

In corridors or stairwells, such as on Wiesbadener Straße, a faint "knock-knock-knock" can be heard – the only reminder that there is constant traffic beneath. This is what the locals call the heartbeat of the complex. There are some 54,000 beats a day; that's the average number of vehicles passing through.

According to residents, nothing can be heard in the apartments, even on the fourth floor just above the roads.

Completed in 1980, the Berlin Snake embodies the fever that gripped the West at the time, and particularly its infatuation with rooftop constructions, which almost without exception remained at the planning stage. Oswald Mathias Ungers (OMU), a well-known name in Western architecture, had proposed the construction of a 20-storey superstructure straddling the 500 kilometre-long motorway between Hamburg and Frankfurt am Main. Berlin was fortunate (or perhaps unfortunate) that money from Western subsidies flowed in during the time Germany was divided, so it was able to build not only a city motorway (which is still in the process of being built), but also the snake.

There is a similar building in Osaka – the Gate Tower Building.

THE LAHORE AHMADIYYA MOVEMENT MOSQUE

20

A jewel of Indo-Islamic architecture

Brienner Straße 7–8, 10713 Berlin
Daily 11am–6pm
U2, 3, 7 (Fehrbelliner Platz)

The magnificent Wilmersdorf Mosque (also known historically as the *Berliner Moschee* or *Ahmadiyya-Moschee*) is the oldest mosque in Germany. Built between 1924 and 1928 for the Ahmadiyya Anjuman Isha'at Islam (AAIIL – Lahore Ahmadiyya Movement for the Propagation of Islam), it consists of two 32 metre-high minarets detached from the main building, and a dome 26 metres high and

10 metres in diameter. The prayer hall can accommodate about 400 worshippers.

Designed by Berlin architect K.A. Hermann, the mosque is reminiscent of the Mughal architecture of the Taj Mahal. Current owner and builder AAIIL financed its construction solely through donations.

As has always been the case, the mosque is "open for worship to Muslims of all Mohammedan nations and all religious currents without distinction." Simply put, it is open to all, every day.

During the Nazi period, the Berlin branch of the AAIIL and its mosque played an important role in helping Jews flee Germany. However, the Nazis had used the mosque for propaganda purposes. For example, the SS received Mohammed Amin al-Husseini – the Grand Mufti of Jerusalem and a known anti-Semite – as a guest of honour.

THE RED LETTERBOX OF THE FEHRBELLINER PLATZ (21)

A discrete souvenir of British occupation

Fehrbelliner Platz 4, 10707 Berlin
U2, 3, 7 (Fehrbelliner Platz)

On the front of number 4 Fehrbelliner Platz, a former Nazi building which was home to the general management of the DAF, the Deutsche Arbeitsfront ("German Labour Front"), a discrete, red letterbox with inscriptions written in English, goes relatively unnoticed ...

The typically English-style telephone box standing proudly nearby, reminds us that the building, which was not damaged in the bombings during the war, was converted into the headquarters of the British occupying forces in 1945.

Named Lancaster House, the building shared the same name as the legendary British Bombardier plane called Avro Lancaster, which was used during World War II. In 1954, the British Army Headquarters moved to the former Sportforum, on the site of the 1936 Olympics. But the British had good memories of the premises on Fehrbelliner Platz, which was full of charm. The subjects of Her Majesty had a reputation. They liked keeping to themselves, for example, at the British officers' mess club located on Thüringer Allee, in the very place where the Berlin's ice skating club had been based before the war broke out. It was the Queen's visits in 1965, 1978 and 1987, that made the British more appealing to Berliners. In May 1987, the year of the city's 750th anniversary, Queen Elizabeth stayed in Berlin for two days with her husband, Prince Philip. She made a speech at the Palace of Charlottenburg, addressing Berlin in German, and had tea at Bellevue Palace with German Federal president Richard von Weizsäcker. She then celebrated her own birthday (the celebrations of which are traditionally held in May instead of April because of the weather) on the Maifeld, which belonged to the Olympic site and which was being used by British troops.

On 5 March 1987, Her Majesty's ambassador, Sir Julian Leonard Bullar, and the British occupation sector's commander in Berlin, Patrick Guy Brooking, had already given the telephone booth and the red letterbox to the Germans. It was an official gift from the British occupying power. In comparison, the Americans had donated an entire library: the Amerika-Gedenkbibliothek.

KREUZKIRCHE

An expressionist masterpiece

Hohenzollerndamm 130a, 14199 Berlin
0 30 / 83 22 46 63
kreuzkirche-berlin.de
Sat 4pm–6pm and Sunday mass at 11am
S41 (Hohenzollerndamm)

Rare are the Berliners, and even more so the tourists, who have been inside the listed Kreuzkirche church, which is a real pity: built between 1927 and 1929, from plans drawn by Günther Paulus, it is a masterpiece of expressionist architecture.

Other than its three-pointed steeple, which can be seen from afar (54 metres high), the church has a surprising front door – in blue ceramic, reminiscent of an Asian pagoda. On either side of the door, on the sides of the main tower, it is interesting to note the zigzag of decorations (in brick), typical of expressionist architecture. Partially rebuilt after the war in 1953, the church was renovated in 1984, respecting the original plans as faithfully as possible. Inside, a corridor leads to a remarkable main hall (octagonally-shaped) whose exceptional decor painted behind the altar is also typical of expressionism.

The original colours, created by Erich Wolde, corresponded to those of a rainbow: the entrance (*Brauthalle*) in yellow, the corridor in red, the main hall in green, the pews for the worshippers in blue (the only original colour that remains today) and the area around the altar in purple.

The harmony and architectural balance which flows from this place is definitely worth taking in for a moment on the pews of this church.

NEARBY

Walking up the Hohenzollerndamm towards the S-Bahn, the front door of the parish offices, some ten metres away to the left of the main entrance to the church, is also endowed with fantastic expressionist decor.

130
a
1929

MUSEUM OF THE BLIND

Six dots that changed everything

Rothenburgstraße 14, 12165 Berlin
Wed 3pm–6pm; guided tour for all every 1st Sunday of the month at 11am
Free entry (donations are welcome)
U9 (Rathaus Steglitz)

Not far from the Town Hall of Steglitz, the discreet Museum of the Blind was founded in 1890 at the Royal Institution for the Blind in Berlin-Steglitz. It focuses on the development of writing systems for the blind, emphasising their role in the integration of the blind into society and their personal development.

If the blind can now read and write, play an instrument, compose music, study or teach, it is essentially thanks to Louis Braille who, in 1894, lost his sight at the age of five. His yearning to express himself and to communicate pushed Braille to invent a type of writing that had never been seen before using six raised dots to represent Schwarzschrift ("writing of the full-sighted"). Later, he also devised a dot for musical notes for the blind.

In this way, Louis Braille opened up a whole new world to fellow sufferers, and a former professor of the Institution for the Blind in Steglitz built the first braille typewriter in 1900.

Despite today's technological advances, such as navigation by GPS and audio books, braille and its typewriter still play a key role in a blind person's life, even in these times of smartphones, tablets and computers.

What existed before Braille?

Before braille was adopted, the blind in Germanic countries used the *Stachelschrift* system (*Stachel* meaning "thorn" in German), which was a form of tactile code writing perfected by Klein.
The system really lives up to its name: the metal dots on the lettering blocks are so finely cut that they can easily make your fingertips bleed.

THE MÄUSEBUNKER

An unknown masterpiece of brutalist architecture

Krahmerstraße 6, 12207 Berlin
Visible only from the outside
S25, 26 (Lichterfelde Ost)

With its building in the form of a giant warship, the Research centre for Experimental Medicine (Forschungseinrichtung für experimentelle Medizin), better known as the Mäusebunker (literally the "mouse bunker"), is one of the most spectacular yet lesser-known buildings in Berlin.

A masterpiece of brutalist architecture, this exceptional building measuring almost 120 metres in length stands between Hindenburgdamm and Krahmerstraße, along the Teltow canal (from which it is hidden by the trees). The derelict building cannot be visited, but there is a good view from Krahmerstraße between the canal and Hindenburgdamm.

The building was designed as the Freie Universität's laboratory for animal experimentation between 1967 and 1970 by the Berlin architect Gerd Hänska, with the help of his wife Magdalena and his son Thomas. The construction project suffered many setbacks and was finally finished in 1981.

The concrete building has an astonishingly truncated pyramid structure. Large, blue, cannon-like tubes on the two lateral sides of the building give visitors the impression that they are looking at a warship and not a simple research centre. In the past, these tubes were used as air ducts, an essential way of maintaining a sufficient level of ventilation inside the building.

The protruding triangular windows, visible on the west façade, let the sunlight in, providing sufficient heating and light for the interior.

Warning: in danger of demolition

Today the building is derelict and in danger of demolition: its owner, the Charité Faculty of Medicine, would effectively like to have it knocked down, even if there are many people who are fighting against this. Negotiations are in progress and may take some time. One idea, which would indeed seem particularly suitable for the building, is for it to be converted into a techno club.

MUSEUM OF ENERGY

Berlin lit by arc lamps

Teltowkanalstraße 9, 12247 Berlin
0 30 / 70 17 77 55/56
energie-museum.de
Dates and opening times of the museum regularly updated on the website.
Guided tours by appointment: Tue 10am–12noon
U9 (Rathaus Steglitz) / Bus 186, 283 (Teltowkanalstraße)

From 1986 to 1994, the building on the site of the electricity workstation of Stromnetz Berlin GmbH (the only one of its kind), housed the largest collection of storage accumulators in the world, built and used by the Berliner Städtischen Elektrizitätswerke AG (BEWAG): 7,080 lead batteries could in fact store 14.4 megawatt-hours. Once the accumulator block had been charged, it could supply 17 megawatts that could support the network for twenty minutes: a necessary precaution during the Cold War.

Converted into a museum after it ceased to operate, it tells the history of Berlin's electricity supply, the first local emergency-storage, electricity power stations, and the evolution of techniques in communication (don't miss the strange pneumatic tubes used up to the 1970s to send messages into town by compressed air).

Also on display here is the control button that was used on 7 December 1994 by Eberhard Diepgen, in Berlin's former city hall, to ensure the famous "interconnection" after the European network supplied electricity to Berlin's network for the first time.

There are numerous demonstrations on offer here, ranging from the activation of the original gas and steam turbines which powered the electricity generators to a demonstration in the lighting section of how an arc lamp from 1905 worked: an opportunity to realise that Berlin's street lamps in the 1920s and 30s could hold their own against today's high-intensity LED projectors.

A TRIBUTE TO THE GROß-LICHTERFELDE TRAMWAY LINE

26

The world's first electric tramway

Corner of Morgensternstraße and Königsberger Straße, 12207 Berlin
S-Bahn: S25, S26 (Lichterfelde Ost)

On the corner of Morgensternstraße and Königsberger Straße, slightly set back from the street, is a paved area of a few square metres. Two railway tracks criss-cross the cobblestones, and on top of a sign next to a public bench is a vintage car wheel. The scene evokes a public transport stop and pays tribute to the world's first electric tramway, whose starting point was located roughly here.

Built in 1881, the line connected the stations of Groß-Lichterfelde (today S-Lichterfelde Ost) and the Prussian Staff College, which was about to be built, and whose premises now house, among other things, a branch of the National Archives – *Bundesarchiv Dienststelle.*

One of the world's first metro systems, thanks to Werner von Siemens

With its 10 lines covering almost 150 kilometres (80 per cent of which are underground), the Berlin U-Bahn is one of the world's first underground rail networks. The first metro line, the U1, was inaugurated in 1902. The reason why Berlin was among the first cities to have a metro system is simple: it was famous industrialist Werner von Siemens, based in Charlottenburg, who invented the first electric motor, i.e. the first dynamo powerful enough to propel a vehicle. However, despite Siemens' persuasiveness, Berlin procrastinated long enough for six other cities to steal a march on it before the project was given the go-ahead.

London had been running steam trains underground since 1863, and electrified its network in 1890, making it the first underground railway in history. In 1896 Budapest inaugurated its first metro line, which is now a UNESCO World Heritage Site. In the same year, Glasgow already had just over 10 kilometres of underground lines circling the city; its network remains the only one to have never been extended beyond its original route. Chicago, then one of the most modern cities in the world, built its metro system as early as 1897. Paris opened its first lines to the public in 1900. Finally, Boston's first metro line preceded the inauguration of Berlin's U1 by one year, in 1901.

There is also an information board about the first tramway in history at the Lichterfelde Ost S-Bahn station, just a few steps from this intersection.

MUNICIPAL WEIGH HOUSE

(27)

Women worth their weight

Charlottenstraße 64, 12247 Berlin
S25, 26 Lichterfelde Ost

"Ratswaage" (municipal weigh house) is written in large letters on the frontage of a small neoclassical construction which stands at the end of Charlottenstraße and Elisabethstraße.

Although it is used today as a place where support groups for women from the local neighbourhood can meet for talks, debates, readings and exhibitions, the building still houses some of the former equipment of the "municipal weigh house", which remained in use up to 1968. Built between 1917 and 1918 by the town's head architect, Fritz Freymüller (1882-1950), to replace a smaller communal weigh house, the municipal weigh house of Lankwitz was the place where farmers and merchants had their goods weighed by driving their vehicle over the weighbridge before travelling to the goods station in Lichterfelde-Ost, a few metres away. The transport cost was calculated on the basis of the weight of the goods that had just been determined.

The protected area in front of the small house is the weighing platform (still in working order today), which was also referred to as the weighbridge for carts and carriages. Its maximum weighing capacity was 11 tonnes, which would prove to be insufficient in the 1970s with the arrival of heavier modern trucks. Whereas today, the tonnage of heavy goods vehicles or railway carriages is calculated electronically and with calibrated load cells, the municipal weigh house of Lankwitz functioned exactly like the antique scales in the stations that weighed luggage using the decimal scales method, only 10 times bigger in size.

From 1927 in Lankwitz, the weighers' jobs were held exclusively by women: women are in fact considered to be generally more accurate ...

A river that is no more

At this time, the source of the Lanke (the river that gave its name to Lankwitz) was located next to the weigh house. Today, it is invisible as its course has been diverted underground towards the Teltow canal. Its mouth is near Oiltanking Deutschland in Gasgrabenweg.

FLIEGEBERG

28

Where there's a will there's a way

Schütte-Lanz-Straße, 12209 Berlin
S25, 26 (Osdorfer Straße)

The mound of Lichterfelde, which now towers over the park from a height of 12.2 metres, was originally no more than a simple mound of rubble which had been created in 1894 by Gustav and Otto Lilienthal, two extremely dynamic brothers from Lichterfelde.

From a very young age, the two men dreamt of building a flying machine with which they would be able to soar into the sky like a bird. Gustav Lilienthal was a student of architecture at the Berliner Bauakademie, whereas Otto Lilienthal, the duo's inventor, was studying mechanical engineering at the Gewerbeakademie (which was to merge with the Polytechnikum of Charlottenburg in 1884).

Thanks to the success of his steam machine, Otto Lilienthal managed to collect the necessary funds and published a pioneering work entitled *Der Vogelflug als Grundlage der Fliegekunst* (Bird flight as a basis for aviation) in Berlin in 1889. In view of all the tests carried out, his gliding machine already fully met the criteria for the construction of a plane. *Segelapparat*, whose wings were made of a cotton canvas that was stretched over the wickerwork structure, was tested for the first time in Derwitz in 1891, and then in the Rauhe Berge. Subsequently, the hill of Fliegeberg in Lichterfelde was built in 1894 using the rubble from the brickworks on site. A photo of these beginnings shows Otto with his machine which, having convinced a handful of buyers, went on to be the first serially produced plane.

In all, Otto Lilienthal took to the air more than 2,000 times, and from his man-made hill, Fliegeberg, he flew 80 metres. In 1896 he crashed to his death on a flight over the heights of Rhinow, where he had flown for a distance of 250 metres. After his death, the Fliegeberg in Lichterfelde nearly suffered the same fate as his house on Boothstraße: it was very nearly flattened to the ground. After the brickworks closed in 1897, the site was converted into a municipal park. A stone staircase was cut into the mound and a viewing point was installed at the top. His friends, pioneers of aviation and aeronautic clubs, regularly began to commemorate the day of his death. With the aviation boom, the reputation and glory of Lilienthal continued to spread over the years and a *Fliegefest* (flying festival) is now organised every year in his memory at the mound, which was inaugurated in 1932.

A beautiful monument was also erected on Bäkestraße in memory of this modern-day Icarus.

4TH OF JULY SQUARE

29

The former "4th Ring" of the Germania project

Platz des 4. Juli, 14167 Berlin
S25, 26 Osdorfer Straße

Not far from the Teltow canal, to the west of the Lichterfeld cemetery (Städtischer Parkfriedhof Lichterfelde), a huge asphalted area suddenly becomes apparent: 460 metres long and 40 metres wide – the size of four football pitches. There is no path or barrier. This square is probably the largest asphalted piece of land in Berlin with no clearly defined purpose.

This is where, in 1994, Bill Clinton, Helmut Kohl and Eberhard Diepgen, the former mayor of Berlin, met to mark the withdrawal of the American troops who had been stationed since 1945 in the old Telefunken factory (a radio electrical company) built at the side of the square.

The American soldiers actually rehearsed marching for American national Independence Day on this large square, and this is why it was renamed 4th of July square, the day on which the USA became independent from Great Britain (4 July 1776).

Today the square is a great playground for bikers and skaters, and is also used for flea markets.

This place used to be called the "4th Ring", the name that Albert Speer gave it when he built the first part of what was supposed to become the fourth motorway ring road (the furthest from the centre) of the capital of the Reich, the future Germania (see page 192).

Hitler was always wary of plans and models and preferred to see models, even partially, at a one to one scale. Whilst visiting the Telefunken plant (with its reminder of the Electra figure at the base of the tower overlooking the square) Hitler gave his approval to the "4th Ring".

The construction project was then shelved due to the Second World War.

The Telefunken factory buildings (which were later to house the McNair Barracks for the Americans and which today offer loft apartments to the wealthier part of the population) were built by forced labour. Where Wismarer Straße crosses the Teltow canal, a pillar-shaped concrete sculpture stands as a reminder of the labour camp barracks and in memory of the prisoners of war.

"THE BERLIN BRAIN"

A spectacular library

FU Philologische Bibliothek
Habelschwerdter Allee 45, 14195 Berlin
Mon–Fri 9am–10pm, Sat & Sun 10am–8pm
(closed on public holidays and on certain special occasions, consult details on: fu-berlin.de)
U3 (Freie Universität/Thielplatz)

Designed by Norman Foster, the exceptional library of the Freie Universität Berlin (The Free University of Berlin) looks from the side like a hot air balloon that has already lost two thirds of its volume after a crash landing.

The famous architect divided up the light-filled space inside into several levels of generously curved shelves, separated in the middle by a furrow (a wide corridor) to the extent that, when entering the library through the yellow funnel, you really feel that you are standing in front of two hemispheres of a brain (hence its nickname, "The Brain").

The heavily laden bookshelves are grouped together and integrated into the workspaces, which form a line following the curve of each level. A light-filled reading room is located on the upper level.

Comfortably seated in a red armchair designed by Egon Eiermann, it feels as if we are in the *USS Enterprise* with Spock, Kirk and Picard.

It is unlikely that the 600 workspaces will ever be empty: 800,000 works fill a surface area of over 6,290 square metres.

For information, readers must remain quiet at all times: "No mobile, no crisps, no small talk!".

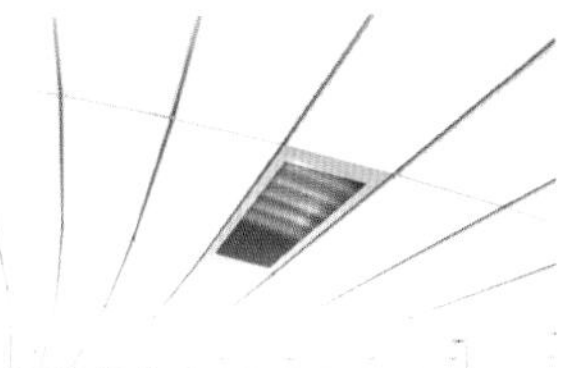

On a technical level, the library is lined on the inside with a non-combustible fibreglass membrane which refracts the daylight. There are also surprises in store with its active acoustics: in high winds, the hot air balloon creaks loudly. From time to time, we get a glimpse of the sky through the transparent (or open, weather-permitting) panels in its skin. The concrete structure is peppered with pipes where an ingenious system regulates the hot and cold water in response to the outside temperature.

THE FORMER EXCLAVE OF WÜSTE MARK

(31)

A former territory of West Berlin in the heart of the GDR ...

Potsdamer Damm 11C, 14532 Stahnsdorf
S7 (Potsdam Hauptbahnhof) then Bus 601 (Güterfelde, Friedenstraße)

Wüste Mark translates as "uncultivated border land". But wüst in German also means neglected, inextricable, untidy... The Wüste Mark is in fact today a large grassy area surrounded by Scots pines. The place's history, however, is surprising: it witnessed the fabulously absurd inter-German territorial sagas. Wüste Mark was in fact an exclave of West Berlin in the GDR.

On the map in the Potsdam Atlas published by the VEB Tourist Verlag in 1978, there is (in the same colour as the border) a dark rectangle in the Parforceheide with the following inscription next to it: "To WB (West Berlin)". The 21.83-hectare Wüste Mark was not an isolated case. Several zones were actually exclaved in GDR territory, but belonged to West Berlin (see box). The Wüste Mark was neither inhabited nor fenced in. Only some signs indicated that the border had been put up. In 1959, Hans Wendt, a farmer from Zehlendorf (GDR) decided to rent this potentially arable land that had been left derelict from the West Berlin administration, and farm it. When the border was closed in 1961, the situation became more complicated, but Hans Wendt did not give up and started farming the land he was renting in 1965. He would drive his tractor down the motorway, with his special passes to gain access to West Berlin, having his papers checked at border control in Dreilinden (see page 432) before going to his field in enemy territory. He even had

passes to allow him to stay there overnight and hire up to five seasonal workers. He grew rye, but also potatoes ("Bostara" and "Clivia" varieties). The Wüste Mark, in spite of its name, was anything but a barren land.

The year 1988 was to witness an exchange of territories between the GDR and West Berlin. In exchange for hard currency and some small plots of land in the GDR (like the Wüste Mark), West Berlin obtained the missing pieces of the puzzle of its urban landscape, such as the Lenné-Dreieck of the Potsdamer Platz, Hottengrund and Große Kienhorst (see next double pages).

This decision was made at the negotiating table without even taking Wendt into consideration, who found it very hard to swallow the change in situation, which meant that he lost all his rights to the land, and he ended up having a heart attack. His son, Christian, had already sown the rye for the winter and had invested heavily with his brothers to ensure a crop rotation with organic vegetables. This was in vain as it was all lost along with the land. Sadly, since then, the Wüste Mark has remained derelict.

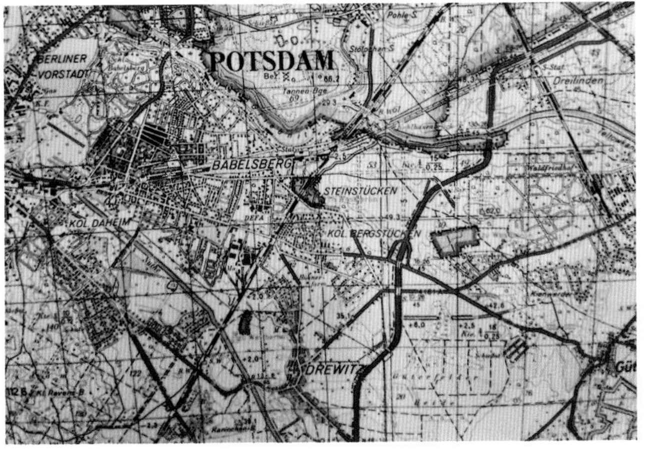

What are an exclave and an enclave?

An exclave is a territory which is under the sovereignty of a country (or of a region) but which is separated geographically from the main territory of the country (or of the region) in question by another country (or region). An enclave is a territory that is completely surrounded by only one other territorial entity (region or country). Lesotho is, for example, an enclave of South Africa.

The extraordinary history of Berlin's exclaves

Today's Berlin is the consequence of the creation of Greater Berlin on 1 October 1920, which brought together around a hundred towns, villages and territories surrounding the old Berlin, leading to the creation of a dozen exclaves which were enclaved in the heart of the neighbouring province of Brandenburg.

In 1945, with the occupation of Germany after the Second World War, the former exclaves of Berlin, dependent on the American and British zones, thus became the exclaves of the Soviet zone, and then from 1949, those of East Germany.

The existence of these exclaves was inevitably the cause of much tension, notably in Steinstücken (see page 436), the only inhabited exclave.

To make travelling between West Berlin and its exclaves easier, three agreements were signed:

- On 21 December 1971, an agreement was made to abolish six exclaves in exchange for territories: East Germany received the exclaves of Böttcherberg, Fichtenwiesen, Große Kuhlake and Nuthewiesen (15.6 ha in total) from West Berlin, in exchange for 17.1 ha: the question of Steinstücken was resolved by attaching the village of West Berlin by a strip of land. West Berlin had to pay 4 million marks to East Germany for this extra territory (2.3 ha).
- On 21 July 1972, East Germany sold 8.5 hectares of land which had previously belonged to Mitte, corresponding to the old station of Potsdamer Platz, for 31million marks.
- On 31 March 1988, a final exchange was made in order to (amongst other things) abolish the last five remaining exclaves: East Germany received Falkenhagener Wiese, Finkenkrug and Wüste Mark in addition to a 50-metre long strip of land running along the front of the goods station of Eberswalder, to the north of Bernauer Strasse (Wedding), which is part of the Mauerpark today (for a total of 87.3 ha). West Berlin was allowed to add Erlengrund and Fichtenwiesen to its territory and it also retreived 14 territories along the border, as well as the Lenné-Dreieck (a triangular-shaped territory near Potsdamer Platz) for 76 million marks (96.7 ha in total). In this way, West Berlin expanded its territory by 9.4 ha with, in particular, the territory of Tiefwerder, East Berlin's former exclave of the west (Spandau), which officially became a territory of Spandau (West Berlin).

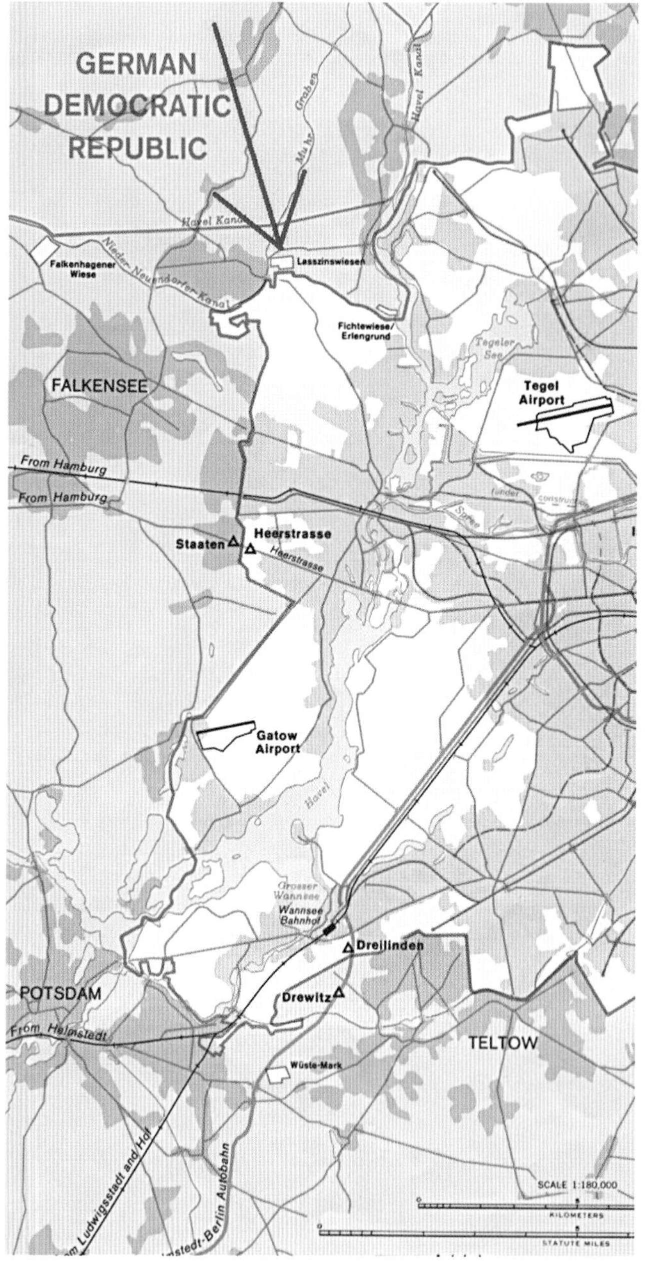
GERMAN
DEMOCRATIC
REPUBLIC
Graben
Havel Kanal
Muhr
Havel Kanal
Falkenhagener Wiese
Nieder-Neuendorfer-Kanal
Lasszinswiesen
Fichtewiese/ Erlengrund
Tegeler See
Tegel Airport
FALKENSEE
From Hamburg
From Hamburg
Spree
Staaten
Heerstrasse
Heerstrasse
Gatow Airport
Havel
Grosser Wannsee
Wannsee Bahnhof
Dreilinden
Drewitz
POTSDAM
From Helmstedt
TELTOW
Wüste-Mark
From Ludwigsstadt and Hof
Helmstedt-Berlin Autobahn
SCALE 1:180,000
KILOMETERS
STATUTE MILES

West Berlin's twelve exclaves in the East were as follows:

- Böttcherberg (0.30 ha): three distinct, uninhabited strips of land ranging from 20 to 100 metres long by a few metres in width, very close to Berlin's south-west border near Königstraße. Given up to East Germany in 1971, they are now part of Potsdam.
- Erlengrund (0.51 ha) and Fichtenwiesen (3.51 ha): two plots of land near Berlin, just north of the Spandauer Forst, near the Havel. These two plots were maintained by West Berlin's gardening associations: to get there, members had to go through a gate in the Berlin Wall, walk down a path, escorted by East German border guards, and then go through a checkpoint. This access, which was reserved for members of the associations, was only possible at certain times. The path in East German territory was fenced in on either side to block access from East Germany. The two enclaves were eliminated in 1988 when East Germany gave up the surrounding land to West Berlin.
- Falkenhagener Wiese (45.44 ha): the largest and furthest of the enclaves, 5 km from West Berlin's borders. This derelict land was given up to East Germany in 1988 and is now part of Falkensee.
- Finkenkrug (3.45 ha): a derelict plot of land, 5 km west of Berlin, was given up to East Germany in 1971 and is now part of Falkensee.
- Große Kuhlake (8.03 ha): a derelict plot of land near Berlin's border, was given up to East Germany in 1971 and is now part of Falkensee.
- Laszinswiesen (13.49 ha): a derelict plot situated immediately north of Berlin's border, given up to East Germany in 1988 and which is now part Schönwalde.
- Nuthewiesen (3.64 ha): an uninhabited marshland area, given up to East Germany in 1971 and which is now part of Potsdam.
- Steinstücken (12. 67 ha): The only inhabited west German enclave (see page 436).
- Wüste Mark (21. 83 ha): Given up to East Germany in 1988, it is now part of Stahnsdorf (see page 426).

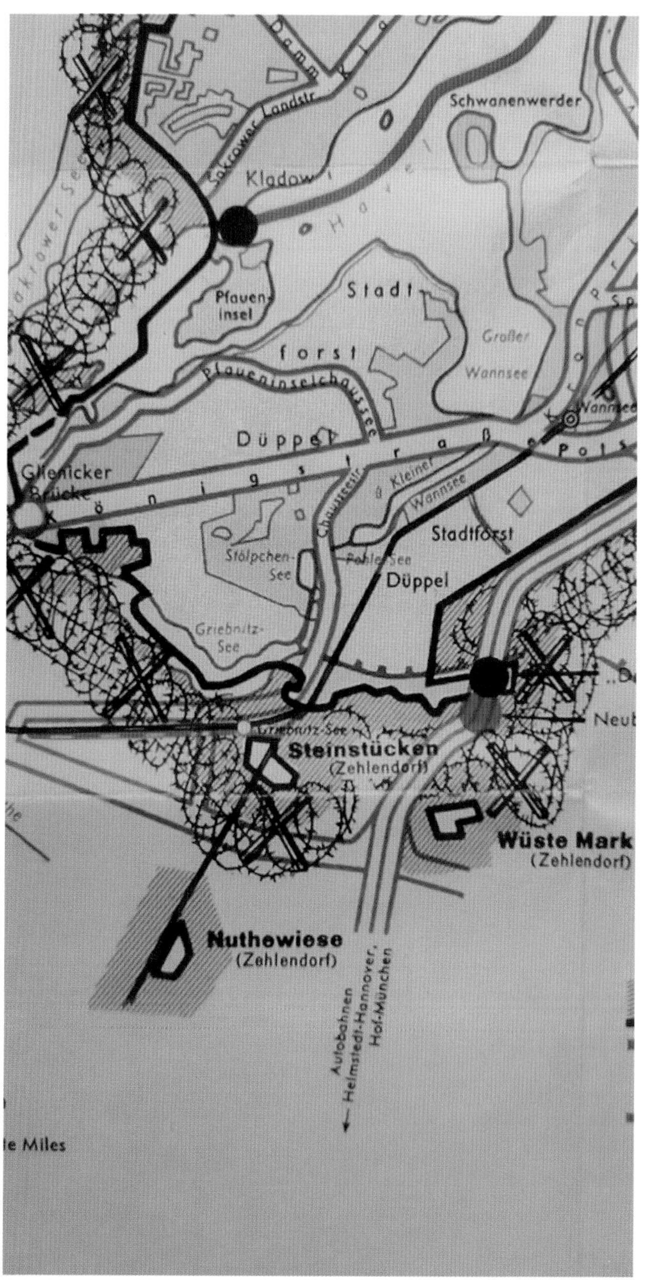
Schwanenwerder
Sakrower Landstr.
Kladow
Pfaueninsel
Stadt
forst
Pfaueninselchaussee
Großer
Wannsee
Düppel
Königstraße
Glienicker
Brücke
Kleiner
Wannsee
Stadtforst
Stölpchen-
See
Düppel
Griebnitz-
See
Steinstücken
(Zehlendorf)
Wüste Mark
(Zehlendorf)
Nuthewiese
(Zehlendorf)
Autobahnen
Helmstedt-Hannover,
Hof-München
le Miles

THE FORMER CHECKPOINT OF DREILINDEN

(32)

The unfortunate route of the former motorway

Kanalauenweg, 14109 Berlin
S7 (Griebnitzsee) / Bus 628 (Stolper Weg)

When looking at the bridge over the Teltow canal from the south, it seems obvious that this derelict construction, which would at first appear to be rather ordinary, is in fact anything but that. On this

large bridge, the worn-out asphalt of which is overgrown with trees, white marks indicate the tracks reserved for various categories of vehicle – BUSES, PKW (cars) and LKW (heavy goods vehicles). The motorway actually used to run through the forest which was an extremely popular place with Berlin's biggest archery club, which practises further down the way.

At the end of the Second World War, the bridge crossed not only the canal but also the border which had just been drawn between the East and the West. (A little piece of West Berlin, Teerofen attached to Wannsee, jutted out into GDR territory and the exact point where the border with the GDR crossed the canal lay directly under the bridge.) The identity of the people travelling between the GDR and West Berlin had already been checked at the Drewitz GÜST, the border control of the GDR. It is for this reason that the first Allied checkpoints, and those of West Berlin's police and customs, were set up on the bridge to check the vehicles travelling to West Berlin. Premises were built to watch over the border crossings from the south bank of the canal. In front of it, flag staffs were placed on either side: (to the south) there were American, British and French flags, and (to the north), the flags of the GDR and West Berlin. The, now flagless, poles are still there today.

However, after the checkpoint of Dreilinden, the journey continued for about three kilometres into the GDR, before crossing the border a second time to get into West Berlin, just before the motorway interchange of Zehlendorfer Kreuz. In 1969, in order to get round the western appendix jutting into its territory (and the problems caused by the infamous three kilometres), the GDR modified this route. The border controls were subsequently carried out just before the Zehlendorf interchange, whilst keeping the old names (Drewitz/Dreilinden/Checkpoint Bravo) intact. Today, the Checkpoint Bravo association ensures the upkeep of the memorial in the former watchtower of the border control (GÜST) of the GDR, situated in the municipality of Stahnsdorf.

Slightly to the north of the former border control of Dreilinden, a few minutes away on foot, the old route of the motorway can be clearly seen from a bridge, giving a good idea of where the motorway actually ran.

THE INSCRIPTION ON THE MACNHOWER STRAßE BRIDGE

33

Remains of the Stammbahn, the first line of Berlin's railway

Machnower Straße, 14109 Berlin
S7 (Griebnitzsee)

A railway that is overgrown with bushes is not such a rare sight in Berlin, but this one is rather special: other than the fact that you will have to climb quite a way to reach it, it is the oldest bridge on the first line of Berlin's railway, the *Stammbahn*.

It has been out of use since 1945, and is difficult to explore much further than the bridge as this section of the first Prussian railway line, which linked Berlin to Potsdam, is so overgrown.

Prussia, usually so rigid in its ways, proved to be particularly quick to build its first railways: the *Stammbahn* was built between 1836 and 1838.

In Potsdam, the station was named "Berliner Bahnhof", and in Berlin, "Potsdamer Bahnhof". It used to stand on what is now Potsdam Square. After the inauguration of this line on 21 September 1838, which had only one track to start with, the newspaper *Vossische Zeitung* described this memorable event: the journey "started on a slow tempo, becoming quicker by the second, until it reached the speed that meant that railways have won a shining victory over all the other means of locomotion."

Situated just before the entrance to the town of Potsdam, the bridge of Machnower Straße is essentially what remains of this legendary line, and a stone on its wall is marked with the year 1838 and the following engraving: "This stone comes from the vaulted work of the first Prussian railway line which was modified in 1926."

What has become of the Stammbahn?

Between Gleisdreieck and Steglitz, the line was closed, but the tracks are still there, in addition to those between Zehlendorf and Kleinmachnow.

Only two sections of the Stammbahn are still in use: the one linking the commuter train stations of Steglitz and Zehlendorf, and the one in Potsdam between the commuter train stations of Griebnitzsee and the mainline station.

THE HELICOPTER OF STEINSTÜCKEN

(34)

Steinstücken, an enclave of West Berlin in the GDR, with its own wall

Am Landeplatz, 14109 Berlin
U7 Griebnitzsee then bus 694 Rote-Kreuz-Straße

It is hard to imagine a more unusual monument: rotor blades from helicopters from the 1960s belonging to the American Army, standing upright like a rifle that you would carry on your shoulder, on the edge of a children's playground ... There is, in fact, a helicopter in the playground: it is made of colourful tubes welded together, and is used as a climbing frame, much to the children's delight, as if helicopters were something special here.

Between 1961 and 1972, American military helicopters did in fact land and take off here, every day, to supply Steinstücken, an enclave of West Berlin in the heart of the GDR, with basic provisions (see page 428).

At that time, the tiny enclave of Steinstücken had a population of around 300 inhabitants and was part of the Wannsee district (Bezirk Steglitz-Zehlendorf), even although it was located in the very centre of Potsdam-Neubabelsberg. In 1920 when Greater Berlin was created, this village had already found itself "out on a limb", but, at first, it had not really mattered to the inhabitants who felt attached to Babelsberg. However, between 1945 and 1971, things were to take an unexpected turn. In October 1951, the GDR failed to annex Steinstücken when, after four days of occupation, the Americans intervened and freed the enclave. In 1952, the

GDR fenced it in. For the inhabitants who numbered no more than 200 people at the time, there was only one possible road left that they could take to get to Wannsee, and it was controlled by the GDR. Visitors and suppliers had to prove that they had a holiday home in Steinstücken. After the wall was built in 1961, three American soldiers remained stationed in Steinstücken and, from that time onwards, helicopters helped out with supplies. However, the GDR was supplying Steinstücken with electricity and water. After the Quadripartite Agreement on Berlin was concluded in 1971, which stated that the "problems of enclaves, including that of Steinstücken, and of other areas of land, can be solved by exchanges of land", Steinstücken was linked to Wannsee by an umbilical cord that was 900 metres long and 100 metres wide. The GDR having relocated the walls, a large road, coming to a dead end, was inaugurated on 30 August 1972 by the mayor of Berlin, Klaus Schütz, which enabled the village to be connected to public transport (Bus 118). From then on, West Berlin could also supply the village with electricity and water. As the helicopters had stopped flying backwards and forwards, the children got bored. Their parents, however, were delighted to see the price of their land soar and to at last be able to park in front of their houses. When tourists began flooding to Berlin, some of the inhabitants, who had enjoyed both the heroic and comical side of their insularity, started missing the past. But, since then, everything seems to have come to a happy end.

LOGGIA ALEXANDRA

35

An exceptional place for a dearly-loved sister

Königstraße, 14109 Berlin
Open 24 hours a day
S 1, 7 Wannsee then Bus 316 Schloss Glienicke

After a short walk from the bus stop in Königstraße in the general direction of Wannsee, you will find yourself in a leafy wood on the right, behind the cemetery of Klein-Glienicke.

The path curves off, going south-west between Berlin and Potsdam. At the first fork, take a left and then a right turn after about 150 metres, which will lead you in a few minutes to the stunning *Loggia Alexandra* that very few Berliners know about.

In 1870, Prince Carl of Prussia had this open-air beauty spot transformed. He appointed the court's sculptor, Alexander Gilli, to design and decorate a tea pavilion.

The prince came here in memory of his sister, Charlotte of Prussia, whom he loved dearly. She had married the Grand Duke Nicolas Pavlovitch in 1817, and then became known as Alexandra Feodorovna. In 1826 she became empress of Russia.

After her death in 1860, Carl initially had a stone bench installed, but it was not enough to express the utter despair he felt when he lost his beloved sister.

From the beauty spot, there was a view of Potsdam as well as of the number three station of the Prussian optical telegraph line, which was situated on the Schäferberg in the opposite direction. When the mourning prince wistfully remembered the romantic stories that he had shared with his sister, the dancing fairies on the painted frescos there helped him to keep dreaming.

The beauty spot was vandalised during the Cold War, but has since been painstakingly restored.

From the bench in front of the loggia there is a wonderful view of what was once "Little Switzerland" (see next double page).

THE REMAINS OF LITTLE SWITZERLAND

36

High up on the mountain, there was once a little chalet ...

Königstraße, 14109 Berlin
S 1, 7 Wannsee then Bus 316 Schloss Glienicke

In Berlin, no mountains. A few round-topped hills. Nothing else. So hearing people talk about a "Switzerland" is rather intriguing. Even more so if the place in question is really a steep slope.

Home to the Loggia Alexandra (see page 448), the mountain of Böttcherberg (66 m) is an exception as it is not a man-made hill, made, as many hills are in Berlin, of rubble from ruins from the war. It was formed naturally and dates back to the Ice Age. This explains why many boulders, the remains of an old glacier, can be seen scattered among ancient oaks.

From 1841, Prince Carl of Prussia had this miniature wilderness made into an alpine rock garden – a "Switzerland" as it was called in those days. As a prelude to this, a mini navigable canal was dug in the valley (the Bäkenkanal) and "Swiss" chalets were built on the slope facing Potsdam, some of which are still standing today.

A small mountain cemetery and a chapel (still standing) lined the road leading to the castle of Klein-Glienicke. This road began with a climb up to an alpine glade, where hikers and walkers could get something to eat and quench their thirst with a glass of milk or beer, before starting the real "climb".

Remnants of former clay extraction activities meant that there was a trench that had been dug here, making it easy to create an alpine Switzerland: the beginning of a narrow mule track was scattered with artificial rock needles and plants from the rock garden. The track led up to the summit of Böttcherberg.

There was also a hillside vine with steps carved into the rock, all contributing to the impression of being at the foot of a mountain.

At that time, this type of landscape architecture, which was created with a good deal of concrete mortar, bricks and limestone from Rüdersdorf, was the first of its kind in Prussia. The rocky outcrops can still be seen, in addition to the high walls that were built for vine growing.

THE TELAMONS OF GLIENICKE PARK 37

They would be called corpses, wouldn't they?

Glienicke Palace,Königstraße 36, 14109 Berlin
S1, 7 Wannsee then Bus 316 Glienicker Lake

In the very heart of the grounds of Glienicke Palace, to the right of the restaurant, at the base of a column near the orangery, facing north, there is what would appear from behind to be merely a pile of stones. However, a walk round the trees will reveal astonishing sculptures of men lying partially concealed in the undergrowth. Take a closer look and you will see the men from the waist up, lying on the ground, yet seemingly still holding something above their heads.

In 1863 Berlin gave these sculptures as a gift to prince Carl of Prussia (1801–1883), the owner and designer of Glienicke Palace and park. He was widely known to be an avid collector: it was common knowledge that he sent for whole sections of monasteries which had been knocked down in Italy to be used in Glienicke Palace on the Havel. He collected everything as long as it was in some way an antiquity: fragments of reliefs, mosaic floors, mural decorations, capitals, sculpted pieces and fragments of balustrades. They were torn from their original settings due to war, decline, volcanic eruptions, or even more banal reasons such as theft. This is how the charmingly named pavilion, "Kleine Neugierde" (Little Curiosity) in Glienicke park, came to be fitted with a mosaic floor from Ancient Carthage.

Prince Carl, however, was not sure what to do with the gift from Berlin: four legless telamons from the Palace am Festungsgraben (near the moat of the fortifications), the residence of Johann Gottfried Donner, who was the personal valet of Frederick II and Elisabeth of Prussia, his estranged wife. The frontage of his palace had been built some hundred years before in the "Hellenistic" Renaissance style. From 1808 onwards, the palace then served as a workplace for 48 finance ministers. The telamons were sculpted in Silesian sandstone from the drawings of a sculptor and porcelain artist, Ernst Heinrich Reichard (died in 1764) who made the KPM royal porcelain factory famous. They still lie here, waiting to go to another place one day. Who knows?

THE COLUMN ON SCHWANENWERDER ISLAND

38

Remains of the Parisian Tuileries Palace

Opposite Inselstraße 5, 14129 Berlin
S1, 3, 7 (Nikolassee)

A 15-minute walk from the beach at Wannsee, on Schwanenwerder Island (which, for a time, was nicknamed Bonzenwerder after key members of the Nazi party who lived there: Goebbels, Speer, Scholtz-Klink and Morell), to the right of Inselstraße there is a tall

column with a Corinthian capital standing against some ruins.

As the plaque on the column tells us, it is a small part of the original façade of the *Palais des Tuileries* (Tuileries Palace) in Paris, which was destroyed during the commune's 1871 uprising.

Hugo von Platen, who owned the island, sold it to Friedrich Wilhelm Wessel, an oil lamp manufacturer in Kreuzberg. The new owner, a speculator, true to the spirit of the *Gründerzeit*, the economic boom which began in Germany after the 1870 war, split the island up into individual plots. In order to make them more attractive for sale, he created a landscaped park bordering onto these romantic places that were greatly sought-after at the time, one of which was near the old column from the *Palais de Tuileries*. He also lived to see his island officially renamed Schwanenwerder (Swan island) by imperial decree in 1901.

In the background, there is an inscription above the bench which is opposite the Havel, reminding us of the transitory nature of happiness: "This stone from the banks of the Seine / transplanted to the land of the Germans, / Warns you, the passer-by: / Oh happiness, how fickle you are!"

This entreaty must have been an oracle not only for Wessel but also for all the other inhabitants of the island. After the war and the departure of the Nazis, the column narrowly escaped being dismantled and taken back to Paris: the French suspected the Germans of having stolen the remains of Tuileries Palace during the 1871 military campaign, and considered them to be the Prussians' perfidious spoils of war.

By collecting all existing evidence, it was possible to prove to the French that the fragments of the columns and other elements from the façade of the Tuileries Palace had, in fact, all been legally acquired by Wessel. They had even been put up for sale to the public in 1882 in Paris as decorative architectural elements.

ACKNOWLEDGEMENTS

Tommy Spree, Philipp Schüneman, Ekaterina Emchenko, Bertrand Saint-Guilhem, Carsten Seiler, Uwe Fabich, Lilith Zink, Andy Altmeier, Karim Ben Khalifa, Nicholas Bamberger, Daniel Heer, Hemma Thaler, Suraj Nathwany, Michaela Lindinger, Frédéric Lucas, Constance Breton, Michael Fuchs, Dr Georg Thaler, Paula Anke, Jan Kleihues, Bodo Förster, Patrick Suel, Veronika Kellndorfer, Elizabeth Markevitch, Daniele Maruca, Oliver Euchner, Mathilde Ramadier, Elodie Bouchereau, Delphine Mousseau, Mathilde Bonbon, Anja Weber, Amélie de Maupeou, Pascale Nicoulaud.

Manuel Roy :
I would like to give my hearfelt thanks to those who so generously supported and accompanied me during my research and explorations of Berlin: my friends Gerhard Schwarz and Sunhwa Lee, Mrs Sandra Rohwedder from the German Foundation for the Protection of Historic Monuments (*Deutsche Stiftung Denkmalschutz*), Mr Hans Riefel from the Regional Office of Historic Monuments (Landesdenkmalamt), Mr Jörg Kuhn from the Berlin Mitte Evangelist Cemeteries Association, Mrs Annette Winkelmann from the Carl-Gotthard-Langhas Society, Mrs Isabella Mannozzi from the Bildgießerei Noak, Mr Yeter Hanefi, as well as the many anonymous Berliners I met at the various places I investigated who so joyfully shared their often astonishing wealth of knowledge. Berlin, ick liebe dir.

PHOTOGRAPHY CREDITS

Photographs by **Tom Wolf**:
Günter Litfin Memorial for victims of the Wall - Rabbit silhouettes on Chausseestraße - Windows of the Invalids' House - Stone of Monbijou Park - Handshake on Sophienstraße - Honi's window - Litfaß column on Münzstraße - Pipes of the wall on Lustgarten riverbank - Dolphin sculpture - Tombstone of Alexander von der Mark - Rosenstraße Memorial - Foundations of the "Alte Synagogue" - Crypt of the Parochialkirche - Wusterhausischer Bär - Commemorative stone of Fischerkiez - Mutter Hoppe restaurant bas-reliefs - Plaque of the Palast der Republik - Allegorical sculpture of the Spree - Memorial to Karl Liebknecht - "Peace be with you" mural - Toll wall - Underground house - Lapidarium - Toad at the Prinzenstraße underground station - Visit to the Malzfabrik - Alfred Hrdlicka's "Danse macabre" - The Three globes of Heerstraße - Archaeology Gallery of Sanitary Facilities - Holes in the pillars of the Leibnizstraße bridge - Binninger's clock - Wedding sand dune - Spa pavilion bas-relief - Walls commemorating Moabit prison - Stairs of the ULAP - Kerbs of Germania - Gas street lamps of the open air museum - Visit to the UT2 - Covered passageway of the Bornholmer Straße border post - Shot tower - Hartung's columns - "Nicaraguan Village – Monimbó 1978" fresco - Remains of the Blankenfelde reception camp - Oldest remains of the Berlin Wall - Cherubs of Pankow - Daimon Museum - Marzahn tower mill - House of Frick - WBS 70 museum apartment - "Gründerzeit" museum - Boeing 707 D-ABOC "Berlin" - Plaque marking John Rabe's last known address - Biberteich - Museum flat in the Haselhorst experimental district - Monument to homing pigeons - Schildhorn Monument - Grunewald forest cemetery - Olympia signal box - Museum of the blind - 4th of July square - "The Berlin Brain" - Former exclave of Wüste Mark - Inscription on the Machnower Straße bridge - Helicopter of Steinstücken - Column on Schwanenwerder island

Photograph by **Élodie Benchereau**:
The old monumental cross of the Berliner Dom

Photographs by **Manuel Roy**:
Concrete pillars of Yorckstraße - Façade of Thomasiusstraße 5

Photographs by **Roberto Sassi**:
James Turrell lighting installation - Water tanks of Prenzlauer Berg

Photographs by **Bertrand Saint-Guilhem**:
James Turrell lighting installation - Hall of the Moabit Courthouse - Fist from the grenadiers' tomb - Façades of Kirchbachstraße 1 and 2 - Entrance gates of the Ceciliengärten - Trudelturm vertical wind tunnel (P. 359) - Tegel Russian Orthodox Cemetery

Photographs by **Thomas Jonglez**:
James Turrell lighting installation - Animal anatomical theatre - The museum of silence - The pavement on Auguststraße 69 - Le décor historique de la Tadshikische Teestube - Signs of resistance on the Umweltbibliothek - Frontage of the old Hofbeamtenhaus Wilhelm II - Geschäftshaus Tietz - The Wusterhausischer Bär - Ermeler House bas-reliefs - Remains of Cölln Town Hall - Plaque of the Palast der Republik (P. 87) - The arm of the statue of the former State Council Building - Historical milestones on Dönhoff Platz - Building at 8 Schützenstraße - Alfandary House bas-reliefs - Diaspora Garden - Staircase of the German Steelworkers Union - Remains of the Stresemannstraße railway line - Old gas station - Grave of

the Mühlenhaupt family - Mausoleum of the Oppenfeld family - Tomb of Erwin Reibedanz - Biedermann tomb - Mural fresco of Fichtestrstraße 2 - Stehfisch sculpture - Ritterhof - Bas-reliefs of the Engelbecken Hof - Slabs of bitumen along the Leuschnerdamm - Reliefs on the façade of Adalbertstraße 79 - Theodor Fontane's pharmacy - Remains of the Brommy Bridge - Abandoned Lohmühleninsel petrol station - Art installations on Reichenberger Straße - Remains of "the parish cemetery labour camp" - Forgotten symbols of the Ideal-Passage - Stones of Alfred-Scholz-Platz - *Café Botanico* garden - Silent Rixdorf garden - Sri Mayurapathy Murugan Hindu temple - Windows of the Church of the Twelve Apostles - Masonic symbols of the Kachelhaus - Mosaic of a cow - "Relocated" tomb of the Langenscheidt family - Visiting the court of Schöneberg - Orte des Erinnerns memorial - Front door of Eisenacher Straße 68 - Museum of Unheard-of Things - Schwerbelastungskörper - Historical collection of the Berlin Police - Visit to the Malzfabrik (P. 205) - Blanke Helle sculpture - Organ of the Martin-Luther-Gedächtniskirche - Natur-Park-Südgelände - House at Niedstraße 4 - Eisack tunnel - Tomb of Heinrich Sachs - Monument to the glory of motorcycle racers - Façade of the building at Pariser Straße 61 - Stained-glass windows of the Church on the Hohenzollernplatz - Anti-Kriegs-Museum air raid shelter - Memorial for deported Jews - Painted ceiling of Alvar Aalto - Buchstabenmuseum - Hall of the Moabit Courthouse - Paper leaves of the Swiss Embassy - Postdamer Brücke ring - Reverse inscription on the Senefelder monument - GDR toy museum - Well in the Jewish cemetery - Tomb of the Riedel family - Tomb of the Pintsch family - Fisherman of Winsstraße - Coat of arms of the Grüne Stadt Gate - Tomb of the Lewinsohn et Netter families - Circular garden of the Georgen-Parochial II cemetery - Columns of Weberwiese - Sign of the horns on the "Craftsman and Son" statue - Former Pintsch AG administrative headquarters - Geological Waall - Luna Bunker - Art installations in Gustav-Adolf-Straße - The Dutch district of Weißssensee - Painter of the Motorwerk - The Herzberge boiler room - Memorial to the Révolution - Trudelturm vertical wind tunnel - Schmetterlingshorst butterfly collection - Corinthian capital in Brix-Genzmer-Park - Water tower in the cemetery of Hermsdorf - Biberteich (P. 375) - Sculpture of a bull - Staakens's old control tower - The fields of Karolinenhöhe - Tower of Beringer - The parabolic mirrors of the "Erschiessungsstätte V" - Dimensions of the Corbusierhaus - Resurrection of Christ Cathedral - A104 motorway tunnel building - Lahore Ahmadiyya Movement Mosque - Red letterbox in Fehrbelliner Platz - Kreuzkirche - Mäusebunker - Museum of Energy - Tribute to the Groß-Lichterfelde tramway line - Municipal weigh house - Fliegeberg - The former exclave of Wüste Mark (P. 427) - The former checkpoint of Dreilinden - Loggia Alexandra - Remains of little Switzerland - Telamons of Glienicke park

Cartography: Cyrille Suss – **Design:** Emmanuelle Willard Toulemonde – **Translation:** Ordentop and Jane Bonin – **Editing:** Matt Gay and Sigrid Newman – **Proofreading:** Kimberly Bess – **Publishing:** Clémence Mathé

It was September 1995 and Thomas Jonglez was in Peshawar, the northern Pakistani city 20 kilometres from the tribal zone he was to visit a few days later. It occurred to him that he should record the hidden aspects of his native city, Paris, which he knew so well. During his seven-month trip back home from Beijing, the countries he crossed took in Tibet (entering clandestinely, hidden under blankets in an overnight bus), Iran and Kurdistan. He never took a plane but travelled by boat, train or bus, hitchhiking, cycling, on horseback or on foot, reaching Paris just in time to celebrate Christmas with the family.

On his return, he spent two fantastic years wandering the streets of the capital to gather material for his first "secret guide", written with a friend. For the next seven years he worked in the steel industry until the passion for discovery overtook him. He launched Jonglez Publishing in 2003 and moved to Venice three years later.

In 2013, in search of new adventures, the family left Venice and spent six months travelling to Brazil, via North Korea, Micronesia, the Solomon Islands, Easter Island, Peru and Bolivia.

After seven years in Rio de Janeiro, he now lives in Berlin with his wife and three children.

Jonglez Publishing produces a range of titles in nine languages, released in 30 countries.

Registration of copyright: September 2023 - Edition: 01
ISBN: 978-2-36195-373-7
Printed in Bulgaria by Dedrax